CLAUSEWITZ'S PUZZLE

The Changing Character of War Programme is an inter-disciplinary research group located at the University of Oxford, and funded by the Leverhulme Trust.

Clausewitz's Puzzle

The Political Theory of War

ANDREAS HERBERG-ROTHE

OXFORD
UNIVERSITY PRESS

OXFORD
UNIVERSITY PRESS

Great Clarendon Street, Oxford OX2 6DP

Oxford University Press is a department of the University of Oxford.
It furthers the University's objective of excellence in research, scholarship,
and education by publishing worldwide in

Oxford New York

Auckland Cape Town Dar es Salaam Hong Kong Karachi
Kuala Lumpur Madrid Melbourne Mexico City Nairobi
New Delhi Shanghai Taipei Toronto

With offices in

Argentina Austria Brazil Chile Czech Republic France Greece
Guatemala Hungary Italy Japan Poland Portugal Singapore
South Korea Switzerland Thailand Turkey Ukraine Vietnam

Oxford is a registered trade mark of Oxford University Press
in the UK and in certain other countries

Published in the United States
by Oxford University Press Inc., New York

German edition published by
Wilhelm Fink Publishers, Munich 2001

This shortened translation first published by OUP 2007

British Library Cataloguing in Publication Data

Data available

Library of Congress Cataloging in Publication Data

Data available

Typeset by SPI Publisher Services, Pondicherry, India
Printed in Great Britain
on acid-free paper by
Biddles Ltd., King's Lynn, Norfolk

978-0-19-920269-0

1 3 5 7 9 10 8 6 4 2

Contents

Part I

Prologue

> War is *more* than a true chameleon that slightly adapts its characteristics to the given case. As a total phenomenon its dominant tendencies always make war a paradoxical Trinity—composed of primordial violence, hatred, and enmity, which are to be regarded as a blind natural force; of the play of chance and probability within which the creative spirit is free to roam; and of its element of subordination, as an instrument of policy, which makes it subject to pure reason.
>
> Carl von Clausewitz[1]

This new interpretation places Clausewitz's analysis of three paradigmatic military campaigns at the centre for an appropriate understanding of *On War* for the first time.[2] It is based on three crucial assumptions: Firstly, *On War* could only be understood with regard to Clausewitz's examinations of the conduct of war in his own times. His analyses of the Prussian defeats at Jena and Auerstedt in 1806, Napoleon's Russian campaign of 1812, and Napoleon's final defeat at Waterloo are the cornerstones of the architecture of *On War*. Clausewitz wrote detailed accounts of each of these three campaigns between 1823 and 1827, the years in which he composed most of *On War*, and he incorporated the core elements of these texts into the book.

Nearly all previous interpretations have drawn attention to the importance of Napoleon's successful campaigns for Clausewitz's thinking. In contrast, I wish to argue that not only Napoleon's successes but also the limitations of his strategy, as revealed in Russia and in his final defeat, enabled Clausewitz to develop a general theory of war. Clausewitz's main problem in his lifelong preoccupation with the analysis of war was that the same principles and strategies that were the decisive foundation of Napoleon's initial successes proved inadequate in the special situation of the Russian campaign (166–7), and eventually contributed to his final defeat at Waterloo. Although Clausewitz was an admirer of Napoleon for most of his life, in his final years, he recognized the theoretical significance that arose from the different historical outcomes that followed from the application of a consistent military strategy. He finally tried desperately to find a resolution that could reconcile the extremes symbolized by Napoleon's success at Jena and Auerstedt, the limitations of the primacy of force revealed by the Russian campaign, and Napoleon's final defeat at Waterloo. Clausewitz's desperation becomes obvious in his desire to rewrite almost the whole text, which is stated in the note of 1827, just three years before he sealed his manuscript for publishing after his death, and in statements like this, from the note: 'I regard the first six books, which are already in a clean copy, merely as a rather formless mass' (69).

Secondly, I proceed from the assumption that *On War* is for this very reason unfinished. Parts of the book can be seen to contradict other parts to a certain extent. However, my final conclusion is that the various concepts of war Clausewitz offers expose the most important contrasting tendencies in each war, and also the unifying common elements of which each war is composed. As will be shown, Books III and IV of *On War* belong, for the most part, to Clausewitz's experiences and analyses of Jena and Auerstedt, along with Napoleon's other decisive successes. The voluminous and frequently underestimated Book VI (about defence) is a reflection on the Russian campaign, and Book VIII (about politics and war plans) is derived from Napoleon's defeat at Waterloo. Only in Chapter 1 and partly Chapter 2 of Book I, and at the beginning of Book II, does Clausewitz succeed in describing a general solution to the overall problem raised by these contrasting historical experiences.

There are four fundamental contrasts between the early and later Clausewitz that need to be emphasized, because they remain central to contemporary debates about his work:

1. The primacy of military force versus the primacy of politics.
2. Existential warfare, or rather warfare related to one's own identity, which engaged Clausewitz most strongly in his early years, as against the instrumental view of war that prevails in his later work.[3]
3. The pursuit of military success through unlimited violence embodying 'the principle of destruction', versus the primacy of limited war and the limitation of violence in war, which loom increasingly large in Clausewitz's later years.

4. The primacy of defence as the stronger form of war, versus the promise of decisive results that was embodied in the seizure of offensive initiative.

Clausewitz's final approach is condensed in his Trinity, which comes at the end of Chapter 1 of Book I. This is my third basic assumption. The Trinity, with all its problems, is the real legacy of Clausewitz and the real beginning of his theory, as he emphasized himself: 'At any rate, the ... concept of war [the Trinity] which we have formulated casts a first ray of light on the basic structure of theory, and enables us to make an initial differentiation and identification of its major components.' I have eliminated in this quotation from the Howard and Paret translation the term 'preliminary', assigned to the term concept, because Clausewitz does not speak of any kind of 'preliminarity' within the sentence in question (*Vom Kriege*, 213, last sentence of Chapter 1).

One particular problem must be mentioned at the outset. Howard and Paret use the term: 'reason alone' in the paragraph on the Trinity, which might suggest a hierarchical interpretation of the three tendencies of the Trinity. This is fundamentally wrong and misunderstands the meaning of the original German wording. In German, Clausewitz uses the term *bloßer Verstand*, which could be best described as 'pure reason' and which I have inserted in the cited paragraph on the Trinity. The decisive difference, which has far-reaching consequences, is that the Howard and Paret translation emphasizes a primacy of reason within the Trinity, whereas in the original phrasing 'pure reason' is only one element among the contrasting tendencies of which war is made up. The Trinity is given consideration under the heading: 'The consequences for theory' (89). Chapter 1 of *On War*, and the Trinity as Clausewitz's result[4] for theory at its end, are an attempt to summarize these quite different war experiences, and to analyse and describe a general theory of war on the basis of Napoleon's successes, the limitations of his strategy, and his final defeat.

Azar Gat might be right, when he argues, that Clausewitz's 'undated note' (70–1), in which he says that he considers only Chapter 1 of Book I as finished, was written years before the author's death and even the note of 1827 (69–71), if we examine only this note itself. But taking into account a broader approach, it must be remembered firstly that Clausewitz included this text (in 1830) into his sealed manuscript shortly before his death

(1831), apparently as a guide for his wife, who was destined to publish it after his death. Secondly, one has to consider, as Marie von Clausewitz wrote in her preface, that her brother inserted the changes, which have been mentioned in the note of 1827, 'in those parts of Book I, for which they were intended (they did not go further)' (67); the conclusion therefore must be that Clausewitz wanted to identify Chapter 1 as his final words, and reworked it just before he sealed the whole text, although the undated note might have been written earlier.[5]

Clausewitz's concept of the Trinity is explicitly differentiated from his famous formula of war, described as a continuation of politics by other means (87). Although Clausewitz seems at first glance to repeat his formula in the Trinity, this is here only one of three tendencies which all have to be considered if one does not want to contradict reality immediately, as Clausewitz emphasized (89). Looking more closely at his formula, we can see that he describes war as a continuation of politics, but with other means than those that belong to politics itself (87). These two parts of his statement constitute two extremes: war described either as a continuation of politics, or as something that mainly belongs to the military sphere. Clausewitz emphasizes that policy uses *other*, non-political means. This creates an implicit tension, between war's status as a continuation of policy, and the distinctive nature of its *other* means. Beatrice Heuser has demonstrated in her overview of Clausewitz's ideas and their historical impact, that resolving this tension in favour of one side has always led to a primacy of the military.[6] This implicit tension is explicated in the Trinity.[7]

It is not accidental, and is indeed a characteristic feature of both of the most emphatic critiques of Clausewitz published in the 1990s by Martin van Creveld and Sir John Keegan, that they nearly always quote only half of the formula, the part in which Clausewitz states that war is a continuation of politics. Their interpretations suppress, often explicitly and always implicitly, the second part of Clausewitz's determination that politics in warfare uses other means. The paradoxical aspect of the criticism of Clausewitz is that he himself is well equipped to respond to it. Keegan is obviously criticizing the early Clausewitz, the supporter of Napoleon's strategy and of the destruction principle as a military method. Van Creveld, on the other hand, is attacking the later Clausewitz,[8] who emphasized the antithesis between limited and unlimited warfare, which became the critical point of his intention to revise his whole work. In this respect, Keegan's criticism could be answered with reference to the later Clausewitz, while the early Clausewitz can respond to van Creveld's criticism. But both critiques show how current attempts to develop a non-Clausewitzian theory of war move within a field of antitheses, the bounds of which were set out by the early and later Clausewitz himself.

Clausewitz's Trinity is also quite different from 'trinitarian war'. This concept is not derived from Clausewitz himself but from the work of Harry G. Summers Jr. Although Summers referred to Clausewitz's concept of the Trinity in his very influential book about the war in Vietnam, he falsified Clausewitz's idea fundamentally. Clausewitz explains in his paragraph about the Trinity that the first of its three tendencies mainly concerns the people, the second mainly concerns the commander and his army, and the third mainly concerns the government.[9] On the basis of this *mehr* (mainly), which is repeated three times, we cannot conclude that 'trinitarian war' with its three components of people, army, and government is Clausewitz's categorical conceptualization of how the three underlying elements of his Trinity may be embodied. Since Summers put forward this conception it has been repeated frequently, most influentially by van Creveld.[10] On the contrary, it must be concluded that these three components of 'trinitarian war' are only examples of the use of the more fundamental Trinity for Clausewitz. These examples of its use can be applied meaningfully to some historical and political situations, as Summers demonstrated for the case of the war in Vietnam with the unbridgeable gap between the people, the army, and the government of the USA. Notwithstanding the possibility of applying these examples of use, there can be no doubt that Clausewitz defined the Trinity differently and in a much broader, less contingent, and more conceptual sense.

Additionally, one can detect a characteristic difference between Clausewitz's Trinity and Summers' and van Creveld's understanding of trinitarian war. While Clausewitz emphasizes explicitly that the three tendencies of his Trinity are 'variable in their relationship to one another' and that no arbitrary relationship between them should be fixed (89), the three elements of 'trinitarian war' are integrated into a hierarchy, with the people as the basis, followed by the army and finally the government at the top.[11] A hierarchy between the three tendencies is in no way the same thing as the relationship Clausewitz had in mind when he wrote that the three tendencies are 'variable in their relationship to one another' (89).

The task therefore is, according to Clausewitz, to develop a theory that 'floats' between these three tendencies.[12] He even emphasizes: 'A theory that ignores any one of them . . . would conflict with reality to such an extent, that for this reason alone it would be totally useless' (89).

The interval between the first and second wars in Iraq (1991 and 2003) has seen a remarkable shift from Clausewitz to Sun Tzu in the discourse about contemporary warfare. Clausewitz enjoyed an undreamed of renaissance in the USA after the Vietnam War and seemed to have attained the status of master thinker. *On War* enabled many theorists to recognize the causes of America's traumatic defeat in Southeast Asia, as well as the conditions for gaining victory in the future. More recently, however, he has very nearly been outlawed. The reason for this change can be found in two separate developments. Firstly, there has been an unleashing of war and violence in the ongoing civil wars and massacres, especially in sub-Saharan Africa, in the secessionist wars in the former Yugoslavia, and in the persistence of inter-communal violence along the fringes of Europe's former empires. These developments seemed to indicate a departure from interstate wars, for which Clausewitz's theory appeared to be designed, and the advent of a new era of civil wars, non-state wars, and social anarchy. Sun Tzu's *The Art of War* seemed to offer a better understanding of these kinds of war, because he lived in an era of never-ending civil wars.[13]

Secondly, the reason for the change from Clausewitz to Sun Tzu is connected with the 'revolution in military affairs'. The concepts of Strategic Information Warfare (SIW) and fourth generation warfare have made wide use of Sun Tzu's thought to explain and illustrate their position. The 'real father' of 'shock and awe' in the Iraq War of 2003 was Sun Tzu, argued one commentator in the *Asia Times*.[14] Some pundits even claimed triumphantly that Sun Tzu had defeated Clausewitz in this war, because the US Army conducted the campaign in accordance with the principles of Sun Tzu, whereas the Russian advisers of the Iraqi army had relied on Clausewitz and the Russian defence against Napoleon's army in his Russian campaign of 1812.[15] The triumphant attitude has long been abandoned, since it is now apparent that there is much to be done before a comprehensive approach of the Iraq War will be possible. Yet it seems fair enough to say that, if Sun Tzu's principles are seen to have been of some importance for the conduct of the war, he must also share responsibility for the problems that have arisen afterwards.

And this is exactly the problem. Sun Tzu's *The Art of War*, as well as the theoreticians of SIW and fourth generation warfare, lack the political dimension with respect to the situation after the war.[16] They concentrate too much on purely military success, and undervalue the process of transforming military success into true victory. The three core elements of Sun Tzu's strategy could not easily be applied in our times: a general attitude to deception of the enemy runs the risk of deceiving one's own population, which would be problematic for any democracy. An indirect strategy in general would weaken deterrence against an adversary who could act quickly and with determination. Concentration on influencing the will and mind of the enemy may merely enable him to avoid fighting at a disadvantageous time and place and make it possible for him to choose a better opportunity as long as he is in possession of the necessary means—weapons and armed forces.

One might win battles and even campaigns with Sun Tzu, but it is difficult to win a war by following his principles. The reason for this is that Sun Tzu was never interested in shaping the political conditions, because he lived in an era of seemingly never-ending civil wars. The only imperative for him was to survive while paying the lowest possible price and avoiding fighting, because even a successful battle against one foe might leave one weaker when the moment came to fight the next one. Mark McNeilly emphasizes the advantages of following a strategy based on Sun Tzu's principles for modern warfare. As always in history, if one wishes to highlight the differences to Clausewitz, the similarities between the two approaches are neglected. For example, the approach in Sun Tzu's chapter about 'Moving Swiftly to Overcome Resistance' would be quite similar to one endorsed by Clausewitz and was practised by Napoleon.

But the main problem is that both McNeilly and Sun Tzu neglect the strategic perspective of shaping the political-social conditions after the war and their impact 'by calculation' (Clausewitz, *Vom Kriege*, p. 196)[17] on the conduct of war. As mentioned before, this was not a serious matter for Sun Tzu and his contemporaries, but it is one of the most important aspects of warfare of our own times.[18] If one wanted to incorporate thoughts from Chinese military culture and especially Taoist theorists into one's own strategic thinking, one would be better served for example by *The Book of Leadership and Strategy* of the 'Masters of Huainan', because the purpose of its implicit strategy is much more relevant to the needs and tasks of our times than that of Sun Tzu.[19]

Finally, one has to take into account the fact that Sun Tzu's strategy is presumably successful against adversaries with a very weak order of the armed forces or the related community, such as warlord-systems and dictatorships, which were the usual adversaries in his times. His book is full of cases in which relatively simple actions against the order of the adversary's army or its community lead to disorder on the side of the adversary, to the point where these are dissolved or lose their will to fight entirely. Such an approach can obviously be successful against adversaries with weak armed forces and a tenuous social base, but they are likely to prove problematic against more firmly situated adversaries. Whereas Sun Tzu was generalizing strategic principles for use against weak adversaries, which may lead to success in particular circumstances, Clausewitz developed a wide-ranging political theory of war by reflecting on the success, the limitations, and the failure of Napoleon's way of waging war. Although he might have reflected merely a single strategy, he was able by taking into account its successes, limits, and failure to develop a general theory of war, which transcended a purely and historically limited military strategy.

Clausewitz's Trinity is the final result of this development and his true legacy, his 'Testament' (Raymond Aron). It offers us an understanding in which there is no longer any need either to view his various determinations of war as inconsistent or to choose only one of them as the fundament of the whole interpretation. This has happened frequently in the history of interpretations of Clausewitz. Nevertheless, Clausewitz explained his methodological approach most clearly in the chapter on defence, in a paragraph that seems to have been inserted at a very late stage and which has been underestimated until now: 'Once again we must remind the reader that, in order to lend clarity, distinction, and emphasis to our ideas, only perfect contrasts, the extremes of the spectrum, have been included in our observations. As an actual occurrence, war generally falls somewhere in between, and is influenced by these extremes only to the extent to which it approaches them' (517).[20] This new interpretation of *On War* tries to restructure Clausewitz's 'unfinished symphony' (Echevarria) on the basis of this methodological approach, as well as his analysis of Jena, Moscow, and Waterloo, and by doing so attempts to outline the foundations of a general theory of war and warfare.

***

Finally, I have to note that I concentrate in this book, for reasons of clarity, on the new interpretation of Clausewitz which is derived from his analysis of different campaigns. Of course, recent developments following the breakdown of the Soviet Union as well as 9/11 have had an implicit impact on my interpretation. Various other important aspects, concerning the relevance of Clausewitz for today and the interpretation of his work, have been dealt with elsewhere. My argument with John Keegan and the contradiction in his critique of Clausewitz can be found in *Defense and Security Analysis: 'Primacy of "politics" or "culture"'* (August 2001) and is partially reproduced in this book. Martin van Creveld's mythological assumptions are described in the previous German edition of this book. Some additional biographical information about Clausewitz is included in my comparison between Clausewitz and Hegel ('Clausewitz und Hegel. Ein heuristischer Vergleich', in *Forschungen zur brandenburgischen und preußischen Geschichte*, 1/2000). Although I agree with Colin Gray about the importance of Clausewitz for the twenty-first century (perhaps he is now even more important than ever before), I think that the different strategic goals in Clausewitz's and our times are of greater relevance than a 'realistic' approach could concede.[21] An attempt to present my own perspective with regard to this matter can be found in my essay, 'Clausewitz and a New Containment: Limiting War and Violence', which is included in the forthcoming volume, *Clausewitz in the 21st Century*, edited by Hew Strachan and myself (Oxford, 2007). The relevance of Clausewitz's implicit dialectical conception for philosophical problems is elaborated in my book, *Lyotard und Hegel. Dialektik von Philosophie und Politik* (Vienna, 2005) (Lyotard and Hegel: Dialectics of Philosophy and Politics). An attempt to use Clausewitz's Trinity and my interpretation of it in order to develop a general theory of war is made in my article, 'Clausewitz's Trinity as General Theory of War and Violent Conflict' (*Theoria*, 2007, forthcoming). A discussion of some of the new developments in the discourse about warfare can be found in my article 'Privatized Wars and World Order Conflicts' (*Theoria*, August 2006).

In reworking the English translation I have become more and more conscious of how much I owe to my colleagues, friends, and my family. First and foremost, I am very grateful for the kind invitation extended to me by Hew Strachan (Oxford) to act as joint convenor of the conference on 'Clausewitz in the 21st Century' (Oxford, 21–23 March 2005) and as co-editor of the resulting volume, and for his support and cooperation in connection with the publication of this book by Oxford University Press and in the funding of its translation, 'The Changing Character of War', by the Oxford Leverhulme programme, of which he is the director. All this encouragement was absolutely essential and without him nothing would have succeeded. Gerard Holden has translated the German text accurately, and was even so meticulous that he eliminated some mistakes that appeared in the German edition. I am still amazed by and therefore very thankful for the extensive editing work of Dan Moran as a Clausewitz specialist, work which he has undertaken purely out of interest and generosity. The ongoing discussions (by email and personally) with Christopher Bassford, Antulio Echevarria II and Jan Willem Honig have been very helpful, and have forced me to look more closely at the consequences of my thoughts. Beatrice Heuser contributed to the project by writing a very positive peer review.

Of course, none of those mentioned is to blame for my mistakes or for my 'strange' insistence, as a mere political philosopher, on this dialectical approach. My beloved wife enabled me to carry on working on this subject in really difficult and unsure times with respect to employment and the funding of my research, for which I am much more grateful than I can express. Finally, I would like to dedicate this book in friendship and thankfulness to the memory of my first academic teacher, Werner Hahlweg (1912–89), the editor of the German editions of Clausewitz's *On War* since 1952 and a lot of his previously unknown writings. He was the first to bring Clausewitz to my attention, and I would like to honour his memory with this book in times when we are seemingly more and more unconscious of the historical dimension of our actions.

Part II

Antitheses and Ambivalences

1

Clausewitz and Napoleon: Jena, Moscow, and Waterloo

> The statements and counter-statements made by Clausewitz 'are like weights and counterweights, and one could say that through their play and interplay the scales of truth are brought into balance'.
>
> Carl Linnebach[22]

Jena, Moscow, and Waterloo. These are more than just the names of towns or cities, more than mere battles and locations of military victories, defeats, and destruction. Napoleon's victories over the Prussian forces at Jena and Auerstedt in 1806 were so overwhelming and comprehensive that they led to the collapse of a whole conception of the world. Moscow (1812) was the turning point of the Napoleonic Wars. The Battle of Waterloo (1815) was the final battle of the wars of liberation and a total defeat for Napoleon. All these places are associated with the name of one man: Napoleon. In the beginning there was Napoleon.[23] For Clausewitz, however, Napoleon, the 'god of war', stood both at the beginning and at the end of his lifelong study of the theory of war.

The literature in this field is united in its assessment that Napoleon's successful way of waging war had a significant influence on Clausewitz's theory. However, no one has yet asked how Clausewitz's theory dealt with Napoleon's later defeats, especially the failure of the Russian campaign and the final defeat at Waterloo. It is true that Napoleon's victorious campaigns led Clausewitz to develop a theory of successful warfare. But it was only Napoleon's defeats in Russia, and then at Leipzig (1813) and Waterloo (1815), that made it possible for Clausewitz to develop a *political* theory of war. Of course, this does not mean that Clausewitz's political theory of war is a theory of defeat. However, it does mean that the successes, limits, and defeats associated with Napoleon's way of waging war forced Clausewitz to reflect on questions that went beyond purely military matters and led him to a *political* theory of war.

For Clausewitz, Jena, Moscow, and Waterloo symbolize more than just events of global historical significance in which he himself had participated (though his military rank was not sufficiently high for him to be involved in taking important decisions). The military historian Stig Förster sees the 1792–1815 period as the first genuine world war in history, because a number of non-European powers were also drawn into the conflicts of these years.[24] These wars were triggered off by the established European powers' attempt to reverse the French Revolution by military means; the Revolution led to Napoleon's seizure of power, his expansionism, and the subsequent European wars of liberation. Napoleon's success, failure, and defeat at Jena, Moscow, and Waterloo form the shifting centre of Clausewitz's political theory of war. Jena, Moscow, and Waterloo symbolize for Clausewitz contrasting experiences of war, which structure his entire body of work. By looking at his analysis of these events we can reconstruct the contrasting elements within his work.

I therefore treat Jena, Moscow, and Waterloo as the three decisive points at which these elements in Clausewitz's political theory can be grasped most clearly. Of course, some aspects of his theory of war are associated with other places, especially the Battle of Leipzig, the experiences of the battles of Borodino and the Berezina, the campaign in Spain, and some of Napoleon's earlier victories. However, I am convinced that these three places, as locations of military encounters and destruction, were the most significant in terms of their effects on Clausewitz's theory. This is because they led directly to the decisive theoretical break in 1827, as Clausewitz formulated it in his author's note written in that year. Within the framework of his numerous historical writings, Clausewitz spent the years 1823–8 occupied nearly exclusively with the history of these three campaigns. The break with his former views, as formulated in the author's note, can therefore be traced directly to the work he did in these years.

1.1. THE TWIN BATTLES OF JENA AND AUERSTEDT: THE CATASTROPHE AND ITS CONSEQUENCES

'When in 1806 the Prussian generals . . . at Saalfeld [and] . . . near Jena . . . plunged into the open jaws of disaster by using Frederick the Great's oblique order of battle, it was not just a case of a style that had outlived its usefulness but the most extreme poverty of the imagination . . . .

The result was that the Prussian army under Hohenlohe was ruined more completely than any army has ever been ruined on the battlefield' (154–5). In a letter to his wife, Clausewitz writes of the soldiers who 'had been destroyed physically and morally'[25] in these battles. The significance of these military defeats can only be appreciated adequately if we remember the words of Frederick the Great: 'Prussia is as safe on the shoulders of such an army as the world on the shoulders of Atlas.'[26] It was this army, on which the entire Prussian state was supposed to rest, that was not only defeated by Napoleon's superior troops but also—as Clausewitz saw it—destroyed by its own generals.

Clausewitz considered the defeats at Jena and Auerstadt to be terrible examples of disasters caused by the weakness of the supreme leadership and by the defects of military and political institutions. In Clausewitz's view, the intellectual poverty and moral cowardice of Napoleon's opponents contributed to the superiority of his troops.[27] In addition, the daily press treated the Prussian defeats as a 'judgement of God', a reminder of the gradual degeneration of the people. The French occupation of much of the country was understood as a 'salutary punishment sent by God', which would have the beneficial effect of leading the people away from the path of flaccid, cowardly laziness. It had taught the country that there was a need for 'learning to use weapons' and 'manly sacrifice' for the fatherland if Prussia and Germany were to be liberated.[28]

In Clausewitz's opinion, these catastrophic Prussian defeats were in the final analysis caused by a combination of two factors: (1) the revolutionary changes in warfare brought about by the French Revolution and Napoleon's genius; and (2) the 'moral cowardice' of the Prussian political and military leadership and their inability to react in an appropriate way to these transformations. One could say, he wrote, that the twenty years in which the Revolution knew nothing but victories were in large measure the consequence of mistakes made by the governments opposed to it. There had been an extraordinarily long delay before the cabinets of old Europe realized that a whole new kind of dynamic had developed in the struggle for political power (609–10).[29]

1.1.1. The Existential Construction of War in Early Clausewitz

Clausewitz's interpretation of the reasons for these Prussian defeats changed his conception of the political subject of warfare in a fundamental way. The focus of his analysis was no longer the Prussian state, but the German nation as a subject waging war. 'We wander, orphaned children of a lost fatherland, and see that the lustre of the state we served, the state we helped to form, has been extinguished.'[30] During these years his goal was, in Paret's words, 'the ideal of German freedom'. 'We nourished the loftiest hopes; never can an army have purchased more noble glory with its blood than we would have done had we saved the honour, the freedom, and the civic happiness of the German nation.'[31] The immediate cause of his reference to the German nation was not simply the Prussian defeats as such, but above all the realization that the French victories were made possible by the mobilization of the entire nation. For the first time in history, conscript armies had been put into the field whose numbers alone made them superior to the armies of the military powers that had been dominant up to that point.[32]

However, the mobilization of the nation did not just affect the young men who were called up to serve in the army. The *levée en masse* decreed that *all* French citizens were considered part of the contingent called upon to perform military service. Young men would join the ranks, married men would forge weapons and be responsible for supplies, women would make tents and clothing and work in the hospitals, children would make bandages, and old people would go to the public squares where they would keep up the soldiers' fighting morale and declare their hatred of the enemy. The declaration went on to say: 'From now on, until the moment when all enemies have been driven from the territory of the Republic, all French citizens are called upon to perform permanent military service.'[33] In his obituary of Scharnhorst, his military teacher and friend, Clausewitz stressed the military potential of the concept of the nation. With their revolutionary measures, he argued, the French had freed the terrible element of war from its old financial and diplomatic restraints. He now saw war marching onwards in the form of raw violence, carrying with it the great forces it had unleashed.[34]

Clausewitz combines this orientation towards a German nation realized outside state institutions with what Muenkler calls an 'existential construction of war'. According to this conception war is not a direct way of pursuing policy goals, but it is a medium through which a political entity is constituted, transformed, and changed. War is thus a medium through which man can rise above his normal condition, go beyond his everyday egoism, and attain for the first time the condition in which the body politic becomes conscious of its identity.[35]

This existential construction of war, as a means of constituting or transforming a political identity, can be seen with great clarity in a letter Clausewitz wrote in 1806: 'You want a revolution. I am not opposed to this, but will it not be much easier to bring about this revolution in the civic constitution, and in the constitution of the state, in the midst of the movement and vibration of all parts that is occasioned by war?'[36] In a letter from 1809 he once again states his belief in the need for a revolution in Europe: 'Whoever is victorious, Europe cannot escape a great and general revolution.... Even a general insurrection of the German peoples...would only be a precursor of this great and general revolution.'[37] What Clausewitz is advocating here is more than just a revolution of civil society and the state constitution. He is also saying that it will be easier to bring about this revolution by waging war.

However, we should not allow ourselves to be deceived by Clausewitz's revolutionary choice of words. At this stage of the development of his thought, he supports the idea of a revolution and orients himself strongly towards the 'German nation' as a political subject. But by arguing in this way he is not primarily pursuing national or revolutionary goals as such; rather, he is using them as means to the desired end of military success. From Clausewitz's perspective, the achievements of the French revolutionary armies necessitated a fundamental transformation of the political subject if Prussia (or Germany) was to be able to offer effective resistance to Napoleon and his army, which had so far been victorious in all its battles. Prussia's old army, and its old political structures, would not be able to do this. However, for Clausewitz the apparently total preoccupation with and privileging of military success also places limits on the extent to which man can rise above his normal condition through war and violence, since this process remains tied to the instrumental value of his actions. By way of contrast, no real limits are set to what I call the disinhibition of man through war and violence, as it was envisaged by Ernst Moritz Arndt and Theodor Körner at the time of the wars of liberation, and later by Ernst Jünger and Max Scheler in the First World War and by Frantz Fanon in the period of decolonization in the 1950s and 1960s.[38]

Clausewitz's new ideas, like those of the Prussian military reformers after Jena, were a double-edged sword. As a reaction to Prussian defeats, military reforms were introduced that were simultaneously oriented towards the example provided by the victorious Napoleonic armies and reflections of specific Prussian conditions. The result was a particular kind of tension. On the one hand, the whole of society was to be mobilized to support the waging of war, with the goal of creating a *soldat citoyen* who would always be ready for patriotic action and prepared to sacrifice himself. On the other hand, the political transformation had to remain limited, as there was no intention of doing anything to endanger the existing structure of rule. Prussia did not have a sovereign nation of citizens, and it did not even have a constitution restricting the powers of the monarch and making it possible for the citizens to participate in drawing up legislation. But how could national enthusiasm, and a readiness to sacrifice oneself for the nation state, be brought about in accordance with the French model without the necessary social basis—the equality of all citizens and the opening up of opportunities for them to participate in political life?

The military reforms were therefore self-contradictory, even though there can be no doubt that they contained a lot of positive elements—in particular, the abolition of degrading and inhuman punishments. The only way the reformers could resolve their dilemma, the need to mobilize the whole of society for war without changing any part of the existing social structure, was an 'educational dictatorship' ('Erziehungsdiktatur'). Before the Prussian defeats the army had been an institution where internal brutality, an absence of freedom, and strict separation between different social ranks were the order of the day. The reformers took the view that it needed to become the 'main school of the entire nation', for war and also for peace, as the Minister of War, Herrmann von Boyen, put it in the 1814 Prussian Law on Defence. In taking this step the reformers went much further than requiring the whole nation to serve during the restricted period in which war was actually being waged. From now on, this kind of service was to be a goal in peacetime as well; during which, as is often observed in civilian societies in the aftermath of wars, what were originally secondary effects became the intended goals: the military were supposed to become more civilized, but the nation was to be militarized. The second of these points was understood by Councillor of State von Raumer principally in terms of the 'beneficial sense of order, subordination, and honour' acquired by citizens during their military service also being applied 'in different circumstances'.[39]

However, it would be a mistake to see Clausewitz as a revolutionary. In reality, what the 1809 letter gives expression to, is the contradiction experienced by all conservatives in revolutionary times (as Aron puts it). If the 'raging turmoil among the people' were one day to endanger the King, writes Clausewitz, he would unquestioningly lay down his life for the monarch. He could not hope to delay a revolution or to reverse it by doing this; that would require very different measures, and heroic self-sacrifice would not be enough. But he would do whatever he could, and proudly, to show what sacrifices he was capable of in order to serve his King. At the same time, Clausewitz emphasizes that the King would be lost if he had to rely on such actions. Clausewitz thus continues to manifest unconditional loyalty to the state as embodied in the King, or rather an almost feudal submissiveness to the person of the King. But he also sees clearly the extent of the revolutionary crisis, and it was this that placed him in the reformers' camp.[40] Clausewitz's existential construction of war thus expresses the tension between loyalty to the old order and the revolutionizing of warfare based on the French model. It must also be seen in relation to changes in those areas of politics and society which presented obstacles to military modernization.

1.1.2. Disinhibition of Violence

At one point in *On War*, Clausewitz argues that it is the duty of theory to 'give priority to the absolute form of war and to make that form a general point of reference'. Anyone who wishes to learn something from theory must consider the absolute form of war so that he 'becomes accustomed to keeping that point in view constantly, to measuring all his hopes and fears by it, and to approximating it when he can or when he must' (581). For much of his life, Clausewitz's thought was guided by the idea of a form of war, which would tend to be absolute and extreme as the goal, ideal, and natural course taken by the conduct of war as it at that time was technically possible and socially acceptable. The early Clausewitz understood the expansion of war and the orientation of the conduct of war towards its absolute form as a way of achieving military success.

The tendency towards unrestrained violence, as a method and instrument for the conduct of war, was something Clausewitz saw as justified by the successes of the French revolutionary and Napoleonic armies.[41] John Fuller, in his study of Clausewitz, emphasizes the way in which he (partially) structures his analysis around the idea of the decisive battle, as in the following passages: Fighting is the essence of war (127), and the decisive battle must always be considered the true focal point of war. The direct destruction of the main enemy forces is always the principal objective. The main battle is the bloodiest way to resolve the situation. Clausewitz continues: this battle is more than just reciprocal butchery, and its effects are more a matter of destroying the enemy's courage than of killing enemy soldiers, but blood is always the price that has to be paid. In this passage Clausewitz says that this kind of action is necessary if the battle is to be won, but he goes on to say that as a human being, the commander will recoil from it (259).[42]

In his chapter on the use of battle, Clausewitz introduces a 'dual law': 'destruction of the enemy's forces is generally accomplished by great battles and their results; and, the primary object of great battles must be the destruction of the enemy's forces' (258). 'Just as the focal point of a concave mirror causes the sun's rays to converge into a perfect image and heats them to a maximum intensity, so all forces and circumstances of war are united and compressed to maximum effectiveness in the major battle' (258). And, Clausewitz goes on, 'it is not simply the concept of war that leads us to seek decisive moments only in great battles; the experience of past wars teaches us the same lesson. Bonaparte himself would not have experienced the outstanding success of the Battle of Ulm (20 October 1805) if he had quailed at the prospect of bloodshed earlier.' Clausewitz continues, in a dramatic tone: 'We are not interested in generals who win victories without bloodshed. The fact that slaughter is a horrifying spectacle must make us take war more seriously, but not provide an excuse for gradually blunting our swords in the name of humanity' (260).

The idea of extreme violence as a means of achieving military success is expressed particularly clearly in Clausewitz's treatment of the pursuit of the enemy after a victorious battle. Destroying the enemy by pursuing them is one of the distinctive characteristics of Napoleon's way of waging war. Clausewitz emphasizes that in earlier wars (the cabinet wars of the eighteenth century), commanders were so preoccupied with the honour of victory that they did not pay sufficient attention to the destruction of enemy forces. They saw this as just one method among many, 'certainly not the main, even less the only one. They were only too ready to sheathe their swords as soon as the enemy lowered his.' Nothing seemed to them to be more natural than to stop fighting as soon as the outcome was clear; they saw any further shedding of blood as unnecessarily brutal (265).

Clausewitz disagrees with this, and stresses that no victory on the battlefield can have any great effect unless it is followed by the pursuit and destruction of the enemy. In recent wars, he says, the pursuit of the enemy has become 'one of the victor's main concerns' (266). The energy devoted to this pursuit is the main factor determining the value of the victory, and in many cases is even more important than the actual victory on the battlefield. As it is pursued, the defeated army suffers a disproportionate level of sickness and exhaustion, and its spirit is so weakened and worn down by constant worry about being lost that it is no longer able to think of resisting effectively. With every day that passes in this pursuit, thousands of soldiers are taken prisoner without any further blows being struck. The aim of pursuit is the destruction of the enemy, especially of his order and morale.[43] What Clausewitz means here is not the physical destruction of the enemy, but the attempt to reduce him to such a state of disintegration that he will not be able to undertake further military action. Clausewitz explains that whenever he uses the phrase 'destruction of the enemy's forces', he means that 'the fighting forces ... *can no longer carry on the fight*' (90, emphasis in original).

There is a reciprocal relationship between the disintegration that sets in when armies are in flight and the increase in military capacities on the pursuers' side. Even if the organized pursuit of an army cannot be compared directly with the behaviour of a pack of hunting hounds, some of the psychological and especially the moral effects are analogous. The decisive point is that flight atomizes social relations on the side of those being pursued, while the hunt multiplies the military potential of the pursuing army. Both the pursuing pack and the pursuers in war appear invulnerable to attack, and they have from the start the advantages of movement and surprise, particularly at night. The violence of the pursuing army is above all the violence of speed, and time is its most important weapon. Pursuing packs think only of attack and the offensive; they have no thought of retreat or defence. The pursuers gain more and more ground on the pursued, and as they get closer to their quarry their feeling of shared power grows. The hunters are eager for success, for the moment that seems to mean absolute freedom for them. It seems as though the impending triumph is casting its spell over them. As the pursuers gain ground on their quarry, the more their energy and eagerness for the kill increase; at the same time the exertions of fight exhaust the courage, strength, and ability to resist of the pursued.[44]

One can see these psychological effects at work with particular clarity in the report of an eyewitness who saw the heavy losses suffered by the remnants of Napoleon's army as it retreated across the Berezina:

> When I arrived at the bridge, I found a scene of dreadful confusion. Many thousands of... stragglers, having heard the sound of the cannon, were now flowing towards the crossing in a mighty stream. There was such a crush that the bridge soon became nothing more than a path over the dead and dying.... Among the crowd of troops squeezed together so closely, I saw men crushed, falling down only to be trampled ruthlessly into the muddy ground of the bank by the masses pressing behind them. Horses and men who had tried to swim across or to cross via the ice floes, and who had managed to reach the bank, struggled to get out, in some cases in vain, and met their deaths there in the swamp.[45]

Clausewitz's commentary on this experience is as follows: 'continuous, uninterrupted flight' is the main action leading to the disintegration of the enemy: 'Nothing is more repugnant to a soldier than hearing the enemy's guns yet again just as he is settling down to rest after a strenuous march. This sensation, repeated day after day, can lead to absolute panic' (267). As Clausewitz put it after Jena in his description of Napoleon's strategy: it is only the pursuit and destruction of fleeing armies that transforms battlefield successes into truly great victories.

Despite this bloodthirsty language, the early Clausewitz still sees extreme violence as a rational instrument and a way to conduct victorious war. The instrumental aspect of this conception also sets immanent limits to escalation, since it must lead to military success. Even though this limitation is only a weak one, and in moral terms quite inadequate, it was probably the reason why Clausewitz later treated war's tendency towards escalation as the antithesis of its limitation. The subordination of the scale of violence to the criterion of military success relativized Clausewitz's attitude towards Napoleonic warfare at the very moment when the latter's strategy of ever-expanding violence ceased to bring him success.

1.1.3. The Primacy of the Attack

Clausewitz believed that the essential elements in the Prussian defeats were not just the mistakes and cowardice of Prussia's political leadership and the numerical superiority of the French; Napoleon's military genius was vital too. In order to identify differences between the possibilities available for the conduct of war at the time of Frederick the Great and in his own time, he says in Book VIII of *On War* (that is to say, in a later part of the whole text) that the opponent against whom Austria and Prussia fought was the 'god of war', in the form of Napoleon. Initially, the view among military strategists (especially the Prussians) of Napoleon's way of waging war was that it was successful, but at the same time simply crude and, above all, lacking in artistry. Only after the crushing defeats at Jena and Auerstedt did these circles realize what gave Napoleon the decisive advantage over all his opponents: the unprecedented force of his offensives, the speed and astonishing boldness of his operations, his striving always to concentrate overwhelming force at the decisive point of the battle, and his way of planning a whole campaign so that it would be decided by one destructive battle, after which the defeated enemy would immediately be pursued until his forces had completely disintegrated.[46]

There is a direct connection between the unleashing of violence and the orientation towards the primacy of the attack. Clausewitz argues that the best strategy consists of always being very strong. This rule is generally valid, but it is particularly applicable to the decisive point of battle. There is, says Clausewitz, no higher or simpler law of strategy than the requirement that a commander should keep his forces together. He supports Napoleon's principle that an army can never be too strong at the decisive point. The law he seeks to develop states, he says, that all forces to be used in pursuit of a strategic goal should be employed simultaneously. This use of force will be all the more absolute if everything is concentrated in one action and one moment (194–7).

1.1.4. The Primacy of Military Force Over Policy

In his interpretation of Clausewitz's letter to Fichte, Peter Paret argues that Clausewitz and Fichte agreed with each other, and differed from their contemporaries, in their analysis of the specific situation relating to Prussia's defeat at the hands of Napoleon and the French armies. They were both convinced that Niccolò Machiavelli's writings could open the eyes of a generation they considered blind and corrupt to the primacy of violence, including military force, in political life.[47]

Clausewitz criticizes those parts of Prussian society which, he believed, had advocated a policy of appeasement towards Napoleon both before and after the Prussian defeats. He attacks large parts of the court and the public: many believed in the need for submission, in the hope that the victors would show mercy, and some people were so impudent that they placed most value on their own security and their right to enjoy their bourgeois property in peace, being prepared to sacrifice the King's rights, honour, and freedom if this could be guaranteed. But anyone who did not believe that the most shameful form of submission was a duty, and held instead that this was dishonourable, was seen as a traitor by the most distinguished circles of society, of which the court and state officials were the most corrupt.[48]

Clausewitz also says that if he must reveal the 'most secret thoughts' of his soul, he is in favour of using the most violent methods possible: 'I would use lashes of the whip to arouse the animal from its lethargy, so that the chain it has allowed to be placed upon it in such a cowardly and timid way would be shattered. I would set free in Germany a spirit that would act as an antidote, using its destructive force to eradicate the scourge that threatens to cause the decay of the entire spirit of the nation.'[49] Clausewitz and Fichte, pointing out that Napoleon had demonstrated the superiority of military power over inadequately armed ideals, placed this in the context of Machiavelli's 'timeless statement' that this was the very essence of politics.[50] However, an orientation towards the primacy of military power presupposes a definite (and limited) concept of policy: that of policy conceived in civil terms, something fundamentally different from military force.[51] This limited concept of politics emerges from Clausewitz's criticism of Prussia's earlier policy of neutrality, which he thought practically reduced politics to diplomacy.

Let us summarize the argument so far. The Prussian defeats at Jena and Auerstedt led Clausewitz to develop four ideas which constitute some of the central elements of the early phase of his theory of war. These were conditioned by Napoleon's success and military genius, and can be characterized as follows: an existential conception of war; the inherently unlimited violence of war; an orientation towards the primacy of the attack at all costs; and, in Clausewitz's early writings, the prioritization of military success over ideals and politics (understood in civilian terms). Overall, one can say that the Prussian defeats prompted Clausewitz to develop an approach that broke through a variety of previously conventional theoretical limits. The existential construction of war necessitates a transformation of the war-waging subject, and so is politically disinhibiting. The orientation towards the decisive battle necessitates an acceptance of extreme violence, and the absolute privileging of military success necessitates the orientation towards the attack at all costs.

1.2. MOSCOW: THE TURNING POINT

With regard to the failure of Napoleon's Russian campaign in 1812, Clausewitz drew quite different conclusions than those he had derived from the Prussian defeats at Jena and Auerstadt. There was no fundamental difference between Napoleon's strategy in Russia and the one he had employed in earlier campaigns. In Clausewitz's view, Napoleon had wanted to wage and win the war in Russia in the same way as he had always waged it: commencing with decisive blows, using the advantage thus gained in order to strike further blows, and using the winnings to stake everything repeatedly on one card until he had broken the bank—this was Napoleon's way of waging war. We must recognize, writes Clausewitz that without this way of waging war Napoleon would not have enjoyed the enormous success he had had in the world.[52]

However, the decisive factor in the case of the Russian campaign was that the enemy behaved quite differently. It was difficult to engage in a decisive battle against an opponent who sought to avoid fighting any kind of battle. Secondly, Russia's almost limitless space presented an insuperable obstacle to Napoleon's strategy.[53] Clausewitz stresses repeatedly that from the purely military point of view, Napoleon's strategy of seeking to destroy the Russian army, occupy Moscow, and then negotiate with Tsar Alexander had been correct.[54] But the Russian army's evasive actions, its scorched earth tactics, and the great spaces of Russia meant that Napoleon's army perished as a result of its own efforts.

In Clausewitz's opinion, Napoleon's campaign in Russia did not fail because he advanced too far and too fast, but because the only methods that could have brought success failed. The Russian Empire is not a country that can be conquered in the conventional way, writes Clausewitz in Book VIII. A country like Russia can only be vanquished as a result of its own weakness and the effects of internal divisions. Clausewitz argues that Napoleon could only hope to shake the courage of the Russian government and the loyalty and steadfastness of its soldiers if he could reach Moscow. In Moscow, Napoleon hoped to find 'peace', and this was the only rational war aim he could set himself (627).

Napoleon did reach Moscow, but in what circumstances! In Clausewitz's view, he could only have attained peace if a further condition had been met: he would have had to continue to inspire dread in Moscow. As Clausewitz's account relates, though, Napoleon's army took over 12 weeks to march from Kovno to Moscow, a distance of no more than 115 miles. Of the 280,000 soldiers who started the campaign only 90,000 reached Moscow. Clausewitz argues that if Napoleon had taken better care of his army the losses would have been much lower. But an army of only 90,000 men in Moscow, with exhausted soldiers and worn out horses, with a hostile army of 110,000 men on its right flank and surrounded by a people in arms, forced to set up defences facing in all directions, without magazines and with insufficient stores of ammunition, connected with the outside world by a single, completely devastated road—a French army in this condition and situation could not survive the Russian winter in Moscow.[55]

There had surely been no other case, wrote Clausewitz, in which 'the evidence is so clear that the invader was destroyed by his own exertions' (385). But if Napoleon was unsure whether he would be able to hold his ground through the whole winter in Moscow, he should have returned to France before the onset of winter. As Clausewitz saw it, Napoleon's retreat was inevitable from the moment when Tsar Alexander refused to sue for peace. The whole campaign had been based on the assumption that he would do so (167).[56] However, the devastating fire in Moscow symbolized more dramatically than anything else the fact that peace could not be found there. The sight of Moscow in flames is seen as a symbol of the vanity of the hope that peace could be found there, regardless of whether the Russian government planned to set fire to the city deliberately or the Cossacks did so unintentionally.[57]

The Russian campaign demonstrated in the most vivid way imaginable the superiority of defence over attack, as Clausewitz emphasized repeatedly from this moment on. Every attack loses impetus as it progresses, as he put it in the final words of one of his last texts (71). The superiority of Russian defensive operations led him to qualify his previous view of the exemplary character of Napoleon's strategy, because the offensive way of waging war he had also employed in the Russian campaign was, in Clausewitz's view, correct as far as it went—but it was not the right strategy now that Russia, rather than Prussia or Austria, was the opponent. It was true that the offensive had been considered at the beginning of the Russian campaign to be a 'true *Arcanum*', the holy of holies in the waging of war, because the French had been victorious everywhere as they advanced and were constantly on the offensive. However, Clausewitz analyses the Russian campaign as follows: 'Anyone who thinks this matter through carefully will say to himself that attack is the weaker form of war and defence the stronger form. He will also see, though, that the former is the positive form, that is to say the greater and more decisive, and that the latter has only negative purposes; this brings about a balance, and makes it possible for the two forms to exist alongside one another.'[58]

This change in Clausewitz's assessment of Napoleon becomes especially clear in one of his late texts, where he no longer sees the boundless violence in Napoleon's strategy as a consequence of his genius; he now treats it as a strategy Napoleon had to resort to in an emergency, an indication of his tendency to 'gamble'. The exceptional circumstances in which France and Bonaparte had found themselves had made it possible to 'overthrow the enemy' and to render him defenceless almost everywhere and on every occasion. And so the idea developed of treating the plans that had arisen on this basis, and the execution of those plans, as the general norm. But this amounted to a summary dismissal of the entire history of war up until that point, and that in turn would be foolish.[59]

One must, of course, ask why Clausewitz neglected historical conditions to some degree when he derived abstract general guidelines for successful warfare from Napoleon's campaigns, and so made these campaigns the link between quite contrasting positions on the universal value of war as an instrument. This explains why so many different people have admired Clausewitz—German generals, Lenin, Hitler, Mao Zedong, and American strategists. Another problem in Clausewitz's writings seems to be that he does not always distinguish between general and historically conditioned criteria in warfare.[60] For this very reason, the development in his assessment of Napoleon is particularly significant.

The tension within Clausewitz's assessment of Napoleon can be seen in the final words of his account of the Russian campaign: 'We repeat, everything that he was he owed to his daring and resolute character; and his most triumphant campaigns would have suffered the same censure as this one had they not succeeded.'[61] Clausewitz finds that Napoleon conducted this campaign as he had conducted all his others. This was how he had made himself the master of Europe, and it was the only way he could have achieved this. Anyone who had admired Bonaparte in all his earlier campaigns as the greatest of commanders should not, therefore, look down on him now. Clausewitz's positive appreciation of Napoleon's achievements must be seen in the context of the fact that in the course of the Russian campaign Napoleon and his army were not really defeated in a single skirmish or battle: 'in every battle the French were victorious; in each they were allowed to achieve the impossible—but when we come to the final reckoning, the French army has ceased to exist.'[62]

Clausewitz continues to admire Napoleon's military genius. At the same time, he realizes that even this genius cannot be successful under all conditions: 'It could not be foreseen with certainty, it was perhaps not even likely, that the Russians would abandon Moscow, burn it down, and engage in a war of attrition; but once this happened the war was bound to miscarry, regardless of how it was conducted.'[63] Clausewitz's later thought, and his hesitant abandonment of the view that Napoleon's strategy was exemplary, reflects the tension between his continued admiration for Napoleon and his insight into the inevitable variability and historical specificity of strategy, which was the consequence of these very defeats: In fact, Clausewitz (and many later Germans) always remained under Napoleon's spell, and he never realized that there was a contradiction between his own definition of military genius and Napoleon's genius: Napoleon lacked the higher virtue needed by a statesman.[64]

According to Clausewitz, the strategy derived from Jena and from Napoleon's early successes reached its limits for the first time in Moscow. After Jena, Clausewitz initially put forward an existential notion of war. In this conception, the transformation of the political subject, the modernization of the army, and limited changes in Prussian political conditions were supposed to provide the means by which warfare could be waged successfully. The new way of waging war Clausewitz envisaged was modelled on the example of Napoleon, but it was the limitations of this very model of warfare that were revealed in Moscow. The decisive factor was that conditions were different in Russia, and so the strategy Napoleon had employed so successfully up to that point failed there.

This had two consequences for Clausewitz's theory. Firstly, he recognized that Napoleon's strategy could not be applied in all conceivable circumstances and that it was not a passport to success in general. Secondly, he begins—despite his admiration for Napoleon—to criticize him for sticking to the established strategy in spite of the changed circumstances and trying to bend fate to his will. What Clausewitz had formerly seen purely as Napoleon's genius, he now re-evaluates as thoughtlessness and negligence. He concedes that Napoleon's goal of defeating and dispersing the Russian army and occupying Moscow was a feasible objective for a campaign, but in order to achieve this something else would have been needed: sufficient strength in Moscow. However, Bonaparte had neglected this, 'solely out of the arrogant recklessness that was characteristic of him'. Napoleon had had 90,000 men in Moscow when he needed 200,000. This would have been possible if he had treated his army with more care and had not been so wasteful of its strength. Napoleon would have lost some 30,000 fewer men in battle 'had he not taken the bull by the horns every time'.[65]

Moscow confronts Clausewitz with experiences that are diametrically opposed to those of Jena. The most conspicuous lesson of the Russian campaign is the superiority of the defence to the attack. A less obvious lesson, but one that is fully developed and repeatedly stressed by Clausewitz in his later writings, is the primacy of policy over warfare. The Russian campaign could not have been won, however it might have been waged. With these words, Clausewitz draws attention to a fundamental limit of warfare. Under the circumstances of the time Russia could not be militarily defeated, not by any conceivable strategy and not even by Napoleon. It is true that in later years, Clausewitz returned repeatedly to the subject of the conditions under which Russia could in fact have been defeated (especially in Book VIII of *On War*). However, these reflections seem to have been prompted by the possibility of war between Prussia and Russia and thoughts about Prussia's prospects of success, rather than by any renewed change of mind on Clausewitz's part about the significance of politics for warfare in the light of the limits of what was militarily possible. While the Prussian defeats had demonstrated the superiority of military force to 'inadequately armed ideals' and to politics in the form of diplomacy, what happened in Moscow was that the limits of attempts to achieve political goals by military means became clear. It was this experience of the immanent limits of even Napoleon's strategy that made it possible for Clausewitz to develop a new basic idea of his theory, the primacy of policy over warfare.

1.3. WATERLOO: MORE THAN THE FINAL BATTLE

In his study of the 1815 campaign, Clausewitz places Waterloo on a par with Jena as an example of the complete destruction of an army on a large scale (Waterloo was known in Germany as the Battle of Belle-Alliance).[66] 'Jena and Belle-Alliance show that any sort of regular retreat becomes impossible if one fights to the last against a superior foe' (272). This time, though, it was not the Prussian army that was defeated but Napoleon himself, the victor of Jena and the personified god of war. Here too, a conception of the world collapsed—this time the unconditional belief in Napoleon's military genius. 'Thus the people's trust in the intelligence that led them collapsed along with the military system that was supposed to secure the borders of France.' Clausewitz stresses that no victory has ever had greater moral force than that of Waterloo, which led directly to Napoleon's abdication.[67]

What was the significance of Napoleon's comprehensive and final defeat at Waterloo for the lessons Clausewitz had drawn from his victories? What were the consequences for the lessons of Jena as they had related to his existential understanding of war, the expansion of violence, the primacy of the attack, and the primacy of military force over civilian politics?

Clausewitz argues that after Jena, different armies had come to wage war in very similar ways. In the 'current wars of civilized nations' there were no great differences any more, neither between the armed forces, nor their conduct of warfare, so the differences in numbers between them would be much more decisive than hitherto.[68] Clausewitz's analysis of the growing similarity between ways of waging war even extends to a criticism of Napoleon for failing to be sufficiently true to his own principles when pursuing the Prussian army. He also praises Blücher and Gneisenau for their pursuit of the French army, which he sees as the realization of Napoleon's original way of waging war.[69] Overall, Clausewitz criticizes and defends Napoleon in equal measure, but there is one exception. He starts by explaining Napoleon's defeat in terms of the political circumstances, but then goes on to the analysis of a fundamental error made by Napoleon. This leads to a decisive revision of Clausewitz's theory.

1.3.1. The Significance of the Domestic and External Political Circumstances

According to Clausewitz's analysis, the growing similarities between the two sides' ways of waging war mean that other, non-military factors are able to exert greater influence on the conduct of war. The most important factors contributing to Napoleon's defeat were, he argues, France's domestic and external political circumstances, which decided in advance the outcome of the campaign and of the Battle of Waterloo. In terms of foreign policy, the French army was confronted—as in the Battle of Leipzig—by a coalition of the leading states of Europe. In addition, because of domestic political circumstances, Napoleon did not dispose of anything like the resources he later claimed (in his memoirs) to have had, and could only rely on the veterans of his earlier campaigns.[70]

Because his army of veterans was experienced in battle, Napoleon had some advantages over Blücher's army and the British forces under Wellington, both of which consisted in part of inexperienced militia regiments.[71] However, this advantage by no means compensated for the French army's significant inferiority to the allied forces, which was a consequence of his domestic political weakness. Clausewitz even goes so far as to accept Napoleon's own argument to the effect that a defensive war was out of the question for domestic political reasons, and the only course of action open to him was an offensive outside French territory.[72]

The military outcome too was decided in advance by considerations relating to foreign policy. At the time of his early victories Napoleon had faced individual states, which he could defeat one after the other; now, though, France was being attacked by a coalition made up of Britain,

Prussia, Austria, and Russia. The armies of these states had not yet all been brought together, but in military terms the Battle of Waterloo was decided by the numerical superiority of the British and Prussian troops fighting together against Napoleon. It was the external political conditions that decided the balance of forces between the sides engaged on the battlefield, and so structurally predetermined the outcome of the Battle of Waterloo in circumstances where the two sides were waging war in similar ways.

In his summary, Clausewitz initially stresses the consequences of the battle. He then goes on directly to state his view of the general primacy of policy over the waging of war, the view we then find in Book VIII and Chapter 1 of *On War*. He sees the causes of Napoleon's total defeat in 1815 in the influence of political elements which pervade all wars to a greater or lesser extent, but which affected this particular war much more strongly and proved to be very much to Napoleon's disadvantage. The conclusion Clausewitz draws is that war can never be regarded as an independent phenomenon; it is only a modification of political intercourse, a way of pursuing political interests, and carrying out political plans 'by means of fighting'.[73] As far as I know, Clausewitz emphasized the primacy of politics in such an accentuated manner for the first time in his analysis of the campaign of 1815 and Napoleon's final defeat at Waterloo.

1.3.2. Napoleon's Mistake: His Inability to Limit Defeat

Clausewitz does not, however, argue that the only causes of Napoleon's total defeat were the unfavourable political circumstances and the fact that the military capacities of the two sides had come to resemble each other. Napoleon also made a mistake that had grave consequences. After criticizing individual aspects of Napoleon's plans and the measures he adopted, but defending their essential features, Clausewitz comes to his decisive point of criticism: after the outcome of the battle had already been decided and all had been lost, Napoleon continued to fight.

He used up his last reserves in a hopeless attempt to reverse the tide of the battle, and in so doing brought about the destruction of his entire army: 'It may be that Napoleon has never made a greater mistake.'[74] After it had become clear that there was no longer any possibility of victory, it was

Napoleon's duty to use part of his reserves to engage the Prussian army; this would have made it possible for the main part of the French army to gain ground for its retreat, which it could then have begun immediately while covered by the rest of the reserves.

'The battle was lost, perhaps a true defeat could no longer be avoided, but for Bonaparte's subsequent dealings it clearly made an enormous difference whether, defeated by a superior force, he left the battlefield at the head of a still-undefeated remnant that fought on bravely, or came home as a true fugitive, burdened with the reproach of having led his whole army to destruction and then left it in the lurch.'[75] Napoleon had sacrificed his reserves in the search for a victory that was no longer possible, and so had failed to cover his own retreat. This made it possible for the Prussians to pursue the French army as it withdrew during the following night, and to destroy it. Napoleon's own principles for the successful conduct of warfare were now applied by his opponents, and he did not have sufficient insight to incorporate this possibility into his calculations and to prepare himself to meet it.

Instead of just losing a battle, Napoleon lost his entire army and returned to Paris like a beggar, without any further power resources. Clausewitz goes on to say that a commander who reacts to the slightest shift to his disadvantage by retreating cautiously will not win many battles, and that many victories are only gained by endurance and summoning up the army's last resources of strength. But even so, he writes, criticism has the right to demand that the commander should not seek for the impossible 'and sacrifice to this impossibility forces that can be better used elsewhere'.[76]

Apart from the question of whether these criticisms of Napoleon are historically justified, and that of whether alternative courses of action really were open to him (to which only a speculative answer can be given), there is one aspect that is of decisive importance for the political theory of war. The crux of Clausewitz's criticism of Napoleon is that he failed to keep his military defeat within limits, and that by adhering to the strategy of unleashing violence and seeking a decision at any price he destroyed his entire army and ruined himself. In Clausewitz's view, it was exactly the same military strategy, exactly the same behaviour, which had hitherto provided the basis for Napoleon's victories and political successes that now led to his downfall. Clausewitz assesses Napoleon's actions at the end of the Battle of Waterloo as those of a 'desperate gambler, indifferent to all rational calculations'.[77]

It is pointless to speculate about whether one can criticize someone like Napoleon, who owed all his successes to a specific strategy, for remaining true to that strategy right up to the end of his life. However, the fundamental conclusion drawn by Clausewitz for his political theory of war was that wars should not only be unleashed for instrumental purposes, but should also be limited.

After Waterloo it becomes very clear that Clausewitz, who had earlier been an advocate of the primacy of great, decisive battles, is now taking a more qualified view. He continues to argue that the destruction of the enemy's forces is always the main priority and the more effective way of waging war, which must take precedence over all other methods. The decisive formulation here, however, is the argument that the extremely high value placed on this destruction 'is balanced by its cost and danger' (97). The danger of seeking a victory in a great, decisive battle is that 'the more intent we are on destroying the enemy's forces, the greater will be the damage if we fail' (97). If the attempt to destroy the enemy forces in one battle fails, Clausewitz sees a danger of self-destruction.

1.4. JENA, MOSCOW, AND WATERLOO IN CLAUSEWITZ'S POLITICAL THEORY

Jena and Auerstedt were, without doubt, the most significant events for Clausewitz: they demonstrated the superiority of the strategies of unleashing violence, the attack, and the decisive battle over the existing belief in the equal status of manoeuvre and giving battle, and also the superiority of military power over policy. In the wake of these changes, Clausewitz developed an existential construction of war according to which the state, as the actor waging war, should be replaced by the nation and the people, as had happened in France. The fundamental change in Clausewitz's thought began with Moscow. The superiority of the defence over attack, the military value of avoiding a decisive battle, and his realization of the immanent limits to what could be achieved by military action at least suggested that policy should be accorded primacy over the military aims. Waterloo in turn demonstrated the primacy of policy in a situation where the two sides were waging war in very similar ways, and at the same time the negative side of Napoleon's strategy of unrestrained violence, which—as could now be seen—had led to self-destruction.

Once Clausewitz had drawn from this battle the conclusion that Napoleon should have tried to limit his defeat, it was not difficult to take the next step and begin to treat strategies for limiting wars as no less important than Napoleon's strategy of maximum force. As we have already seen in connection with the conclusions Clausewitz came to after Moscow, even after Waterloo his attitude to Napoleon remained a mixture of admiration and criticism. One can still see traces of this contradictory assessment of Napoleon in the concept of war Clausewitz uses in Book VIII of *On War*, where he speaks of the antithesis between absolute war as an ideal and real war (579–81).

We can therefore identify four fundamental antitheses in Clausewitz's theory, which were based on his experience and examination of war campaigns and can be found in his analyses of Jena, Moscow, and Waterloo: the expansion or limitation of violence, the existential as opposed to the instrumental understanding of war, the primacy of military force or policy, and the priority of the attack as against the superiority of the defence. We must, of course, distinguish between the chronology of Jena, Moscow, and Waterloo as historical events and Clausewitz's interpretation of these events. The Battle of Jena in 1806, the turning point of the Napoleonic Wars in Moscow in 1812, and Waterloo, Napoleon's final battle, in 1815, belong to a period in which Clausewitz was himself on active military service and had hardly any time to work on his theory of war. The interpretation of Jena can be pieced together from Clausewitz's correspondence of the time and, in its essentials, from the early parts of *On War*—Book III on strategy, and Book IV on the engagement as well from his late analysis: 'From observations on Prussia in her great catastrophe' (1823–5).[78] The interpretation of Moscow and Waterloo, on the other hand, is to be found in Clausewitz's later work.

During 1823 and 1824 Clausewitz devoted himself once again to the analysis of the disaster of Jena, as mentioned above. During 1824 and 1825 he wrote his history of the Russian campaign, and during 1827 and 1828 the history of the 1815 campaign and the decisive Battle of Waterloo. It is highly likely that there is a direct connection between the theoretical shift that took place in Clausewitz's work during the 1827–30 period and the analysis of these three campaigns, since that analysis was carried out in 1823–7 and so directly precedes and accompanies the theoretical shift. Clausewitz's intention to revise his work, which he announced in his author's note of July 1827, was directly related to two of the points just mentioned—the primacy of policy over war and Clausewitz's change of mind about the exemplary function of Napoleon's way of waging war, since the treatment of the two forms of war (war to render your enemy powerless or limited war) places them alongside one another and gives them equal status (69–70).

Jena, Moscow, and Waterloo conditions different stages of *On War*. Books III and IV, on strategy and the engagement, and especially the chapters in Book IV on the battle, belong to the Jena stage. Book VI is completely dominated by the idea of the superiority of the defence, which is characteristic of Clausewitz's reflections on Moscow. Book VIII, on the other hand, attempts after Waterloo to present the expansion and limitation of war as principles enjoying equal status. After he had completed the analysis of the three campaigns symbolized by Jena, Moscow, and Waterloo, Clausewitz began to revise his entire work on the basis of the insights he had reached. Jena, Moscow, and Waterloo symbolize the antitheses of Clausewitz's political theory of war, and his fundamental reflections on these questions are to be found in Chapter 1 in which Clausewitz developed a synthesis of his diverse experiences of war and made the antitheses within these experiences into the constitutive basis of his theory of war.

2

Violence, Fear, and Power: The Expansion and Limitation of War

> It is his ambivalence, the way in which incompatible postulates merge with one another within one overall body of thought that makes Clausewitz so fascinating to us and makes his ideas so attractive. It also gives us the certainty that he has observed very carefully, and has not forced his observations into a pattern so that they conform to a particular view of the world.
>
> Wilfried von Bredow and Thomas Noetzel[79]

According to Clausewitz, the 'three interactions to the extreme' of war are the most important factors accounting for the escalation and expansion of war. In his exposition of one of the three interactions, he expresses this as follows: 'war is an act of force, and there is no logical limit to the application of that force' (77). What Clausewitz says about the interactions to the extreme provides the basis for the assumption that he is the theorist of destruction and the precursor of the idea of total war. Since the three interactions are to be found in Chapter 1 of Book I of *On War*, which is indeed the only book Clausewitz later considered finished, a problem of interpretation arises.

In my previous chapter, I responded to Clausewitz's critics by saying that it was only the Clausewitz of Jena who advocated the unleashing of escalatory war, but this seems to be contradicted by the fact that the three interactions to the extreme appear in Chapter 1, which was written last. However, Chapter 1 must be seen as Clausewitz's attempt to bring together the antitheses of Jena, Moscow, and Waterloo. It follows from this that Jena, as the symbol of the expansion of warfare, has its place in Chapter 1, but it is not characteristic of war as a whole.

There are some additional points that have always been overlooked in interpretations of Clausewitz. Firstly, the interactions to the extreme apply only to war aims, not to war as a whole. Secondly, these escalatory interactions are placed in opposition to the three interactions that tend to limit war, which are hardly ever taken into consideration.[80] And thirdly, whatever first appearances may suggest, the concept of war is by no means determined by the three interactions to the extreme alone. In the past, attempts have been made to respond to the arguments of Clausewitz's critics by explaining that the tendency towards the expansion and escalation of war 'to the extreme' only relates to his concept of war. But this proposal created more problems than it solves. Additionally, one must draw attention here to the decisive point that at the end of Chapter 1, Clausewitz also describes the Trinity as his concept of war (89). In this chapter, I do not treat the three interactions to the extreme primarily as a concept of war; rather, I analyse them initially as real problems and tendencies characterizing developments in war.

2.1. THE INTERACTIONS TO THE EXTREME AS ATTEMPTS TO OUTDO THE ENEMY

In the first of the interactions to the extreme, Clausewitz argues that anyone who uses force 'undeterred by the bloodshed it involves' will gain the upper hand in war if the enemy does not do the same (75–6). In this passage, Clausewitz is reflecting on the escalation of warfare by the French Revolution and Napoleon, and also on the further attempts to outdo this unleashing of force in partisan warfare in Spain.

In his 'Political Declaration', Clausewitz partly argues in favour of a strategy of unrestrained violence as a means to the desired end in partisan warfare. The starting point of the argument is the question of what happens if the side fighting with regular troops treats the rebel prisoners with such cruelty that the population no longer has sufficient courage to continue this kind of war. Responding to reservations about the use of this form of warfare, he says that 'it is obvious that we can be just as cruel as the enemy'. The cruel nature of this kind of war works to the disadvantage of the side which has fewer people at its disposal, that is to say the side fighting with standing armies and so unable to deploy the entire population. Clausewitz continues: 'Let us take a chance and repay cruelty with cruelty, reply to acts of violence with more acts of violence! It will be easy to outdo the enemy and to lead him back to the path of moderation and humanity.'[81]

The concept of outdoing the enemy, which is applied here to the concrete situation of partisan warfare, acquires central importance in Clausewitz's later writings. He uses the terms outdoing and interaction as synonyms: 'Thus interaction, the effort to outdo the enemy, the violent and compulsive course of war, all stagnate for lack of real incentive' (604). What does this attempt to outdo the enemy in the use of force mean for the strategy of escalatory warfare?

Clausewitz's statements about outdoing the enemy are particularly instructive as indications of the tensions and internal contradictions within his work. To begin with, they reveal how far Clausewitz the theorist was removed from real events, as we can see a few sections later with particular clarity. Clausewitz argues that there has been a tendency to believe that the use of extreme force involves much greater danger than is in fact the case. In relation to the guerrilla war in Spain, which was one of the models for the Prussian struggle for liberation he advocated, he claims that even there 'things were not as terrible as they were imagined to be'.[82] In fact, Francisco Goya's drawings *Desastres de la guerra* and his painting of the execution of rebels in the 1808–14 Franco–Spanish War prove that force was completely unrestrained in this conflict, and give the lie to the way in which Clausewitz plays down the cruelty of this kind of war.[83]

However, it is also clear that Clausewitz has an instrumental understanding of the unleashing of force and even sees it as a way of restoring a limited, regulated, and professionalized way of waging war. He bases this argument about restoring a regulated form of war on the suggestion that after the first atrocities committed by both sides, the opposing side will be forced to treat the insurgents, the partisans in the same way as the regular combatants. In this passage, Clausewitz seems close to being most concerned about the recognition of the members of the Prussian militia as equal partners in the liberation struggle. He expresses the view that the worst excesses of unrestrained warfare, as had happened in Spain, could be avoided if the Prussian government were to give the protection provided by its authority to every armed man among the Prussian people. The escalation of force could be limited, in Clausewitz's view, if the Prussian government were to threaten to take revenge on prisoners for every atrocity committed against its honourable defenders.[84]

Clausewitz's views on unlimited war have three main aspects, which are partly in tension with one another:

1. As a pure theorist, Clausewitz underestimates the ferocity of war between regular and irregular troops. He underrates both the moral significance of extreme violence and the effects of this kind of warfare on politics and society.[85]
2. Although escalation is used as a way of waging war successfully, it remains restricted by the emphasis upon military success. The escalation of war was not an end in itself for Clausewitz, but a rational method to be used for the purpose of successful warfare. However, if the extreme violence of Napoleonic warfare and, in theory, of any escalatory strategy, could in principle always be outdone and raised to a higher level, it could no longer be useful as a way of waging war. After *Jena* Clausewitz saw escalation as a way of waging war successfully, but in Moscow and in the Spanish partisan war it became clear that such extremism could in turn be outdone, and could not guarantee military success. Cora Stephan makes a similar point when she argues that whoever breaks the rules within a strictly regulated culture of war, such as existed in the eighteenth century, always enjoys the advantage that accrues to the aggressor. However, everyone paid the price in the form of a never-ending spiral of violence.[86] One can make this point even more strongly, since with respect to Napoleon the side that initiated the escalation ended up as one of the heaviest losers, because the other side followed suit and was able to raise the stakes higher still. The same phenomenon occurred in the First and Second World Wars: on each occasion Germany was the first to move up the ladder of escalation, and on each occasion it ended up losing most.
3. Outdoing the enemy by means of partisan warfare is for Clausewitz a 'paradoxical' way of returning war to the limited forms prescribed by custom, professionalization, and mutual respect.

The conclusions Clausewitz draws from the Spanish partisan war remain mixed. He speaks of total war, of outdoing the enemy's use of force as a way of combating a regular army in partisan warfare. At the same time, though, this is supposed to help bring about the exact opposite, returning war to its limited and ritualized forms.

However, this idea of outdoing an earlier escalation does not just refer to the use of force as such. The *levée en masse* declaration during the French Revolution made war into 'the business of the people', and, as Clausewitz puts it, the 'resources and efforts now available for use surpassed all conventional limits' (592). The expansion of war via the revolutionary mobilization of the entire nation removed the distinction between military specialists and ordinary citizens. From 1793 onwards war was all of a sudden an affair of the people, of 30 million people, all of whom considered themselves to be citizens. However, the pressing into service of the whole nation did not yet do away with the distinction between combat troops and the civilian population as such. But it is this very distinction that loses its significance in partisan warfare, because everyone—man or woman, child or old man—is a potential participant in this form of war.

Another thing that is 'outdone', though, is the political restraint operating on the subject who is waging war. Even though the French Revolution removed the personal sovereign and the aristocratic factions and put the people and the nation in their place, war was still being waged by the state. In the Spanish partisan struggle, on the other hand, the state was of secondary importance. In this case there is no longer any kind of unified political subject whatsoever, just decentralized resistance by peasant partisans which derives its virulence from unorganized spontaneity and cruelty. The struggle of the Spanish peasant partisans 'outdoes' war as a struggle between formal political communities and transforms it, at least on one side, into a struggle for the recognition of traditional cultural and social forms of life.

If the unleashing of war and force by the French Revolution and Napoleon could, in principle, be outdone by the spontaneous cruelty of the Spanish partisan struggle and in the war of extermination fought by the Russian army, the expansion of war could no longer, for the later Clausewitz, be a means that could be employed at any time. The unrestrained violence of the partisan struggle is not something that can be easily instrumentalized.

In the three interactions to the extreme, Clausewitz addresses the final consequences that follow from the attempt to outdo the enemy. If the way in which the French revolutionaries and Napoleon, the 'god of war', waged war was characterized by extremities of violence when compared with warfare in the earlier part of the eighteenth century, it was still not absolutely, completely unlimited. Initially, it was outdone in the partisan struggle and in the Russian army's war of extermination against the French troops. At that time, no one could yet imagine the catastrophes of the First and Second World Wars, the Holocaust, or the overkill capacities of the nuclear age. However, one of Clausewitz's own decisive experiences of war led to his realization that the expansion of warfare that had taken place up to that point could be outdone once again. The treatment of the interactions to the extreme is where Clausewitz addresses this very question, the fact that escalation can always be outdone by the enemy, and can in principle be taken as far as a notionally extreme and absolute point (77).

Clausewitz summarizes the three interactions to the extreme in a few pages, and provides no complete explanation of how this mutual outdoing works. This is why commentators on Clausewitz have usually referred to the concept/reality antithesis, which he deals with in the following section. Clausewitz seems, therefore, to treat escalation to the extreme as something that is restricted to the conceptual sphere. But what is he really saying here? It is clear that in this passage, the extreme is for Clausewitz a notional extreme point. The three interactions to the extreme are a clarification of the way in which any escalation of warfare can be surpassed once again. This process of outdoing the enemy corresponds to the world Clausewitz experienced and the wars of his time. But the extreme as only a logical consequence of unrestrained warfare, on the other hand, is purely notional and abstract. The more decisive categories are the ones Clausewitz identifies as the driving forces of the process of outdoing the enemy—violence, fear, and the striving for power.

2.2. PURPOSE, AIM, AND MEANS IN THE THREE INTERACTIONS TO THE EXTREME

Clausewitz begins his revised version of Chapter 1, and so the whole book, with a definition in three parts: 'War is thus an act of force to compel the enemy to do our will.' Force is the means used to impose one's will on the enemy, and this is the (political) purpose of war; disarming the enemy is the actual aim of military action. Immediately after this definition of war, Clausewitz introduces the three interactions to the extreme: firstly 'the maximum use of force', secondly 'disarming' the enemy, and thirdly 'the maximum exertion of strength' (75–7). Because the three interactions to the extreme come immediately after the definition, one might conclude that what Clausewitz is doing here is setting out the consequences of his three-part definition as a whole. But this is not the case.

The three interactions to the extreme refer exclusively to the aim of warfare, the disarming and overcoming (or overthrowing) of the enemy. In the three interactions to the extreme, the (military) aim takes the place of the (political) purpose, and one could say that it pushes the purpose into the background as something that is not part of war itself (75). In all three interactions to the extreme, Clausewitz treats the overcoming of the enemy as the aim of military action. Clausewitz makes this methodological restriction clear when he says that a subject he had left out of section 2, the political purpose of war, is now forcing its way back into consideration (80). If he left the political purpose out up to this point of consideration, it is clear that it can play no role in the three interactions to the extreme.

In the exposition of the second interaction, Clausewitz says: 'So long as I have not overthrown my opponent I am bound to fear that he may overthrow me.' The worst that can happen to someone waging war is that he finds himself in a situation where he is completely unable to defend himself. Disarming or *overcoming* the enemy, whatever one may choose to call it, is always the *aim* of an act of war. Clausewitz also uses the argument about overcoming the enemy in the third interaction to the extreme: 'If you want to overcome your enemy you must match your effort against his power of resistance' (77). 'Overcoming' the enemy is, for Clausewitz, the aim of warfare.

In the three interactions to the extreme, Clausewitz addresses exclusively the question of the aim of the act of war. However, this aim is differentiated further on the basis of the original three-part definition of purpose, aim, and means. In the first interaction, Clausewitz examines the overcoming of the enemy in relation to the consequences that result from the use of force as a means of warfare. In the third interaction, the strength of the enemy's will and his motive for fighting are placed at the centre of the discussion about the consequences of overcoming the enemy.

In the first and third interactions, force as the means, and imposing one's will on the enemy as the political purpose of war, are treated as subordinate aspects of the overcoming and disarming of the enemy, that is to say of the aim of the act of war. What can one say about the second interaction to the extreme? This examines overcoming as such, in its purity and its internal differentiations. Clausewitz begins the exposition of the second interaction by saying that disarming the enemy is the aim of the act of war, and goes on to say that he now wants to show that this is necessary, at least as part of the theoretical argument (77).

In Clausewitz's three interactions to the extreme each part of the initial three-part definition is discussed, but in each case it is the aim of the act of war that remains primary. In all three of the interactions, the intensification to the extreme and to the absolute point of war results from the momentum of each side's attempts to overcome and disarm the other. This means that the extreme point of war, to the extent that it is discussed in the exposition of the three interactions, results not from the totality of the initial definition but exclusively from the isolated treatment of one of its three elements, the aim.

2.3. THE INTERACTIONS TO THE EXTREME—VIOLENCE/FORCE, FIGHT, AND WILL[87]

2.3.1. The First Interaction: 'The Maximum Use of Force'

In the first of the three interactions, Clausewitz argues that there are no limits to the use of force, so each side 'will force the other to follow suit' and drive its opponent towards extremes, the unlimited use of force (76). Mutual escalation in war between two opponents therefore leads to an extreme point. 'That side will force the other to follow suit; each will drive its opponent toward extremes, and the only limiting factors are the counterpoises inherent in war' (76). The restraint exercised by internal counterbalances on a tendency that strives towards infinity can already be found in Fichte's writings on science.[88]

How should we understand Clausewitz's statement to the effect that there are no limits to the use of force? It is certainly not meant to be understood in the moral sense, because Clausewitz never discusses the moral case for or against force and war. However, he in no way justifies or makes the case for any abstract, limitlessness of force; rather, what he does is to examine the escalation of force in his initially isolated treatment of victory and defeat. When one looks at this argument more closely, it is not yet conclusive. Why should an escalation, an intensification to the extreme by means of uninhibited force, result from the sheer desire of each of the two opponents to defeat the other? If both sides do the same thing, this does not necessarily mean that each of them is trying to outdo the other in the use of force.

It is also possible to reach a quite different conclusion: one of the two sides could abandon its aim. An interaction could be derived from this too, but it would lead to de-escalation rather than escalation. After his treatment of the interactions to the extreme, Clausewitz in fact examines three aspects that inhibit this tendency to escalation and which can be understood as 'interactions to limited war' (Münkler). In one of these, he argues that any action that either side may omit because of its weakness becomes a real, objective reason for the other to reduce its efforts, and so the striving towards the extreme is returned via this interaction to a certain more limited level of effort (80). This means that intensification to the extreme cannot be derived from the process of interaction as such.

Clausewitz's argument to the effect that there are no limits to the use of force could, however, be substantiated with the help of the assumption that violence itself involves a removal of inhibition. It is true that both in the initial three-part definition and in the famous formula (war as the continuation of policy by other means), Clausewitz's basic understanding of the use of force in war is an instrumental one. In the first of the three interactions to the extreme, however, he observes that the use of force involves the removal of restraint in itself. The combination of the polarity of the duel and the principle of destruction on both sides, together with the disinhibiting effect of the use of force, leads to a real tendency in war: the intensification towards extreme and limitlessness force.

Disinhibition through force, the transgression of personal and societal limits by violence, has been documented in many different contexts—and not only in recent times. Immanuel Kant captured this aspect of escalatory warfare 200 years ago, when he wrote: 'What is bad about war is that it creates more evil people than it destroys.'[89] One can see the negative consequences of extreme violence, both for individuals and for social groups, very clearly when one looks at the fate of child soldiers in civil wars. Wolfgang Sofsky has provided a striking account of the way in which people are disinhibited by violence. His examples show us the violence of the passions which drive people, the triumph of survival, the sovereignty of transgressing one's own limited identity, and the desire to liberate oneself: 'Violence intensifies itself. Absolute violence requires no justification.... Its only aim is its own continuation and intensification.... It no longer obeys the laws of creative production, of *poiesis*. It is pure *praxis*. Violence for the sake of violence.'[90]

One can trace this disinhibition through force in wars themselves, especially in the First and Second World Wars, and also in the period between them. There is a large amount of literature from this period dealing with war and death. It seems that there was an audience for writing dealing with large-scale death because the survivors were unable to find peace. This death cult was the result of 'a feeling of being lost', despondency, of 'losing oneself' in war, in which civilization's defences against barbarism were torn down and there were no longer any limits to the toleration or exercising of force.[91]

2.3.2. The Second Interaction: 'The Aim Is to Disarm the Enemy'

In the second interaction to the extreme, Clausewitz turns his attention to the question of the polarity of the duel as a zero-sum game: if one of the two opponents wins, the other loses. Escalation is not primarily caused by the intention to destroy the enemy, but by the desire to avoid being destroyed oneself. As long as neither of the two sides has been overthrown, both must fear being overthrown, defeated, and destroyed. From this perspective, it is only the destruction of the enemy that can prevent one's own destruction. In the second interaction to the extreme, the fear of being destroyed before the enemy has been defeated leads to an escalation without limits (77). Dread and the fear of one's own death can lead to a wide variety of forms of violence, all of which have the aim of self-preservation. Usually, one can assume that dread and the fear of one's own death will lead to caution and to greater restraint in war. However, in the second interaction Clausewitz describes how the desire for self-preservation can have precisely the opposite effect, and lead to an intensification of war and to attempts by both sides to outdo the enemy.[92]

One level of the intensification of war to the extreme, for the sake of self-preservation, is individual combat. Unlimited fear of one's own death, the fear of being killed by another person, can in individual combat often only be endured if one kills that other person. This disinhibition is intensified even further when the instinctive and culturally imposed restraints that normally prevent us killing are rendered ineffective by fear of one's own death.[93] In this way the adversary seems to be responsible for the painful way in which one's own inhibitions in relation to killing are overcome in this process. Finally, unlimited anger directed against the immediate opponent wells up, because it is his behaviour that results in the overcoming of one's own inhibitions. One has the subjective impression that it is the opponent who causes one to kill and so is the source of one's own guilt. In the immediate life-and-death struggle, with its blind killing as the result of fear of one's own death, the fury and frenzy of violence exceeds all bounds. On the individual level of the duel, there is a direct antithesis between the first and second interactions to the extreme. In the first interaction it is the individual's disinhibition through force that leads to escalation, whereas in the second it is fear of one's own death that sets in motion the mechanism of outdoing the enemy.

A second level is characterized by fear of the death of one's own community. This community seems to be a comprehensive symbolic *Self*, a symbolic ego, which has formed itself as a community for the purpose of self-preservation. In order to preserve this community, it can be necessary for individuals to risk their lives. In addition, the opponent is seen as a threat to one's own (collective) identity. Fear that the symbolic community will 'die' can lead in this case too to the perception that one's own community can only be kept alive if the enemy community dies. A central factor here is that one's own community is already conceived as something that exists for purposes of self-preservation—as a nation, state, etc. One's own aggression and force can therefore be justified by a threat to the community or the possibility that it might fall apart, because it is the community that is supposed to guarantee the self-preservation of the individuals who belong to it.

If the identity that goes beyond the individual is additionally understood as a religious community, something which has significance beyond the individual's death, a further expansion of force follows from fear of death. In this case, the collective consciousness is supposed to make possible survival in a way that provides meaning, and transcends the individual in a collective conceived in political-religious terms. On this level too, force becomes a raging frenzy, and any kind of cruelty seems to be justified by the 'sacred cause'. This is more than just a life-and-death struggle; it is a struggle over the significance of life and death.[94]

In all three cases, fear of death as an individual or as a political-religious collective leads to a greater willingness to kill. Fear of individual destruction, or of destruction that goes beyond the individual, leads to an automatic escalation of violence, which Clausewitz expresses vividly in the following sentence: 'Thus I am not in control: he [the opponent] dictates to me as much as I dictate to him' (77).

2.3.3. The Third Interaction: 'The Maximum Exertion of Strength'

In the first two interactions there are two identifiable factors which give rise to the tendency towards extreme violence in war: the psychology of force in itself, and fear of defeat, destruction, and death. In the third interaction there is, at first glance, no such unambiguous factor that could explain the intensification to the extreme.[95] Here, Clausewitz examines the consequences that are bound to follow from the principle of destruction and outdoing the enemy by military means in circumstances where both sides want 'the same'. He argues that if we assume a certain level of resistance on the part of our opponent, we must either make our own efforts so great that they will exceed those of the enemy or at least ensure that they are equally great. 'But the enemy will do the same; competition will again result' (77). Even though the analysis here is a brief one, there can be no doubt that this interaction too depicts a real tendency in any violent conflict.

In the third interaction, escalation comes about because each side attempts to impose its will on the other. Clausewitz refers to the power of the opponent's resistance, but this covers both the means at his disposal and the strength of his will (79). Max Weber defined power as 'the possibility of imposing one's own will upon the behaviour of other'. In the definition he provides at the outset, Clausewitz defines war as an act of force committed in order to compel our enemy to do our will. The third interaction to the extreme thus addresses the tendency for war to escalate as a result of two opponents' striving for power.[96]

2.3.4. Fear of Loss of Power in the Second Interaction, as Against the Striving for Power in the Third

Clausewitz's account of the third interaction can be illustrated with the help of Plato's analysis of the causes of the Peloponnesian War. Plato argues that any policy designed as a show of force will, for structural reasons, lead to war. The Peloponnesian War between Athens and Sparta was, according to this analysis, the inevitable result of a dynamic set in motion in Athens by maritime trade. This meant the end of the old customs and the modest principles that had been in operation up until that time, and set in motion a dynamic process of material covetousness that would, in theory, be endless. From this moment on, there was bound to be a struggle between Athens and Sparta for supremacy in Greece. Plato says that the decisive factor, in addition to greed and avarice, was the power struggle between two opponents. This led to a situation in which, when war broke out, neither of the two sides had any freedom to decide or freedom of manoeuvre. As I have shown, Clausewitz expresses this point in the second interaction when he says that neither side is any longer master of its own actions; in other words, they are no longer free in the decisions they take.[97]

There is another comment that can be made in relation to Clausewitz's argument, in the second interaction to the extreme, about the escalation of war and force as a result of fear of destruction. Thucydides, the chronicler of the Peloponnesian War and one of the Ancient world's most important historians, also sees the initial cause of the war in the growth of Athenian power: 'What made war inevitable was the growth of Athenian power and the fear which this caused in Sparta.' Unlike Plato, though, Thucydides argues that it was not the striving for power in itself, but rather fear of loss of power and, in the long term, fear of being oppressed, robbed of one's freedom, and enslaved that caused the competitive interaction leading to war. In Thucydides's account, fear was the cause of war on both sides: Sparta was afraid of the growth of Athenian power, and Athens was afraid of what might happen if it gave in to an escalating series of demands and threats, the end result of which could not be foreseen. Thucydides thought the war was inevitable, not because both sides were pursuing aggressive, expansionist, or imperialist aims but because both governments were afraid of losing power.

According to Clausewitz it is the fear of defeat that sets political-military escalation in motion, while for Thucydides fear of losing power has the same effect. However, Thucydides does not treat the loss of power in an abstract way. In the long term, losing power would mean that Sparta would take away Athens's power and rob the Athenians of their freedom, as long as the Spartans themselves are striving for power.[98] In this respect, Thucydides's analysis operates on two levels. As in Clausewitz's second interaction, it is primarily fear of the destruction of one's own political community as the result of a loss of power that sets off the escalation. At the same time, though, Thucydides's analysis—just like Plato's analysis of the causes of war and Clausewitz's third interaction—sees the dynamics of the striving for power as responsible for the outbreak of war.

2.4. THREE INTERACTIONS LEADING TO THE LIMITATION OF WAR

In the three interactions to the extreme, Clausewitz describes real tendencies in real wars. In the second and third interactions he even goes further and mentions two fundamental causes of war. Clausewitz however, argues that the three interactions only lead to an extreme 'in the field of abstract thought'. One could conclude from this that Clausewitz's concept of war is determined by the three interactions to the extreme, which, however, he says 'would be an abstraction and would leave the real world quite unaffected' (78). The part of the argument that is much more convincing than the straightforward comparison between concept and reality[99] is Clausewitz's treatment of the three *antitheses*, which he contrasts with the three tendencies to the extreme. These are three restraining, 'moderating interactions' (Muenkler) leading to limited war.

Clausewitz sets out these antitheses to the escalating interactions as follows. Real war, he says, would only correspond perfectly to the three interactions to the extreme:

'(a) if war were a wholly isolated act, occurring suddenly and not produced by previous events in the political world;
(b) if it consisted of a single decisive act or a set of simultaneous ones;
(c) if the decision achieved was complete and perfect in itself, uninfluenced by any previous estimate of the political situation it would bring about' (77).

Clausewitz initially accounts for the tendency to limited war in purely negative terms. There are three things which ensure that the extreme point of escalation will not actually be reached. Firstly, 'Man and his affairs, however, are always something short of perfect and will never quite achieve the absolute best.' These shortcomings are to be found on both sides, and therefore constitute a moderating force (78). Secondly, Clausewitz emphasizes that because it is contrary to human nature to make an extreme effort, 'the tendency therefore is always to plead that a decision may be possible later on' (80). Whatever one side omits to do because of its *weakness* will be an objective reason for the other to reduce its efforts. Thirdly, a decision in a battle is also seen as a transitory evil (80). The shortcomings and weaknesses of human beings are thus 'negative' reasons for the tendency towards moderation.

2.4.1. Limitation of War by its Duration

What further conditions for the limitation of war does Clausewitz identify in the three 'moderating interactions'? He says that the two opponents are not unknown to one another. War does not break out wholly unexpectedly, and it cannot 'spread instantaneously' (78). Both sides are able to assess the other by considering the way in which it has acted in the past, not on the basis of the actions that would be dictated by theory. Furthermore, the decision in war does not consist of one single action or several actions occurring simultaneously, but of a set of 'successive acts'. An action that has just been performed is the measure of one's own action, and in this way the striving towards the extreme is moderated. Finally, Clausewitz speaks of the possibility of a later 'remedy', which can moderate the violence of the tension and the intensity of the effort that needs to be made (79–80).

All three criteria relate to the way in which war is embedded in history. Clausewitz's initial explanation of the non-identity of the concept of war and real war distinguishes between concepts and historical development. This connection becomes clear when the three criteria are seen in their relation to the three modes of history—past, present, and future. Clausewitz begins by emphasizing the historical advancement of war, its connection with earlier developments. He then goes on to explain in detail the significance of the duration of the act of warfare (in war, the present is not determined in the Aristotelian way as a brief moment in time that cannot be broken down further, but as something continuous), and finally deals with the repercussions of the (possible or desired) future for the present.

This final train of thought may not seem directly illuminating at first glance, but Clausewitz illustrates it in a very vivid way: the political situation that will ensue after the war affects the way the war is waged because it is part of the warring parties' calculations. As past, present, and future, the duration of the war, and future developments are integrated, certain factors that are not directly part of the concrete war in question become decisive.

Clausewitz argues that wars between 'civilized nations' are much less cruel than those between 'savages'. He bases this judgement on the differences between the respective social conditions within states and in the relations between them. However, these societal determinants are not part of the war itself. The principle of moderation could never be introduced into the theory of war itself without absurdity, says Clausewitz (76). This position means that war would lead to an extreme point if it depended on nothing but its own immanent laws.

The temporal dimension is the connecting link between internal laws and external conditions. By introducing the temporal dimension, Clausewitz departs from a purely internal treatment of war and places it in the context of external determinants. The most important of these are the earlier history of the state and its future political condition. In the extensive treatment of the second moderating interaction, a number of other determinants are noted. Here, Clausewitz refers to the imperfect organization of humanity and the impossibility of summoning up and exerting all one's strength at the same time. He says that it is in the very nature of these forces, and the way they are used, that they cannot all come into operation at the same time.

These forces are: the fighting forces proper, the country with its physical features and population, and the state's allies. These factors also explain the temporal dimension of war. In this context, Clausewitz also mentions space, 'the country, with its physical features' (79) as a reason why moderation is possible. Strictly speaking, though, the effects of space are only indirect, in the sense that the opposing forces cannot all go into action simultaneously, so time remains the immediate reason for moderation.[100]

The very early Clausewitz nevertheless makes the point that he thinks time is of very little significance for warfare. In his later writings, the duration of military action and time become the decisive elements in the limitation of the three interactions to the extreme of force. In an early draft of *On War*, he argues that it is self-evident that time is irrelevant to the act of warfare.[101] This point, the question of what time has to do with the way in which war is waged, is the very issue Clausewitz addresses in his treatment of the three moderating interactions. In Chapter 1, Clausewitz also explains how an interruption of military activity can come about during a war. He argues that the possibility of inaction introduces a new moderation into the act of warfare. As Clausewitz puts it in his crucial formulation, 'the possibility of inaction has a further moderating effect on the progress of the war by diluting it, so to speak, in time' (85).

2.4.2. The Individual Duel and the Duel on a Larger Scale

As the temporal dimension is introduced, the external conditions of war come to the fore. War is a 'duel on a larger scale', rather than an individual duel. Even before he provides his actual definition of war, Clausewitz says: 'War is nothing but a duel on a larger scale' (75). What are the differences between an individual duel and a duel on a larger scale?

The development of Clausewitz's argument in Chapter 1 of *On War* can be seen as a progressive differentiation between the duel in the strict sense and war as a duel on a larger scale. This extension of the duel has two aspects. The first of these is the category of time, but there is a second aspect which can in turn be divided into three parts: the material means of waging war; the fact that this duel takes place between states rather than individuals; and the fact that the war occurs in certain political conditions.

Let us examine first of all the differences between war as a duel on a larger scale and the individual duel. These are described as follows:[102]

- War expresses hostile intentions, whereas the duel expresses hostile feelings.
- Up until now there has hardly been a case in which a war has consisted of a sole armed clash, while the duel is a single encounter in which everything depends on only one moment.
- In war the overall result is what matters, not the fate of any individual, whereas in the duel the individual's fate is the decisive factor.
- Because of its geographical extension and the large numbers of people and masses of material involved, war cannot spread instantly, so that it is not possible for there to be fighting everywhere at the same time; the duel, on the other hand, is fought at a moment's notice, with all available weapons and against all the vulnerable parts of the body—a single blow can mean victory or defeat and can even cause death.
- War never occurs all of a sudden, because the enemy is known as a neighbour or as someone from the past, whose behaviour is reasonably predictable; a duel, however, often happens out of the blue, and the opponent is just as frequently unknown, so that in these cases neither his strength nor his willingness to fight can be assessed in advance.
- The outcome of a war is never absolute—as a continuation of policy by other means, its results are modified by the policy that follows; the result of an (individual) duel, on the other hand, can be final for the party that is under attack and can end in death.

In the secondary literature on Clausewitz, insufficient attention has been paid so far to the question of what changes as a result of the extension of the duel and of the distinction between the individual and the communal duel. Clausewitz argues that the main factor which accounts for the transition from the interactions to the extreme to the interactions to limited war is the duration of the war. The temporal aspect of war is also decisive for the distinction between the individual and the extended duel. If we follow Clausewitz in understanding war as an extended duel, this concept of extension certainly means something more than just the adding together of individual duels.

In war, there are duels at different levels. These may be individual, but they can also take place at the level of the engagement, tactics, or strategy. Even so, all these duels do not add up to the whole war. The extension of the duel brings with it temporal duration in the present and integration into the past and future, so that differences in terms of content can be derived from this, but the immediate, individual duel, which is a matter of life and death, is almost timeless.[103] The most important distinctions between the individual and the extended duel are determined by the category of time.

2.4.3. Differences in the Category of Time

Up until now I have accounted for the most important aspects of the differences between the individual and the extended duel, and between the internal and external determinants of war, in terms of the significance of time for Clausewitz. The three interactions to limited war are also, in decisive respects, based on the temporal dimension. One could conclude from this that the three interactions to the extreme are characterized by 'timelessness'. However, because there can be no timelessness in real war, this would make the three interactions to the extreme nothing more than an abstraction—something abstracted from time, space, and the material means needed to wage war.[104] I have tried to demonstrate that this conclusion would be a mistake, because the three interactions to the extreme are real tendencies in real wars, even though they do not determine war as a whole.

The antithesis between timelessness and the temporal duration of war can be compared with the antithesis between a point and a line. What defines a point is that it is not extended. In reality, though, there are no unextended points; every point can be treated as a line, even if it is a very short one. The individual duel and the three interactions to the extreme only seem to be timeless in an analogous way, but this is not the case in reality. Every action, however brief it may be, has duration, and an interaction in particular cannot be thought of without duration.

As Clausewitz stresses: 'Like everything else in life, a military operation takes time' (597). How, though, should we understand the difference between apparent timelessness and temporal duration? The decisive point is that temporal duration rests on a succession of distinct actions, while apparent timelessness marks continuous, complete acts. This means that the three interactions towards moderation which Clausewitz introduces are determined by the temporal dimension, because the original unity of the action is broken down into temporally distinct acts. Clausewitz states explicitly that a 'decision in war consists of several *successive* acts' (79).

The fury of the fight and the immediate violence of the duel are understood by Clausewitz as standing outside time. The blind killing and struggle to preserve one's own life seem to be timeless because they are unified actions. In this case, the time horizon disappears from the consciousness of those involved because their actions consist of nothing but violence. The immediacy of the life-and-death struggle thus transcends the consciousness of time, and moments seem to last an eternity. For this reason the immediacy of war captured in the three interactions to the extreme seems to be timeless.

The antithesis between the three interactions to the extreme and the three interactions to moderation mentioned by Clausewitz is, contrary to initial appearances, not determined by timelessness as against temporal duration. Rather, what is involved is the antithesis between a unified action within a period of time and time with a distinct dimension, and this makes it possible to distinguish between different kinds of action. The possibility of using the category of time to introduce differentiations between 'unified' and successive actions is what motivates Clausewitz to attach such great significance within Chapter 1 to the possibility of 'an interruption of military activity' (81–3). The temporal dimension of war and its integration into past, present, and future, features which are emphasized by Clausewitz, rest on this distinction. However, this does not mean that the individual duel and the interactions to the extreme are absolutely timeless and therefore abstract.

2.5. THE CONFLICT BETWEEN THE INTERACTIONS TO THE EXTREME AND TO LIMITED WAR

What is the relationship between the interactions to the extreme and those tending towards limited war? Is the category of time the sole explanation of the difference between them, or are there further differences? There is a tension between them, even if it is not an immediate tension, and they conflict with one another to some extent. The mechanics of escalation are explained in the three interactions to the extreme with the help of the categories of force, fear, and power. Even if these three categories are not taken up directly in the interactions to moderation, the overall context suggests quite strongly that they are the most important factors here as well.

2.5.1. Fear: Escalation and Limitation

The contrast between moderating and escalatory tendencies is brought out most vividly in the second interaction. This is where Clausewitz identifies fear of one's own destruction as the most important motive leading to escalation. If the destruction of the enemy is the only guarantee that one will not be destroyed oneself, the logic of the situation means that an unlimited spiral of violence cannot be avoided. In the second moderating interaction, however, Clausewitz qualifies his position on the logic of escalation and argues that this would only apply in cases where the war consisted of a single decisive moment or a number of such moments occurring simultaneously. However, an absolute bringing together of forces 'in time' (by which Clausewitz means at the same time) is contrary to the nature of war. The possibility of a later decisive moment means that human nature, in its weakness, would not just pursue a single outcome (79–80).

Clausewitz sets out this antithesis to escalation out of fear, which is conditioned by the weakness of human nature, in the section on the use of the battle:[105] 'But the human spirit recoils even more from the idea of a decision brought about by a single blow.' Throughout history, governments and commanders have sought to avoid the decisive battle. An 'economization' of war results from the temporal duration of the war and from the risk that defeat in a single battle may mean losing the whole war (259–60). It is 'fear in the midst of fearlessness', the survival instinct, that accounts for all the vacillation, hesitation, and calculated weighing up of options in war, and which explains the tendency to limited war as it is described in the second moderating interaction.[106] In Clausewitz's view, this fear of one's own destruction has quite contradictory consequences.

2.5.2. The Shortening Versus the Extension of the Time Horizon

In the interactions to moderation, the category of time limits escalation. In the interactions to the extreme, on the other hand, the shortening of the time horizon tends to be escalatory—both in Clausewitz's system of thought and in historical terms. Ever since the time of Helmuth von Moltke, the German Chief of General Staff during the three wars of German unification between 1864 and 1871, it has been a central concern of military strategy in industrialized states to fight shorter and more limited wars. There were repeated debates about the argument that the waging of war and the stage of industrialization that had been reached were mutually exclusive. However, the answer given was an attempt to find a third alternative. Both the fear of a two-front war and, in particular, the problem of the likely destruction of industrial capacity led, via the later Chief of General Staff in Wilhelmine Germany, Count Schlieffen, to the blitzkrieg strategy developed by Hitler and the German General Staff in the Second World War.[107]

In all its variants, the blitzkrieg sought to use mobility and increased destructive capacity to overwhelm the enemy with the first wave of attack, in order to avoid prolonged positional warfare as in the First World War. However, these conceptions had the opposite of the intended effect and contributed to the totalization of war, since, as Clausewitz puts it, 'the enemy will do the same' (77). If one side attempts to defeat its enemy at the outset by developing new weapons technologies and military strategies, it is only a matter of time before the other side does the same. Hitler's blitzkrieg was therefore successful to begin with because the other side was unprepared for the new way of waging war. As in the case of Napoleon's victories, the main reason for the success of this strategy was the disintegration of the morale of an opponent who was unable to react quickly enough to 'tactics based so overwhelmingly on speed, concentration, and surprise'.[108]

After the Second World War, however, this form of warfare became generally accepted. The shortening of the time horizon reached its peak during the nuclear age. In order to prevent incalculable damage to one's own side, it was necessary to try to anticipate the enemy's actions and to destroy his nuclear missiles before they could be launched. Both sides' attempts to destroy as much as possible of the enemy's destructive potential before it could be used led both to warning times and conceivable exchanges lasting only a few minutes and to a high level of overkill.

Paradoxically, both wars with *knives and machetes* (Herberg-Rothe) and high-tech wars are characterized by a loss of temporality. Although the shortening of the time horizon in modern wars is an integral component of military success (time is not only money here, but also power), a quite different phenomenon can be observed in the case of civil wars. In civil wars, the significance of time is diminished: all expectations directed towards the future are put to one side and attention is focused on immediate survival. The continuation of the 'economy' of civil wars comes to depend on the radical exploitation of presently available resources and the abandonment of investment in future development. The prospect of future peace gradually disappears as the spirals of violence and survival escalate.[109] The difference between the two forms of war is that in high-tech wars military actions become shorter and shorter, while in civil wars the present is extended and the future ceases to exist. Fear eats the soul and the future.

The comparison between the interactions leading to escalation and to limited war might suggest that a shortening of the time horizon in warfare contributes to escalation and the extension of that time horizon contributes to limitation. However, this fails to take into consideration the first interaction to the extreme. I have argued that violence itself has disinhibiting effects. Indeed, we can use Clausewitz to speak of a postponement of the use of military force into the future, which has limiting effects. At the same time, though, this also extends the use of force and eliminates restraints on the actions of both sides. One can find examples of this in almost all the civil wars currently in progress. The limiting effect of an extension of the time horizon is diametrically opposed to the escalatory effect of a more prolonged use of force.

2.5.3. The Contrasting Tendencies of Power

Clausewitz's third interaction to the extreme, the striving for power, leads to unlimited escalation, to an automatism in which neither of the two sides is master of itself. In the three moderating interactions, Clausewitz qualifies this analysis by introducing the category of time. The next question is: does the category of power itself have an exclusively escalatory character in Clausewitz's conception?

The 'antitheses' on escalation as a result of the striving for power on both sides are to be found in Book VI of *On War*, which deals with defence. Here, Clausewitz examines the scale of the resources available to a defender, and in this framework treats the defender's allies as his 'ultimate source of support'. The European balance of power system is, he says, not systematically regulated. Even so, he goes on, there can be no question that 'major and minor interests of states and peoples [are] interwoven in the most varied and changeable manner'. Each of these points of intersection forms a fixed point which serves to hinder the initial striving for power. The sum of these points constitutes a more or less large totality which must be overcome whenever anyone seeks to bring about change. In this way, the overall network of relations between all states tends to maintain the totality in its present form rather than to produce changes (373).

Setting aside the problematic question of whether an international balance of power system always contributes to the maintenance of peace,[110] it should be emphasized that Clausewitz understands the category of power here as a means of 'maintenance of the status quo'. Without this 'common effort toward maintenance of the status quo, it would never have been possible for a number of civilized states to coexist peacefully over a period of time'. If Europe has been in existence for a thousand years, this is due to the dominance of the system as a whole. It is true that the primacy of 'collective security' has not always been sufficient to ensure the preservation of each individual state, but—argues Clausewitz—these incidents are irregularities which were not able to destroy the European states system as a whole. The 'maintenance of the status quo', as a historical tendency, is a 'philosophic truth' which does not, however, regulate each individual case (374). In this context, Clausewitz's concept of power should be understood as self-preservation in situations of competition.

If the striving for power leads to escalation in the third interaction to the extreme, Clausewitz's category of power is characterized in exactly the same way as a means to be used in striving for the 'maintenance of the status quo'. A balance of power understood in this sense must assume that exercising power is the best way to acquire further power and to preserve oneself. In this respect Clausewitz belongs to the tradition of Machiavelli and Hobbes, both of whom understood the monopoly of force within the state and the external balance of power as the precondition of avoidance of a 'war of all against all', and so as the guarantee of internal and external peace. It therefore emerges that just as fear can, in Clausewitz's analysis, have both disinhibiting and limiting effects, so too are contradictions to be found in the category of power. On the one hand, the striving for power and fear of the loss of power lead, in the second and third interactions to the extreme, to escalation without limits. On the other hand, Clausewitz's conceptualization of power is simultaneously characterized by the striving to preserve what exists and the goal of self-preservation. Clausewitz thus conceives of power as caught between competing impulses towards expansion and self-preservation.[111]

2.5.4. Certainty Versus Uncertainty

In addition to the concept of interaction, the three interactions to the extreme rest principally on elements that could be paraphrased in terms of the unrestrained use of force, combined with fear of and ignorance about the enemy's intentions. They are therefore characterized by an absence of communication, uncertainty, and ignorance about the enemy. The interactions to limited war are a different matter. Clausewitz accounts for the limiting interactions by saying that neither of the two sides is an abstract person in the eyes of the other, and the other side's will is not entirely unknown either. As war does not happen all of a sudden, each of the two sides can to a considerable extent already judge the other on the basis 'by what he is and does, instead of judging him by what he, strictly speaking, ought to be or do' (78).

Clausewitz continues: 'Such shortcomings affect both sides alike and therefore constitute a moderating force' (78). When, in the second interaction to limited war, Clausewitz concludes that whatever one side omits to do because of its weakness becomes an objective reason for moderation on the part of the other, this presupposes that each side knows about the other's weakness. Without this knowledge on both sides, each would—in accordance with the third interaction to the extreme—have to increase its own efforts to the maximum possible in order to overcome its own weakness.

It was possible to observe these effects of certainty and uncertainty about the intentions of the other side with particular clarity during the era of the bipolar nuclear arms race. The only thing that was certain was uncertainty about the scale of the mutual destruction and about the enemy's actions. The avoidance of war with nuclear weapons of mass destruction was essentially based on a combination of certainty and uncertainty in relation to the waging of war. In 1991, in spite of all the rhetoric and the launching of medium-range missiles against Israel, Iraq was put in a position where it could not attack Israel with weapons of mass destruction. This too is likely to have been based on a combination of certainty and uncertainty about Israel's likely response. It was claimed that Israeli planes armed with nuclear bombs had been on the way to Baghdad, but were ordered back just before they reached their target. Regardless of whether this report was accurate, it is precisely this combination of assumed certainty and uncertainty about how one's opponent will react that can have a self-deterring effect and prevent escalation.

However, Clausewitz qualifies the equation which states that uncertainty about the strength and will of the opponent leads to the expansion of war while certainty leads to its limitation. The commander's 'imperfect knowledge' of the strength of the enemy's forces and will is, in the section on periods of inaction in war, a decisive reason for the moderation of war. It is only in relation to his own situation that each commander is fully informed, and his knowledge about the enemy is based on incomplete information. This imperfect knowledge is, says Clausewitz, one of the 'natural causes which, *without entailing inconsistency, can bring military activity to a halt*' (85, emphasis in original).

A tendency to overestimate rather than underestimate the strength of the enemy is also part of human nature. It must therefore be admitted that 'partial ignorance of the situation is, generally speaking, a major factor in delaying the progress of military action and in moderating the principle that underlines it' (85). This means that the categories of certainty and uncertainty do not provide us with a generally reliable way of getting to grips with the question of escalation or limitation of warfare. These categories may have had escalatory or limiting functions in individual cases, but this does not allow us to draw any generally valid conclusions.

2.5.5. Violence/Force as a Means

According to the interpretation of the first interaction to the extreme I have put forward, escalation in war is explained by the fact that the use of force itself is by nature disinhibiting. However, the issue Clausewitz addresses is not the use of force as such, but force as a means to be employed in waging war successfully. The disinhibition of force reaches its limit in war at the point where it becomes dysfunctional. Thus hand-to-hand combat produces rage and aggression as a result of the direct experience of violence. Perhaps these emotions even have a biological function, as a way of stimulating the body so that the muscles are exerted to the maximum. But rage and aggression are no longer useful when complex weapons systems have to be operated. Even in the case of simple long-range weapons such as the bow and arrow, any emotional excitement can be a disadvantage; the important thing is to remain calm and relaxed in order to be able to aim and hit the target. The development of firearms in the fifteenth and sixteenth centuries even led to a change in the personality of the 'ideal warrior'. If 'wild aggression' had been needed before, what was now required was a passive, cautious contempt for the enemy so that the new weapons systems could be operated effectively.[112]

The production and supply of weapons and uniforms, the setting up of ammunition stores, the upkeep of the army, the establishing of supply lines, training, the construction of fortifications, and numerous other activities needed to supply the material requirements of warfare: these aspects too make evident the differences between modern war and war in its narrower sense as an individual duel and trial of strength. This problem became especially clear in the eighteenth century, when the European states were investing such a large proportion of their budgets in the army that it no longer made any sense to use the army in war for fear of bankrupting the state.

In the modern period, however, the limitation of warfare through the fact that only limited material means were available was transformed into its opposite, as the material possibilities grew more and more immense (by comparison with earlier conditions) with the development of the economy, industry, and technology. Even so, here too a tension remains between the expansion and the limitation of war as a result of the material capacities available. The use of force in war is and remains a disinhibiting factor. On the other hand, the subordination of its use to criteria of effectiveness leads to limitation, because completely unrestrained force in warfare would be dysfunctional.

2.6. THE CONTRASTING TENDENCIES IN THE NATURE OF WAR

Clausewitz articulated the contrasts between unlimited and limited war, but he did not just do this in the different stages of development of his thought. The expansion/limitation antithesis is a constitutive part of his definition of war in Chapter 1 of *On War*, the last work he completed. The 'escalation and moderation of force' (Muenkler) can be seen in Clausewitz's theory as opposing principles of war which conflict with one another. Clausewitz did not insist exclusively, in any doctrinaire fashion, on either escalation or moderation; he thought of these two principles as contrasting forces, both of which affect war to the same degree.[113]

If we follow this train of thought further, we can see that the antitheses of Clausewitz's theory can be explained with reference to the object of that theory, war itself. For Clausewitz, the fear of being destroyed in a single encounter has an 'economizing' function, but it also leads to increasing violence. Force is conceived of as disinhibiting, but it is also defined as instrumental, and its instrumental role tends to limit its scope. The category of power also remains tied to the antitheses of disinhibition and self-preservation. These antitheses are not just aspects that are assigned to different types of war; they are not simply expressions of war's 'dual nature' ('War can be of two kinds'; *On War*, p. 69), but are conflicting antitheses that exist within every war.

Violence, fear, and power are the central categories in the three interactions to the extreme, but they simultaneously have limiting effects in warfare. Clausewitz also sees the temporal dimension of war in terms of contradictory factors. What these categories share is the fact that one cannot unambiguously associate escalatory or limiting effects with any one of them. This even applies to the category of force itself. There may be cases in which force must be used rationally, in order to ensure that force cannot escalate beyond certain limits. At the same time, every act of violence runs the risk of setting in motion a spiral that cannot be controlled, because the use of force as such has disinhibiting effects. The conclusion to be drawn from this discussion of the three interactions is a sobering one. In Clausewitz's thought, violence/force, fear, and power can have both escalatory and limiting effects.

What follows from this? One possibility would be to investigate the categories identified in order to see when, and under what conditions, which causes have led to either the expansion or the limitation of wars. One could then try to develop a typology of escalation and limitation of warfare. However, it could be that while this kind of investigation would find numerous examples to support one interpretation or the other, it would do nothing to resolve the question of the contradictory consequences of these categories for warfare in general. Although of course this kind of investigation might succeed in outlining some significant probability, the same categories can have quite different effects in real wars. The tendency towards escalation in Clausewitz's conception brings the opposing force of moderation into play immediately. In a case of mutual outdoing leading to extreme force, however, 'consideration for the scale of the political demands would be lost', the means employed would lose all proportion in relation to the aim, and in most cases this intention to 'make an extreme effort would fail as a result of the counterweight represented by one's own inner condition'.[114] In this way, emphasizes Clausewitz, the 'belligerent' is driven to adopt a middle course between escalation and moderation (585).

Because of the tension between escalation and moderation, theory must—in Clausewitz's understanding of the term—leave the area of strict science as represented by logic and mathematics. Theory becomes an art, the skill required to identify the most important and decisive objects and relationships within a vast number of these, by using the 'power of judgement'. 'Responsibility and danger do not tend to free or stimulate the average person's mind—rather the contrary; but wherever they do liberate an individual's judgement and confidence we can be sure that we are in the presence of exceptional ability' (585–6). Clausewitz takes the view that human beings are internally torn, and that this inner conflict emerges most noticeably in war. This, however, is also for Clausewitz the condition which makes it possible for human beings to take their own decisions, and so renders them free and responsible.

3

Concepts of Absolute and Real War

Clausewitz begins *On War* with an instrumental definition: 'War is thus an act of force to compel our enemy to do our will' (75). He then derives a concept[115] of war based on its escalatory interaction (75–7). Finally, in his 'consequences for theory', he arrives at the 'wondrous Trinity' (89). A problem arises here: these three conceptualizations are incompatible with one another. Indeed, Clausewitz's definition, his initial concept of war, and his 'consequences for theory' are to some degree at odds with each other—and this in the only one of all the chapters he considered finished. Was Clausewitz no longer able to capture the complexity of his experience of war, or does his exposition have a structure that is not immediately visible? Is there a puzzle here that needs to be solved?

It is often the case that complex concepts are perplexing and cannot be defined unambiguously. We know what is meant, but are unable to express it directly. What, for example, is freedom, or infinity? Such concepts lack a precise definition, though this does not mean that we could manage without them. This absence of clarity is a problem, but it is also one of the strengths of these concepts, because it means numerous differentiations, nuances, and further developments are possible. Clausewitz's theory of war is one such concept: its many-sidedness makes it more of a puzzle than an exact conceptualization. Despite the uncertainty of his theory of war, Clausewitz's aim is to develop 'clear ideas'. The human mind, he says, has 'a universal thirst for clarity, and longs to feel itself part of an orderly scheme of things' (71).

Concepts are not just words, mere descriptions of objects. They are attempts to express something, the essence or function of an object. But what is essential in the case of a complex matter such as war, the subject of Clausewitz's work? And when we speak of his theory of war, do we mean the sum of all possible meanings he attached to the word, which may themselves have changed over time, or do we mean the unchanging qualities identified through abstraction? Another factor which influences the way some concepts are understood is their relationship to other concepts. If war is distinguished from other forms of violence, for example, the focus of attention is on the political context. War can also be distinguished from other forms of fighting, on the grounds that it is a use of force organized by the state or a community; or from other forms of politics, on the grounds that it is violent. Moreover, concepts are not the same thing as reality. They simultaneously capture reality and provide grounds on which we act. Conceptualization has reflexive effects. The way we form concepts has consequences for our actions.

The reality of war changed in fundamental ways during Clausewitz's own lifetime. Clausewitz joined the Prussian army at a time when it still operated exclusively on the basis of the principles laid down for warfare in the eighteenth century. He experienced the expansion of war by the armies of the French Revolution, the new dynamism of Napoleonic warfare, and partisan warfare. He was involved in the military reforms of the era, defended the Prussian militia as an important achievement even after it had effectively been abolished in the Restoration, and analysed the attempts to limit warfare after the Wars of Liberation. In his early work he criticized the schematic nature of the military writings of authors like von Bülow, and from this time on his theoretical work focused on changes in warfare and the changeability of war. Changes in the image of war were important pillars of Clausewitz's theory, and they also influenced his conceptualizations.

In order to bring into focus the various dimensions of the concept of war in Clausewitz's work, it is useful to consider some existing interpretations. One particularly important issue in the literature on Clausewitz, for example, is the problem of the difference between 'absolute war' and 'total war'. Clausewitz additionally assigns different functions to conceptualization at different times, and gives different accounts of what concepts should do. As discussed earlier, it is possible to explain such contrasts with the help of the contrasting experiences of war represented by Jena, Moscow, and Waterloo. But Clausewitz did not just note these contrasts and leave it at that. He tried to develop a unified theory of war in the shape of the 'wondrous Trinity'. This is the point of departure for Clausewitz's formulation of his theory, but in order to develop and substantiate this concept he needs the whole of Chapter 1 of *On War*. It is therefore logical that the 'wondrous Trinity' should be introduced at the end of this exposition.

3.1. CONTRASTING INTERPRETATIONS OF CLAUSEWITZ

Raymond Aron argues that, towards the end of his life, Clausewitz arrived at a position that is not to be found in any of the books he did not revise: a conception of the 'abstract, unreal, philosophical, ideal character' of war that is 'in conformity with its concept'.[116] Aron is attempting to refute the view that 'absolute war' is the true theory of war for Clausewitz, from which some have concluded that the idea of extermination is at the heart of his thought. Interpretations along these lines can be found not only in the work of Clausewitz's harshest critics, such as Sir Basil Liddell Hart and John Keegan, but also in the writings of German military thinkers who concluded that absolute wars, or wars of extermination, were the only true form of war.

Count von Schlieffen, for example, claimed that Clausewitz had made a significant contribution to keeping the idea of 'absolute war', the war of extermination, alive in the thinking of the German officer corps. Clausewitz's critics have often taken the same view. They have argued that Clausewitz must bear part of the responsibility for militarization in Europe, and especially in Germany, during the nineteenth and twentieth centuries. As Liddell Hart expressed this criticism, 'the generals became intoxicated on the blood-red wine made from Clausewitz's grapes'.[117] Some even saw connections between Clausewitz's conceptualization of the absolute and extreme and the idea of 'total war' as formulated by Erich Ludendorff, and echoed by Joseph Goebbels in his famous *Sportpalast* speech in which he demanded to know: 'Do you want total war? Do you want it, if necessary, in a more brutal and more radical form than we can even imagine today?'[118] Aron is arguing against the idea that Clausewitz was a theorist of the war of extermination, and is seeking to bring out the analytical potential of his conceptualization of war. The question that has to be asked, however, is whether this can be done with the help of Clausewitz's antithesis between theory and real war. Does his conceptualization itself perhaps remain contradictory?

In Chapter 1 of Book I of *On War*, Clausewitz argues with respect to the interactions to the extreme that 'in the field of abstract thought' such interactions mean that the mind 'can never rest', and cannot find a fixed point until it has reached the extreme. Clausewitz bases this claim on the argument that extremes result when 'absolute terms' are deduced as a consequence of the continual interactions. These extremes, however, are nothing but interplay of ideas, produced by a barely visible sequence of logical subtleties, Clausewitz emphasizes (78). Aron argues that in this context Clausewitz's concept of war is purely abstract, and has nothing to do with reality. Would the theory of war then be 'the opposite of its reality'?[119] Aron's understanding of 'absolute war' in Clausewitz places him in a long succession of commentators (Rothfels, Kessel, Ritter, and Hahlweg), of which he is the culmination.

One can summarize the position of these authors by saying that they see the concept of war put forward by Clausewitz at the beginning of Chapter 1, and specifically the tendency towards the absolute and the extreme that is examined there, as unreal. Clausewitz's theory, these commentators argue, is an ideal type lying beyond the bounds of reality, a purely theoretical notion which should not be confused with real war. And indeed, Clausewitz does emphasize the difference between the conceptual, abstract tendency towards the escalation of violence and real war immediately after he has dealt with the escalatory interaction. If one had to make 'the greatest effort' every time in war, he says, this would be 'an abstraction and would leave the real world quite unaffected' (78).

One still has to ask, though, whether Clausewitz's theory of war should not in the end be interpreted as an idea that regulates reality, at least to some extent. Hans Rothfels stresses that Clausewitz treats absolute war as an ideal in the philosophical sense, as something that has given unity and objectivity to a range of very different phenomena. Accordingly, Rothfels goes on to argue that there can be no doubt that for Clausewitz, 'absolute war' only means war as an abstraction, 'war on paper'. However, Rothfels also identifies another aspect of Clausewitz's argument. He says that Clausewitz tries to resolve the antithesis between absolute and real war with the help of a further concept, the idea of the 'battle' as a focal point—even in wars in which no such battle is actually fought. Rothfels' stress on the battle, while maintaining formally the distinction between absolute and real war, thus tends to shift attention back towards the absolute character of war.[120]

Panajotis Kondylis argues that Aron's 'liberal' interpretation of Clausewitz involves focusing on two pairs of contrasting concepts: 'abstract war—blind violence' as against 'real war—rational political action'. According to Kondylis, Aron is arguing that 'blind violence' is characteristic of war only in theory, whereas real war is determined by rational political actions. This 'liberal' position, he says, is based on a dichotomy between 'undiluted violence', which is restricted to the realm of abstraction, and the whole of reality, where only moderate action is possible. In the end, the idea of 'moderate action' implies the existence of far-sighted civilian actors who are conscious of their own responsibility; but as a result the specificity of military action and the momentum of war disappears. Aron's interpretation of Clausewitz, according to Kondylis, also makes a widespread and fatal mistake: it confuses the antithesis between abstract and real war with the one between wars of extermination and limited wars.[121]

Nevertheless, with the exception of one distinction (the theoretical status of the concept of war), Kondylis's position is not really very far removed from Aron's. Kondylis defines war on the basis of Clausewitz's three interactions to the extreme, which are held in check by factors that are not themselves part of war. But this is not totally different from what Aron says when he argues that there is a moderating force which is opposed to the intensification to the extreme. This force is, according to Aron, alien to war in its narrow meaning as a simple trial of strength; but it is implicit in the overall definition of war as part of politics as a whole. The only real difference between Aron and Kondylis relates to the question of what it is that prevents war unfolding in an 'unchecked' way. For Aron it is politics, and for Kondylis it is culture: in the state of culture, says Kondylis, war is diluted with other elements of existential factors.[122]

Clausewitz himself explains the difference between the strict logic of the concept and real war in terms of the barrier between the two: 'The barrier in question is the vast array of factors, forces, and conditions in national affairs that are affected by war. No logical sequence could progress through their innumerable twists and turns as though it were a simple thread that linked two deductions.' Real war gets stuck in these 'twists and turns' (579). The unresolved question—and this is a significant difference—is that of the status Clausewitz accords to the concept and to the abstraction. Kondylis and Aron answer this question in different ways. For Kondylis, war in Clausewitz's thought is predominantly determined by the duel, struggle, existential combat, and hostility (which leads Kondylis to interpret Clausewitz in terms of cultural anthropology). Aron sees this aspect too, but he places more emphasis on an 'overall definition' of war as part of politics as a whole. One can also note that Aron distinguishes between subjective and objective politics, and that the boundaries between objective politics and society or culture are not as clearly drawn as one might think from reading Kondylis's criticisms of Aron.

The reduction of Clausewitz's concept of war to the 'absolute and extreme' has problematic consequences both for uncritical admirers and for critics of this conception. This applies to German military thinkers in the world wars of the twentieth century, who on the basis of this apparent concept of war came to the view that extermination was the general aim of warfare, and also leads to internal contradictions such as can be seen in Aron's interpretation. On the one hand, Aron says that politics has a fundamental tendency to moderate the kind of war that would correspond to Clausewitz's concept. At the same time, though, Aron argues that it is politics itself which determines the tendency towards total war (obviously bearing in mind the disasters of the Second World War), as well as the relative, limited character of war.

Clausewitz indeed distinguishes between a war that leads to the extreme because of its own internal logic[123] and limited war, in which the three moderating interactions come into play. One of these is in fact the 'political situation' after the war, which has an effect on the way the war is waged and moderates absolute or abstract war (78). One could conclude from this that in Clausewitz's view war leads to an extreme when it follows only its own internal laws. Clausewitz emphasizes that an extreme is therefore reached in 'the field of abstract thought' because the concept is confronted with a 'clash of forces' which only follows these internal laws. Policy, on the other hand, is something different from and external to war, and sets fundamental limits to this tendency to the extreme. In Chapter 1 of *On War*, however, Clausewitz repeats the distinction with which we are already familiar from the Note of 1827, saying that war can be either unlimited or limited, and stressing that, contrary to appearances, *both kinds of war* are determined by policy.[124] There is indeed a major problem with Clausewitz's concept of war, but Aron and Kondylis are not as far apart as Kondylis has suggested.

If we want to find a position that is genuinely opposed to Aron's, it is to be found in John Keegan's work. Keegan too argues that war is characterized by a more comprehensive totality which he identifies as culture. But he is convinced that war does not necessarily lead to absolute or extreme violence when it follows its own laws, is left to itself, and is only moderated by something external and other. According to this view, there are other limitations applying to the intensification of the *furor belli*, which are immanent to war itself.

Keegan's position could be summarized as follows. War is a life and death struggle, but there are *immanent* limits and counterweights which restrict the intensification to the extreme. These include the survival instinct, the fear of being killed, anthropologically conditioned inhibitions that make us reluctant to kill other people, professionalization, ritualization, and conventionalization. This interpretation does not account for escalation in terms of the development of an immanent logic of war, but rather explains it with reference to diametrically opposed, external factors: politics and socio-cultural development, the overcoming of inhibitions about killing with the help of developments in weapons technology and industry, and the production of socio-moral inequality. All these factors contribute to a perception that the enemy is no longer equal in principle. One aspect of the creation of spatial, temporal, and socio-moral distance is the transformation of the enemy as a human being into an object within range of a weapon. This transformation can be seen with particular clarity in the case of spatial distance, for example in the use of modern weapons systems such as missiles.[125]

We can treat Keegan and Aron as ideal types, opposite extremes in the interpretation of Clausewitz. The difference between their views can be made clear with the help of a simplification. In the first interaction to the extreme, Clausewitz seems to be arguing that immanent laws of war lead inevitably to an extreme, because war is a form of violence and fighting. Through fighting and the use of force, war gradually goes beyond the existing boundaries. According to Aron's interpretation, this tendency is moderated by external factors such as politics, society, and culture. Clausewitz stresses: 'We must not allow ourselves to be misled into regarding war as a pure act of force and of destruction.... Instead we must recognize that war is a political act that is not wholly autonomous; a true political instrument.'[126] Characteristically, here too Clausewitz repeatedly lays stress upon the tension between contrasts, even when his argument appears to be unambiguous: war is a political act, and it therefore does not carry wholly its own law in itself. Keegan, unlike Clausewitz, takes the view that it is external conditions such as politics and industrialization, rather than immanent factors, which lead to the increasing disinhibition of violence in war.

3.2. 'ABSOLUTE' AND 'TOTAL' WAR

For an appropriate understanding of Clausewitz's various concepts of war, we need to take a closer look on the relation between 'absolute' and 'total' war. Clausewitz's critics accuse him of using the concept of absolute war to advocate total war. His defenders claim that there is a fundamental difference between the two concepts. Aron, for example, argues: 'Anyone who equates absolute war with total war . . . is not interpreting, he is falsifying.' Later on, though, Aron examines the connections between the two concepts. Here, too, he says that the 'abstract need for intensification to the extreme' is at no time a 'praxeological imperative', but even so he concludes that as soon as one examines real wars, one sees that *both* the possibility of moderating behaviour *and* the abstract need for intensification are decisive.[127] The only difference between these two ways of looking at the question is that, according to Aron, the conceptual level is only determined by the absolute and extreme, whereas at the level of real wars the tendency to the extreme is one of two contrasting possibilities.

The early Clausewitz and the Prussian military reformers took the view that if war was to be waged successfully and if the Prussian state was to survive, the entire nation's potential would have to be mobilized. There is certainly an affinity between this idea and the conception of total war. This idea too is about using all conceivable resources and means of military strength when waging war. As early as 1922, Erich Ludendorff, the commander of German land forces in the First World War, wrote that 'irrevocable facts' meant that the imminent war would take on the character of a 'total war'. Ludendorff accounted for this development by referring to the introduction of compulsory military service at a time when the population was increasing throughout Europe, and to the development of new weapons systems with ever-increasing destructive power.[128] This 'total war' was characterized by the fiction that it would be waged to ensure the 'survival of the people'. In other words, it was not just something that concerned the armed forces but directly affected the life and 'soul' of each individual citizen. It followed that policy too would have to take on this total character.

Ludendorff's conception of the totalization of war owed something to Clausewitz, but at the same time Ludendorff disassociated himself from Clausewitz's ideas. All of Clausewitz's theories, he wrote, should be thrown out. War was, in Ludendorff's view, the highest expression of the people's will to live. Policy should therefore be at the service of warfare, rather than the other way round. In Ludendorff's writings the elevation of the 'people's will to live' as a moral absolute, and the idea of extermination to which it is linked, leads logically to a renunciation of the primacy of policy. This position is diametrically opposed to Clausewitz's. Ludendorff's renunciation of Clausewitz indicates that the primacy of the idea of extermination, which Clausewitz's critics attribute to him, is not easily compatible with the primacy of policy.

As mentioned before, one has to acknowledge that Clausewitz's initial use of one of his diverse concepts of war is introduced in connection with the three interactions to the extreme. Here, though, as demonstrated, it is not war as a whole that is meant, but only the 'aim of warfare' within the initial three-part definition of war. For Clausewitz, the 'pure theory'—concept as well as the concept of 'absolute war' refers essentially to the aim of warfare. Although this seems to be reductionism on Clausewitz's part, it can explain the difference between 'absolute' and 'total war'. Total war gives the impression that it is a situation in which the military aim has become independent and been transformed into a higher purpose. The reversal of the military aim and purpose of war seems to be the decisive criterion for 'total war'.[129]

The sociologist Hans Freyer, for example, summed this up during the 1920s when he argued that all politics was a matter of 'threatening to wage war, preparing for war, postponing or bringing forward war, instigating or preventing war'. In Freyer's view, the state came into being as a result of war and sustained itself through preparedness for war and actual war. Furthermore, the state needed 'something else, something that demonstrates its reality as one among many states: a sphere of conquest'. The state must 'conquer in order to exist'. This turning of the military aim into something autonomous in itself transforms the idea of absolute war into that of total war. War is not a means or an instrument for Freyer; it finds its purpose in itself. The state is 'at its purest as a state when it most openly embodies war'.[130] In Clausewitz's writings, by way of contrast, we find an acknowledgement of the theoretical and historical expansion of military aims, and also (in his early work) an existential conception of war, but nothing resembling this complete reversal of aim and purpose.

3.3. THE DIFFERENT FUNCTIONS OF THE 'CONCEPT' IN CLAUSEWITZ'S WORK

Clausewitz's statements about the difference, and even the opposition, between concept and reality at the end of his analysis of the three interactions are well known and have often been quoted. At this point, he speaks repeatedly of the 'field of abstract thought' and of the difference between this and real war.[131] In one of the three interactions, however, Clausewitz also says that theory and reality correspond to one another. He emphasizes the fundamental difference between them, but also argues that 'the advance of civilization has done nothing practical to alter or deflect the impulse to destroy the enemy, which is central to the idea of war' (76).

At the beginning of Book VIII Clausewitz interprets the *concept* of war as something absolute, an ideal, a general guiding principle which reality only approaches to a limited degree. The differences between theory and real war cannot be removed, he says, but 'theory has the duty to give priority to the absolute form of war and to make that form a general point of reference, so that he who wants to learn from theory becomes accustomed to keeping that point in view constantly, to measuring all his hopes and fears by it, and to approximating it *when he can* or *when he must*' (581, emphasis in original).

This orientation towards the absolute form of war is stated so emphatically that, at this point, Clausewitz describes real war as 'something incoherent and incomplete... something quite different from what it should be according to theory'. Seen from this perspective, real war even seems to Clausewitz to be a contradiction in itself. However, there is an exception. One could doubt, says Clausewitz, whether the idea of the absolute in war could become reality at all, 'were it not for the fact that with our own eyes we have seen warfare achieve this state of absolute perfection'. Napoleon's way of waging war was for Clausewitz (at the beginning of Book VIII) the realization of the concept of war. After the short prelude of the French Revolution, 'Bonaparte brought it swiftly and ruthlessly to that point'. It is therefore natural and necessary, says Clausewitz, that this manifestation of war 'should cause us to turn again to the pure concept of war with all its rigorous implications' (580).

But we must bear in mind that Clausewitz's concept of war is integrated into three basic antitheses, and that the definition of the concept varies from antithesis to antithesis. The first antithesis can be seen when Clausewitz acknowledges the difference between theory and reality but gives priority to the ideal of 'absolute war', which has become reality in the form of Napoleon's kind of warfare. At the beginning of Book VIII (581), Clausewitz develops this idea of the absolute of war in order to bring theory and reality as close together as possible despite their difference. At several points therefore Clausewitz uses the concept of something as a regulatory idea, from which it is possible to derive consequences for reality and for political practice, including warfare. In one passage, for example, he explains the concepts of the theatre of war, the army, and the campaign, but then concludes that they cannot be specified any more precisely because, '[u]nlike scientific or philosophical definitions, they are not basic to any rules' (281).

This means that, in Clausewitz's view, practical consequences for warfare follow from 'philosophical definitions', although in other contexts Clausewitz says that this line of argumentation based on the concept of war is an abstraction. We can find the second antithesis in Chapter 1 of Book I, in which he treats the three interactions to the extreme as a further concept of war, but only in order to render the great difference and distance between theory and practice visible.

The way in which Clausewitz alternates between these two positions can be seen particularly clearly in Book VIII, too. Here he says that it is not permissible to construct an idea of war as it should be on the basis of theory alone. Rather, we should provide space for all the outside elements which intervene in war, especially the profound inconsistency, imprecision, and timidity of man. We must therefore confront the truth: war and the form it is given are produced by ideas, feelings, and circumstances that immediately precede it. This, says Clausewitz, was the case even in the period when war took on its absolute form 'under Bonaparte'. Immediately after this restriction of the function of the theory, however, he argues that the theory must continue to orient itself towards the absolute form of war (580).

The third and final point relates to the contrast between the narrow concept of war as fighting and trial of strength, and to the overall concept of war as part of a more comprehensive whole. At one point, Clausewitz says: 'Essentially war is fighting, for fighting is the only effective principle in the manifold activities generally designated as war. The need to fight quickly led man to invent appropriate devices to gain advantages in combat, and these brought about great changes in the forms of fighting' (127). The only means that can be used in war is fighting. Although this may take many different forms, may have come a long way since its origins as a brutal discharge of hatred and enmity, and many other forces may intrude which are not themselves part of fighting, the concept of war always means that everything that occurs must originally derive from fighting (95).

Clausewitz characterizes this narrow concept of war with the help of terms such as 'abstract thoughts' (79) and the 'pure concept of war' (90). At the beginning of Book VIII, he understands the 'general concept of war' in the sense of fighting with the aim of destroying the enemy forces (577). In this book, though, he stresses repeatedly that war 'cannot follow its own laws' but must instead be treated as part of a more comprehensive whole—and that whole is policy (606). Here too, the concept performs two fundamentally different functions for Clausewitz. On the one hand, he uses a narrow, immediate concept of war which is oriented towards fighting. On the other hand, he emphasizes that the concept of war refers to the whole of war and must be understood as part of this totality.

3.4. THREE CONCEPTS OF WAR: JENA, MOSCOW, AND WATERLOO

How can we resolve these tensions, contrasts and even sometimes contradictions in Clausewitz's various concepts of war? A combination of historical and systematic factors accounts for Clausewitz's wavering and uncertainty in relation to a clear concept of war. The early Clausewitz assumed that there was a direct correspondence between concept and reality. Taking up the ideas of Kiesewetter (a follower of Kant), whose lectures Clausewitz had attended, he distinguished between two forms of truth. Formal truth was correspondence between ideas and the laws of thought, logic. Material truth, on the other hand, was correspondence between the idea and the object it represented.[132] It may be that as Clausewitz's theory grew more complex, he found that it was no longer possible to formulate it in terms of the correspondence between idea and reality only, which nevertheless remained his goal.

However, there were also historical and systematic reasons why Clausewitz retained the idea of correspondence between theory and reality while simultaneously stressing differences. Real war around the time of Jena was determined by Napoleon's way of waging war, which Clausewitz, like his contemporaries, experienced as the 'absolute form' of war. The dominant elements here were the principle of extermination, the waging of war regardless of the losses suffered, and the use of the resources of the entire nation. By comparison with this absolute form of war, the earlier cabinet wars had been extremely limited; during the eighteenth century, no one could imagine the possibilities of warfare Napoleon was to demonstrate. In Clausewitz's eyes, the call for correspondence between theory and reality meant that conceptualization must orient itself towards this new form of warfare. While the wars of the eighteenth century had remained limited for reasons unrelated to military factors, such as consideration of the financial means available, Clausewitz saw Napoleon's way of waging war as war in its naked, 'pure' form. Precisely because Napoleon used all the resources and means available to the French nation when he waged war, war came near to revealing its 'true face', and was no longer circumscribed by the need to take non-military factors into consideration.

The great success enjoyed by Napoleon's new way of waging war must also be taken into account. In a few short years he defeated nearly all the European powers, and expanded France's sphere of influence to include almost the whole of Europe. The twin battles of Jena and Auerstedt showed that this new challenge was too much even for the military state of Prussia. If the state was to survive politically, there seemed to be only one option: Prussia's own army must be reorganized in accordance with the new way of waging war. The Prussian military reforms were an attempt to do this, but so too were the early Clausewitz's writings on the new kind of warfare. The theory of war had to be oriented towards the new way of waging war in order for it to correspond to reality, and the same requirements were dictated by the need to ensure the state's political survival. It followed that all consequences for the practice of warfare must be derived from the new concept of war. By combining correspondence between theory and reality with the orientation towards Napoleon's way of waging war, Clausewitz arrived at the following formula: we only need to remember the concept of war in order to be able to say with conviction that 'destruction of the enemy forces' is the main principle of war (258).

Moscow, and Clausewitz's analysis of Napoleon's Russian campaign, is the turning point. Napoleon, the 'god of war', and his strategy are still Clausewitz's ideal. At the same time, though, the failure of the Russian campaign makes him realize that this strategy cannot be employed in all circumstances and that obstacles can arise. Clausewitz calls these obstacles to the waging of war 'friction'. Everything in war is very simple, he says, but the most simple thing is difficult. These difficulties mount up and give rise to a friction that no one who has not seen war with his own eyes can really imagine. Friction is the only concept that distinguishes real war from war fought on paper: 'This tremendous friction, which cannot, as in mechanics, be reduced to a few points, is everywhere in contact with chance, and brings about effects that cannot be measured, just because they are largely due to chance' (120). One example of these chance effects is the weather, which can slow down a battalion on the march or hide the enemy from view.

This friction causes war to become 'like movement in a resistant element'. The dangers war brings with it and the bodily exertions it requires cause such an increase in the evil of friction that they can be seen as its most significant causes (120). Clausewitz's remarks about friction in Book I of *On War* originate in his analysis of the Russian campaign, from which he took the relevant passages almost verbatim.[133] Clausewitz continues to treat Napoleon's way of waging war as an ideal and as a regulatory principle, but from now on only in the realm of theory—which he contrasts with the limitations imposed by reality, friction.

In Clausewitz's day, the concept of friction was a major problem in the natural sciences. The established eighteenth-century view of the physical world offered explanations in terms of gravitational attraction between heavenly bodies. However, the rubbing together of two bodies, or friction, could not be accounted for within this worldview. What happens when a body is placed on an inclined plane? Sooner or later, when the friction is overcome, it slides down. The calculation of the moment when this would happen, and the speed at which it would happen, was impossible as long as one relied on the laws of celestial mechanics. The concept of friction shattered the prevailing view of the world, because the inclined plane of friction was incompatible with the laws governing the supposedly frictionless motion of the planets. In Clausewitz's writings after Moscow, absolute war can be seen simultaneously as a borderline case and point of construction. Reality circles around this point but cannot reach it. The same problem was debated in mathematics at the time, in the form of the transition from infinitely small distances into the limits used in infinitesimal calculus.[134]

The difference between the concept of the absolute of war as an 'ideal', after Jena, or as a regulatory idea that is limited by friction, after Moscow, can be made clear in the following way. In the first case, it is a matter of keeping hold of the absolute and overcoming friction: 'Iron will-power can overcome this friction; it pulverizes every obstacle, but of course it wears down the machine as well.... The proud spirit's firm will dominates the art of war as an obelisk dominates the town square on which it stands' (119). In the second case, one has to bear in mind what is possible and sensible. It is now 'instinct and tact' which make it possible for the experienced officer, like a 'man of the world', always to take the appropriate decision whatever the situation and to give the necessary orders. Many years of experience and practice mean that an officer knows, without really thinking about it, that sometimes friction can be overcome and sometimes this is impossible (120).

Although the difference in conceptualization after Moscow may seem small, it is in fact fundamental. In the first case, friction is overcome with the help of 'iron will-power'—Clausewitz is describing Napoleon's military genius here, though without mentioning him by name. However, the decisive problem has already been mentioned indirectly. The price that has to be paid in the long run is that although the obstacles are worn down, the 'machine' is worn down as well; that is to say, Napoleon's own army, which was to be destroyed in the Russian campaign. We can already see the shadow of Moscow, and perhaps that of Waterloo as well. After Moscow, it is no longer a matter of overcoming the obstacles whatever the cost; instinct and tact decide the correct course of action in each individual situation.

Keegan, who is Clausewitz's harshest critic, has a formulation which is equivalent to the latter's idea that the conceivable extreme of war is limited by the 'friction' of real life. However, Keegan is evidently unaware that he has provided this same formulation. He says that war is always limited not because man wishes this to be so, but because nature decrees it. King Lear, railing at his enemies, may have threatened to 'do such things—what they are yet I know not—but they shall be the terrors of the earth'; as other potentates in straitened circumstances have found, however, the terrors of the earth are hard to conjure up. Resources are insufficient, the weather worsens, the seasons turn, the will of friends and allies fail, human nature itself may revolt against the hardship that strife demands. This statement may appear quite cynical when facing the actual 'terrors of the earth' that even warlords in straitened circumstances are able to conjure up. Keegan's conclusion that war and violence are always limited by natural determination should be understood in the following way: the extreme violence that is conceivable in theory is limited by external conditions in reality. Clausewitz takes the same position by emphasizing the difference between the extreme required by theory and the limitations in real war.[135]

Clausewitz is more specific than Keegan, because he takes into account the human and societal conditions limiting violence, as well as the 'natural' ones. For Clausewitz, the crucial aspects which distinguish the conceivable extreme from real war are the restrictions imposed by time and space, the connection with previous events in the political world, and the calculation about the political situation desired after the war. Here too Clausewitz speaks of an interaction, but this time it is an interaction to moderation rather than to the extreme; this brings the striving towards the extreme back within certain bounds of effort (78).

But it was the battle of Waterloo that forced Clausewitz to offer a fundamentally new conceptualization of war. As we have demonstrated, he did this in his analysis of the 1815 campaign in Belgium, which ended with Napoleon's final defeat. In this text, written in 1827–8, Clausewitz criticizes Napoleon for failing to limit his defeat at Waterloo, and from this moment on Clausewitz emphasizes the dual nature of war, especially in his Note (dated 10 July 1827). The transitions between one type of war and the other must still be considered, 'but the fact that the aims of the two types are quite different must be clear at all times, and their points of irreconcilability brought out' (69).

It is nearly impossible to overstate the significance of this statement for Clausewitz's theory of war. When, in the Note, he makes the 'two types of war' the point of departure for the projected revision of his work, this means that he no longer considers warfare to be a unity and so no longer has a unified theory of war. War can no longer be defined via the concept of fighting alone, because the analysis of Waterloo has shown that there are two fundamentally different forms of war, which need to be waged in different ways. In the later parts of Book VIII, Clausewitz sets out the conclusions he draws from the differentiation between the two types of war. He says that he has, up until this point, examined the difference between war and the other interests of individuals and societies. The reasons for this difference, he says, are to be found in human nature itself.

His objective now would be to identify the unity that brings these contradictory elements together in practical life. Clausewitz explains that it was necessary to proceed initially by emphasizing these contradictions clearly and examining separately the different elements of warfare. Their unity, though, is captured in the concept that states that war is only one part of political intercourse; which is to say that it is by no means autonomous. After making this point, Clausewitz introduces the famous formula: war is nothing but a continuation of policy by other means. He says 'by other means', and so claims at the same time that this political intercourse is not brought to a halt by the war; its essence continues to exist and is not transformed into anything different. The main lines along which events proceed in war, and to which they are tied, are 'political lines that continue throughout the war into the subsequent peace' (605).

Let us summarize the argument so far. Clausewitz originally thought there were no limits to the revolutionary warfare of Napoleon, but once he saw that this was not the case he became aware of the significance of political conditions as they influenced the outcome of the Battle of Waterloo. After Waterloo, Clausewitz no longer employs a concept of only one kind of warfare because his theory must now incorporate two fundamentally different forms of warfare; as he puts it in the Note, those irreconcilable elements must be separated from one another. If fighting no longer provides a unified conceptualization, Clausewitz needs a category that will enable him to conceptualize war as a whole. He finds this in the concept of politics. In spite of the internal contrast between different forms of warfare, it is the overarching role of policy that makes a unified theory of war possible again: 'Only if war is looked at in this way does its unity reappear; only then can we see that all wars are things of the *same* nature' (606, emphasis in original). These two aspects of Clausewitz's declared intention to revise his work, the two types of war and the primacy of policy, belong together in terms of their contents. The way in which the two forms of warfare are opposed to each other forces Clausewitz to find a theory of war that incorporates this contrast. But there remains a difference between Clausewitz's Book VIII and Chapter 1 of Book I, which now has to be treated separately.

3.5. THE 'WONDROUS TRINITY' AS A DIFFERENT CONCEPT OF WAR

All previous interpretations of Clausewitz's concept of war have treated it as something that must be understood in connection with the three interactions to the extreme, as set out at the beginning of Chapter 1 of *On War*. On this basis, students of Clausewitz have gone on to examine, in diverse and varied ways, the status of this concept for Clausewitz and the relationship between the theory of war and 'real war'. The latter concept has sometimes (Aron) been associated with the 'wondrous Trinity', which is introduced at the end of Chapter 1 with the three tendencies to primordial violence, the play of chance and probability, and the primacy of policy. Because absolute and extreme violence have been exclusively assigned to theory, and the 'wondrous Trinity' to real war, the Trinity has been thought to have not such a significance of its own for the concept of war. This interpretation overlooks an important point: Clausewitz speaks explicitly of the 'wondrous Trinity' as his concept of war. The final sentence of Chapter 1, referring to the 'wondrous Trinity', stresses that the 'concept of war which we have formulated casts a first ray of light on the basic structure of theory' (89).[136]

There is room for different interpretations of this sentence: should the words Clausewitz uses here be taken to refer to the 'wondrous Trinity'? My own view is that the connection is clear. Clausewitz says that he must examine separately the difficult question of how the theory of war 'maintains a balance', floats between the three tendencies that make up the 'wondrous Trinity'. His goal is a theory that satisfies the requirements of reality. It is in this context that he speaks of the concept of war he has formulated (89). There are therefore two quite different concepts of war in Chapter 1 of Book I. Clausewitz develops the first of these concepts in order to make clear the difference and distance between absolute war as an abstraction and war as a historical reality. The second concept of war, the 'wondrous Trinity', is an attempt to conceptualize war as a whole.

Immediately afterwards, in Chapter 2 of Book I, Clausewitz says that he now wants to examine the relationship between purpose, aim, and means. In order to do this, he wants to 'for the moment ... consider the pure concept of war' (90). When he refers here to the 'pure concept of war', he does not mean the 'wondrous Trinity' but rather the concept of war he had used at the beginning of Chapter 1. By speaking of the concept of war at the beginning and again at the end of Chapter 1, Clausewitz gives the 'wondrous Trinity' another dimension: it acquires theoretical status in itself. Chapter 1 begins with considerations which Clausewitz describes as 'definition' and with the following conceptualization of war in connection with the three interactions to the extreme. At the end of this chapter, though, he speaks of the consequences for theory and of the 'wondrous Trinity' as his concept of war.

What is the relationship between the 'wondrous Trinity', the definition that Clausewitz offers at the beginning of this chapter, and the three interactions to the extreme? In Chapter 1, the only one Clausewitz revised, he attempts to summarize in a concentrated way his theoretical ideas, reflections on the history of warfare, and his own experiences of war. His objective here is to map out the direction that will be taken by his work as a whole.

It makes sense to assume that the definition, the concept of war within the three interactions to the extreme, and the model presented as the consequences for theory (the 'wondrous Trinity') are supposed to be compatible with one another, at least to a certain degree. However, we find that in Clausewitz, the definition, the initial concept, and the 'consequences for theory' are simply incompatible with one another. The definition opens up an instrumental horizon, the initial concept of war (in the three interactions to the extreme) cannot be separated from the extreme of violence and fighting, and the wondrous Trinity understands war to be made up of different tendencies, some of which conflict with one another.

Clausewitz's conceptualization remains ambivalent. We must conclude that he never succeeded in bringing together the conflicting elements of his conceptualization as parts of a unified whole. In particular, the characterization of the absolute and extreme of violence as the concept of war has caused two problems: it has had bad consequences for interpretations of

Clausewitz's work, and it contradicts what he says elsewhere in Chapter 1. If we add to this the famous formula, which is not explicitly presented as a definition but has all the characteristics of one, we can see that there is no way in which Clausewitz's definition, the initial concept within the three interactions to the extreme, the formula, and the consequences for theory can be made compatible with one another.

The solution to this dilemma that has been presented here is as follows. If we assume that the concept of war Clausewitz wishes to employ is only formulated when we get to the 'wondrous Trinity', we can read the whole of Chapter 1 in fact as *leading up to* this concept of war. It follows from this interpretation that Clausewitz cannot be accused of introducing a concept of war in a dogmatic way right at the beginning of his book. What he does is to introduce the definition, the interactions, the distinction between 'pure' and real war, the debate about political purpose, and all the other material in Chapter 1 as a way of developing the concept of war he really wishes to bring into play. On the basis of this understanding it is perfectly logical that this concept of war, which provides the basis of Clausewitz's work, should be found at the end of Chapter 1 where it serves as the revised starting point for the book as a whole.

Part III

Using Clausewitz to Go Beyond Clausewitz

4

Clausewitz's Legacy: The Trinity

> The essential difference is that war is not an exercise of the will directed at inanimate matter, as is the case with the mechanical arts, or at matter which is animate but passive and yielding, as is the case with the human mind and emotions in the fine arts. In war, the will is directed at an animate object that *reacts*.
>
> Clausewitz, *On War* (149)

Clausewitz's theory is based on a dynamic understanding of war and force. A central theme in his later work is the question of 'whether a conflict of living forces as it develops and is resolved in war remains subject to general laws, and whether these can provide a useful guide to action' (149–50). There is no suggestion in Clausewitz's thought of any form of essentialism, or of any tracing of war back to a core founded on anthropology or game theory (as van Creveld believes). The 'state of crisis in which the forces find themselves during periods of tension and movement' is not an anomaly during fighting; rather, 'the state of crisis is the real war' (222).

Clausewitz lived in an age of fundamental change, and he did not try to abstract any kind of unvarying essence of war. He emphasized the dynamic character of war, and made the changes that he observed the focus of his analysis. In one of the last texts he wrote, he sums up by saying that 'most people' say it is impossible to 'construct a scientific theory for the art of war', since 'it deals with matters that no permanent law can provide for' (71). This dynamic understanding is what characterizes Clausewitz's theory of war, and it is to be found in Chapter 1 of *On War*, the chapter that is considered his 'Testament' (Aron), his true legacy.

Clausewitz's Chapter 1 does not invalidate the antitheses he had already established in his theoretical conceptions. In Chapter 1 of Book I, he tries to bring together the four basic antitheses of his political theory so that they form part of one coherent approach: extremism and escalation as against limitation, an existential as against an instrumental understanding of war, the antithesis of attack and defence as avatars for disinhibition and self-preservation, and the primacy of force or policy. As he attempts to do this, Clausewitz develops a conception in which he makes the contradictory nature of his experiences of war into the immanent point of departure for his theoretical conceptualization of the phenomenon. In the present chapter and the following one, I offer the detailed interpretation needed in order to give an explicit account of the system which is implicit in this approach.

Throughout Chapter 1, Clausewitz is addressing a fundamental problem: the 'conflict of living forces', he says, cannot be grasped by means of the 'mechanical arts', instrumental thought in the narrow sense. In this kind of thought, the activity of the will is directed against 'inanimate matter' (a subject–object relationship). Nor can the conflict be examined with the help of nothing more than the 'fine arts'. In this case, the activity of the will is directed against a living object, but this object is 'animate but passive and yielding'. Here, the enemy in war is treated like an object (this kind of approach could be best described as thinking in strategic categories (149)).

For Clausewitz, therefore, action in war is 'like movement in a resisting element' (129), because it involves two opponents who are alive, who act, and who react to one another, and whose respective actions can never be fully predicted. The interactions to the extreme and to limitation underline the significance of living actions in war, all of which are influenced by the actions of the enemy. The internal logic of Chapter 1 therefore incorporates different forms of action, which can be deciphered in terms of the antithesis of action and counteraction.

I proceed in the present chapter by examining what gives Clausewitz's Chapter 1 its special character. After that, I provide an exposition of the 'wondrous Trinity' and its immanent limits. I then go on to look at the relationship between this Trinity and the (three-part) definition of war. The contrasting conceptualizations of war in Chapter 1 can be accounted for as a sequence of action and counteraction. After this fundamental difference has been introduced it is possible to conceptualize war in a unified way, in accordance with Clausewitz's account but also going beyond what he says, by bringing together the initial three-part definition and the tripartite nature of war.

4.1. ON THE SPECIAL CHARACTER OF CHAPTER 1 AND OF THE 'WONDROUS TRINITY'

In the last of the notes he wrote commenting on *On War*, Clausewitz stressed that his work remained unfinished: 'The manuscript on the conduct of operations that will be found after my death can, in its present state, be regarded as nothing but a collection of materials from which a theory was to have been distilled. I am still dissatisfied with most of it' (70). In the same text, however, Clausewitz emphasizes that Chapter 1 of Book I is an exception: 'Chapter 1 of Book One alone I regard as finished. It will at least serve the whole by indicating the direction I meant to follow everywhere' (70).

In the literature on Clausewitz, there has been a debate about the significance of Chapter 1: does it provide the key which enables the reader to understand the whole work? Reinhard Stumpf, for example, tries to argue that Clausewitz would probably never have completed his work because of the structure of his personality. What Stumpf is saying is that because his character was internally torn, Clausewitz would never have managed to finish the book. Raymond Aron takes a quite different view of Clausewitz's assessment of his own work, placing this in the context of the Note of 1827, in which Clausewitz speaks of his intention to carry out a fundamental revision.[137]

The planned revision was intended to involve two main aspects: the two types of war, and the formula that 'war is nothing but the continuation of policy with other means'.[138] Clausewitz writes that if this is 'firmly kept in mind throughout', it will bring unity to the whole treatment of the question. Referring to the two types of war, 'unlimited' and limited, Clausewitz stresses that: 'Transitions from one type to the other will of course recur in my treatment; but the fact that the aims of the two types are quite different must be clear at all times, and their points of irreconcilability brought out' (69). When we see Clausewitz's Chapter 1 in perspective, it becomes clear that it is the one he really did revise as he had said he intended to, which meant that he was able to treat it as the only completed chapter.

The debate about whether Clausewitz's character meant he would never have finished his work, and whether he intended to carry out a fundamental revision of it, does have significance in relation to the content of *On War*. The question is not just the abstract one of whether the book we have is complete or not; something quite different is at stake. If we accept Stumpf's argument, we must 'harmonize' the evident contrasts between the different parts of the whole book. In terms of content, this interpretation sees fight, combat and battle as the basis of war's essence, its unity, and unchanging nature. In Stumpf's edited volume which includes excerpts from the writings of Clausewitz and of the Chief of the Prussian General Staff, Helmuth von Moltke, he tries throughout to present Moltke as the more important military theorist. This amounts to a flagrant distortion of Clausewitz's significance, and Stumpf also reduces his work to nothing more than an instructional work on how to wage war. *On War* is a great deal more than this. It is only by reducing the book to a work on this question alone that Stumpf can see Moltke as a more important author than Clausewitz.[139]

If we proceed differently, by demonstrating that there are contrasting aspects of Clausewitz's work which can be located in the different stages via which his thought developed, it becomes possible to emphasize the two main points he makes in the Note: the two types of war, unlimited and limited, which form different poles, and the primacy of policy. As I have shown, these two aspects of Clausewitz's intention to revise the book cannot be separated from one another. If the later Clausewitz's conception of war saw it as determined by the antithesis between the two types of war, war can no longer be characterized by the uniformity of fighting. Consequently, a third element is needed in order to re-establish the unity of the theory of war. Clausewitz presents this in Book VIII, in the form of the theory of war as the continuation of state policy by other means.

My argument is the same as Raymond Aron's in this respect: Chapter 1 of Book I provides us with the guiding principle, the main thread and immanent structure of Clausewitz's theory of war, and we can use this to establish the relationship between the different parts of the work as a whole. I differ from Aron, however, in seeing a significant difference between the 1827 Note and Chapter 1, which was at least partly written later. This relates to the difference between the Note and the 'wondrous Trinity', which is introduced at the end of Chapter 1. While the Note stresses that war is nothing but the continuation of policy by other means, this conceptualization is only one of three tendencies within the later 'wondrous Trinity', and these tendencies are in principle of equal importance.[140]

It is not only the fact that *On War* remained unfinished that has led to a wide range of competing interpretations and 'half-baked criticism', as Clausewitz himself feared would happen (70). In addition, Chapter 1 includes almost all the important elements of Clausewitz's theory of war in a condensed form. In that chapter, one of Clausewitz's approaches is to take up again the contrast between the theory and the reality of war, which has already played such an important role at the beginning of Book VIII. The assumption that policy decides whether war will have a limited character or a tendency to become absolute is also documented in earlier texts. The significance of the antithesis between attack and defence, which is emphasized by Clausewitz in the undated note (70–1) and in Chapter 1, and the conceptualization of their true logical antithesis, which I will suggest is central, is also to be found in the relevant chapters of Book VI of *On War*. Other texts also sketch the rationality of purpose, aim, and means, and there is a version of escalatory interaction in an early draft of this chapter which is almost identical to the published text.[141]

My suggestion therefore sees these aspects of Chapter 1 as providing the thread that guides us through Clausewitz's theory of war. However, we cannot leave it at that. If we want to take Clausewitz's own assessment of his work seriously, we must also ask: what is the special character of Chapter 1 in terms of its content? There is *one* element which is only mentioned explicitly in Chapter 1, although the problem associated with it is one that preoccupied Clausewitz right from the start of his study of the theory of war. This is the 'wondrous Trinity' of war. Clausewitz summarizes the discussion at the end of Chapter 1 by introducing this concept, which must be understood as his 'last word' and Testament, his true legacy. There are some additional comments made by Clausewitz at a later date, but these do not come anywhere near the conclusion of Chapter 1 as a theoretical reflection on war.

The considerable extent to which Chapter 1 was revised can be seen most clearly when we compare the last known draft version with the published text. This draft is almost identical to the published version where it deals with the duel, the initial three-part definition, escalatory interaction, and the difference between theory and real war; but other points are only mentioned briefly: the significance of policy, the tendency towards moderation, and the difference between attack and defence. However, there is no mention at all in this last draft of the conception of the 'wondrous Trinity'.[142]

How, then, does Clausewitz conceptualize the 'wondrous Trinity' as 'consequences for the theory of war'? War is not simply a 'true chameleon that slightly adapts its characteristics to the given case'. As a 'total phenomenon its dominant tendencies always make war a remarkable Trinity'. This, says Clausewitz, is 'composed of primordial violence, hatred and enmity, which are to be regarded as a blind natural force; of the play of chance and probability within which the creative spirit is free to roam; and of its element of subordination, as an instrument of policy, which makes it subject to reason alone' (89).

Clausewitz then emphasizes that:

> These three tendencies are ... deep-rooted in their subject and yet variable in their relationship to one another. A theory that ignores any one of them or seeks to fix an arbitrary relationship between them would conflict with reality to such an extent that for this reason alone it would be totally useless. Our task therefore is to develop a theory that maintains a balance between these three tendencies, like an object suspended between three magnets (89).[143]

The first thing one notices about the 'wondrous Trinity' is that Clausewitz speaks of the subordinate nature of war as an instrument of policy (as in the famous formula of war as a continuation of policy by other means), but he also characterizes this as only one of three tendencies within war, each of which has a status that is in principle equal to that of the others. Not only do these three tendencies enjoy equal status within Clausewitz's conception, but two of them also give expression to a fundamental antithesis: war is, on the one hand, made up of primordial violence, hatred and enmity, which are to be regarded as a blind natural force, and, on the other hand, it is a subordinate instrument of policy. Primordial violence combined with hatred and enmity, like a blind natural force, and war as an instrument of policy, a rational instrument—these equal tendencies form an antithesis and cannot be combined directly with one another. Indirectly, the 'wondrous Trinity' includes a further antithesis. Clausewitz combines the first of the three tendencies—primordial violence, hatred, and enmity—with the statement that these should be seen as a 'blind natural force'. The second of the three tendencies is, by way of contrast, described as the play of chance and probability (89).

We can rule out the possibility that Clausewitz, although his language was sometimes rich in images, saw the 'wondrous Trinity' as nothing more than a metaphor or was unaware that at least two tendencies among the Trinity were antitheses. It is also unlikely that this conception simply reflects the fact that he is sometimes imprecise in his use of concepts. Nor can I agree with Stumpf's view that the use of this religious concept is only intended to be understood descriptively, and that Clausewitz qualifies it by adding 'wondrous' in order to deny it any legitimate function. I also reject the possibility that this conception is no more than a remnant of earlier ideas. It is clear from Clausewitz's assessments that none of these assumptions are correct: 'consequences for the theory', 'deep-rooted in their subject', 'Our task therefore is . . . '.

Most importantly, though, Clausewitz emphasizes the need for this theoretical approach to correspond to real war. A theory that did not take into account any one of the three tendencies, or tried to establish an arbitrary relationship between them, would 'conflict with reality to such an extent that for this reason alone it would be totally useless' (89). The way in which the conceptualization of war as the continuation of policy by other means (in sections 24–7 of Chapter 1) is followed immediately by the integration of this formula into a more comprehensive whole (in section 28) is further evidence against the suggestion that Clausewitz was no longer able to cope with the complexity of his own argument. The break between these sections is so clear that Clausewitz must have been aware of it. The most one could concede would be that most commentators on Clausewitz's work have also overlooked this break, because they have concentrated too much on the interactions to the extreme as set out at the beginning of Chapter 1 as well as on the famous formula.

The way in which Clausewitz stresses the 'wondrous Trinity' and its three tendencies is so obvious that one really has to ask why the existing literature has paid so little attention to it. Some authors have argued that Clausewitz has a purely instrumental view of war, even though this is expressly stated to be only one of three equal tendencies within the wondrous Trinity. This contradiction is especially noticeable in Aron's interpretation. Although Aron places particular stress on the 'wondrous Trinity' and treats Chapter 1, which concludes with a summary of the Trinity, as Clausewitz's Testament, he simultaneously argues that Clausewitz's ultimate position is characterized by a general primacy of policy.[144] These interpretations can be explained with reference to Clausewitz's expression of this position in the famous formula in the immediately preceding sections (87). But if war is, as the formula puts it, a continuation of policy by other means, this stands in direct contradiction to the conceptualization of war as only one of three tendencies in the 'wondrous Trinity'.

It is not possible to bring the 'wondrous Trinity' into harmony with a general conceptualization of war as a continuation of policy by other means. In the 'wondrous Trinity', war is made up of the antithesis of its primordial violence and its subordinate nature as an instrument of policy. One could put this the other way round by saying that the primacy of policy is by no means annulled in the 'wondrous Trinity'; it retains its place and is re-emphasized. But it must also be admitted that Clausewitz neither explains how he arrives at the 'wondrous Trinity' nor provides any detailed account of it. Nevertheless, it must be stressed that the 'wondrous Trinity' represents Clausewitz's summary of the findings of Chapter 1.

Even if we proceed on the basis of the assumption that the 'wondrous Trinity' is the fundamental key to understanding Chapter 1 of *On War*, we still need to look more closely at the concept itself. Clausewitz expresses the basic tension between the three tendencies of the Trinity very clearly when he says that the theory must be 'like an object suspended between three magnets'. He also emphasizes that the three tendencies are equally important, and says that war is made up of these different and contrasting tendencies. The question is whether this will suffice as a description of Clausewitz's method. How can we characterize this state of being 'suspended' between opposed tendencies?

There is certainly a religious background to the 'wondrous Trinity', but it also has an analytical dimension.[145] In one contemporary philosophical dictionary, '*Dreieinigkeit od. Dreifaltigkeit*' (i.e. Trinity) is defined as the idea of one being which is also three. It is possible to go beyond the religious significance of this conception by interpreting it in terms of God seen first as the creator (the generating principle, i.e. the father), then second as the one who sustains (the reproductive principle, i.e. the son), and finally as the one who rules (the guiding or holy principle, i.e. the spirit).[146]

As far as the methodology is concerned, there is a direct link between the trinity in religious terms and Clausewitz's 'wondrous Trinity'. He characterizes the first of these three tendencies as *primordial* violence. This can be treated as a 'generating principle' of war. The third of these tendencies in Clausewitz's work is war's subordinate nature as an instrument of policy, which means it falls into the realm of pure reason. Clausewitz goes on to say that this tendency belongs exclusively to the *government*. The dictionary definition speaks of the 'ruler as spirit' as the guiding principle. In each of these definitions, the third element is characterized by government and reason or 'ruler and spirit'. What about the second tendency? Clausewitz initially describes this as no more than the play of chance and probability—which means, however, that war becomes an activity within which the creative spirit is free to roam. He assigns this tendency to the commander and his army. The commander and his army can be identified as those who actually wage war; they are its sustainers.

Clausewitz stresses that these three tendencies are of equal importance within the 'wondrous Trinity', and that each war is made up of these different tendencies. However, this does not mean there are no differences between them. By comparing them with the religious Trinity, we can draw the direct conclusion that the 'generative', 'sustaining', and 'guiding' principles are not identical. Without wishing to place undue emphasis on the differences between these principles, we can conclude that the three tendencies of the 'wondrous Trinity' describe three quite different dimensions of warfare which, in each individual war, act together as a whole.

4.2. TENSIONS BETWEEN THE 'WONDROUS TRINITY' AND CLAUSEWITZ'S 'DEFINITION' OF WAR

The whole of Chapter 1 is integrated into two three-part conceptualizations of war which appear at the beginning and end of the chapter; Clausewitz describes these as a 'definition' and the 'consequences for the theory'. At the end of this chapter he characterizes the 'wondrous Trinity' as the consequences for the theory, and at the beginning he defines war as follows: 'War is thus an act of force to compel our enemy to do our will' (75). If we compare these two conceptualizations of war, we find some common features but also fundamental differences. In my view, the 'wondrous Trinity' at the end of this chapter takes up and develops the initial three-part definition. The initial definition is enriched and differentiated, and the 'wondrous Trinity' is accounted for in terms of the way the argument has been developed throughout the chapter. Raymond Aron criticizes the initial three-part definition, but his analysis provides indirect support for my interpretation. He argues that the initial definition is still contained within all three elements of the 'wondrous Trinity'. I also agree with Aron's view that a differentiation and enrichment of the initial definition takes place as Chapter 1 develops.[147]

Unlike Aron, however, I do not think the initial definition is a definition in two parts, and I do not believe that all the concepts used in the first few sections of this chapter refer exclusively to the unreality, abstractness, or absoluteness of the extreme of war. It is understandable that Aron should seek to correct misinterpretations of Clausewitz which present him as an advocate of extreme and absolute interactions as the ideal form of warfare, but he fails to appreciate the differentiated nature of Clausewitz's analysis. Let us have a closer look at the relationship between the two three-part conceptualizations of war that we find at the beginning and end of Chapter 1. Both of them address the same three conceptual fields, but in each case a specific antithetical relationship is identified. In the initial three-part definition, Clausewitz says that force is the means we use, while compelling the enemy *to do our will* is the (political) purpose of war. In order to be sure of attaining this purpose we must disarm the enemy, and this is—according to the theory—the actual aim of military action in Clausewitz's view. Force as rational means, the will as political purpose, and *compelling the enemy* to do one's will and disarming him as the aim: these are the three elements that make up the initial definition (75–7). This means that the three conceptual fields shared by the initial definition and the 'wondrous Trinity' at the end of Chapter 1 are violence/force, *compelling the enemy*, and political purpose that the enemy complies with one's will.[148]

In the initial definition force is conceptualized as an instrument, but in the 'wondrous Trinity' Clausewitz speaks of primordial violence, which must be seen as a blind natural force. The elements we find in respect of compelling the enemy to do one's will in the definition are the interactions to the extreme and the necessity and logic of escalation; in the Trinity it is the 'play of chance and probability'. Two of the three equal conceptual fields involved here are thus characterized by a fundamental antithesis: the instrumental rationality of force as against primordial violence, and the necessity and logic of escalation as against the play of chance and probability. The third conceptual field, that of policy, does not seem at first glance to be characterized by any such antithesis.

When Clausewitz examines the two three-part conceptualizations he does not argue explicitly that there is an antithesis in the conceptual field of policy, but much of the literature on Clausewitz sees him as having at least a dual concept of politics.[149] Without wishing to anticipate the more extensive analysis of the concept of politics that follows in Chapter 6 of the present book, two of its dimensions can be mentioned here. The first of these is subjectively determined policy as against an understanding of politics based on objective social conditions, and the second is politics understood as a struggle for power as against a position that rests on the ability to compromise and a balance of interests. If we want to use Clausewitz to go beyond Clausewitz here, we can see each of the conceptual fields of the initial definition, the interactions to the extreme and to limitation, and the 'wondrous Trinity' as relating to the conceptual fields of violence/force, fight, and politics; war is made up of the conflict and interplay between these fields.

Let us try to summarize what has been said so far about the structure of Chapter 1. It is framed by 2 three-part conceptualizations of war, which Clausewitz presents under the headings 'definition' and 'consequences for the theory'. We can note that the famous formula is not stressed in a comparable way in Clausewitz's text. Each of these two conceptualizations, at the beginning and end of Chapter 1, articulates the same three conceptual fields—violence/force, fight, and policy. Each of these three conceptual fields is characterized, explicitly or implicitly, by a specific antithesis:

1. Violence/force as an instrumental means, as against primordial violence.
2. The tendency towards the absolute and extreme, the need for and logic of escalation, as against the play of chance and probability in fight and combat.
3. Subjective policy as against objective conditions. In addition, policy is determined here within the tension provided by the antithesis of gaining power as against agreement or law, and finally of an instrumental as against an existential understanding of war.

The poles in each of these antithetical relationships can be understood as opposing borders; war is determined by these borders, but it also moves and develops as the point half-way between them. The antitheses set out by Clausewitz in the whole of Chapter 1, and the way he differentiates them, are his real conceptualization of war. The way they are made up and the oppositions between them determine every war, though they do so in such a way that they are shaped differently in each case and one pole of the specific antithesis may be dominant. The extremes of these antitheses are the borders within which each concrete war is located. We can sum up the relationship between the initial three-part definition and the 'wondrous Trinity' by saying that although there is a correspondence between the two in terms of the content of the conceptual *fields*, each of their elements is characterized by a specific antithetical relationship. In addition to this, there are some limited cross-references between the individual determinations in some of the different conceptual fields.

However, this is where the true tension in Clausewitz's approach is to be found. Thus it is the very conceptualization of force as a means that accounts for the initial definition of the instrumentality of war, but in the trinity it is located in the conceptual field of policy rather than force. The tendency towards the absolute and extreme in the conceptual field of compelling the enemy corresponds to hatred and hostility as a blind force of nature, but at the end of the chapter these appear in the conceptual field of force. The cross-references between the two definitions indicate that the three elements within each definition do not simply stand alongside each other without having any relationship to one another, as may seem to be the case at first glance. It is true that there is no direct connection between the three elements within each of the two determinations of war, but there is a connection between the conceptual fields identified in each.

4.3. A RECONSTRUCTION OF CHAPTER 1, WITH THE HELP OF A DISTINCTION BETWEEN ACTION AND COUNTERACTION

How can we resolve the antitheses between the conceptualizations of war I have identified at the beginning and end of Clausewitz's first chapter? Could it be that they cannot be resolved? Even if we were able to assume that Clausewitz felt intuitively, or by following the 'instinct of the object' (by analogy with his well-known 'instinct of judgement') that war was treated in Chapter 1 as a unity within which competing antitheses were opposed to each other, this would not amount to an endorsement of his position by itself.

I propose to offer an account of the contrasting conceptualizations of war in Chapter 1 with the help of the idea of action succeeded by counteraction.[150] Although I do not share Ernst Vollrath's view that action in war can be reduced to counteraction or his integration of the instrumental character of war into this conception, his distinction between action and counteraction provides the key to understanding the contrasting conceptualizations of war in Clausewitz's Chapter 1.

Clausewitz does not formulate this distinction explicitly, but he uses it as the implicit basis for the development of his theoretical approach. The fundamental significance of this distinction becomes clear right at the beginning of Chapter 1. The initial definition assumes a sovereign and independent subject which imposes its will on the enemy through the use of force. In the interactions, on the other hand, the will is not seen as sovereign at all. 'Thus I am not in control: he [the enemy] dictates to me as much as I dictate to him', Clausewitz emphasizes (77). This restriction of the sovereign will comes about in two steps. The first of these is Clausewitz's statement that the interactions mean that no one is 'in control': no one is autonomous. The second is that each side dictates to the other, and neither party can escape this.

In Chapter 2, Clausewitz expresses this thought even more clearly: 'If he [the enemy] were to seek the decision through a major battle, *his choice would force us against our will to do likewise*' (98, emphasis in original). In the initial definition, Clausewitz defines war by saying that it is a matter of compelling the enemy to do one's will. In Chapter 2, however, he says that actions which are even opposed to one's own will can be necessary in war.

For Clausewitz, 'action' is determined by the autonomy and responsibility of one's own will. Counteraction is a response to an assumed or real action on the part of another person, and only comes into being 'against our will' as a result of this action. Every action within a context of human activity is determined by both dimensions of action: the autonomy and responsibility of one's will, which cannot be given up, as against the 'interaction' of various counteractions, which operate according to their own logic and which are reciprocally related to one another. In war it is impossible to separate these two types from one another, so this distinction is not a matter of discrete forms of action. It expresses different dimensions or 'tendencies', as Clausewitz puts it, of one and the same context of action.

I take this distinction between action and counteraction from the work of Ernst Vollrath, but it needs to be developed further and differentiated. Vollrath argues that action can be treated as part of politics, whereas war is essentially determined by counteraction. Not all counteraction is warlike, but all action in war belongs to counteraction, Vollrath emphasizes. Action as a whole is primarily a matter of disputes rather than agreement. He argues that this is why the need to reach agreement arises. In action, all action encounters the action of others. The result of this 'acting together' is also determined by the fact that human beings have not sought it together—rather, one action has been directed against another.

Vollrath understands the possibility of counteraction as the fundamental precondition of every society's existence. It is theoretically conceivable that this possibility could be eliminated, but there would then be a danger that the many special features that make man what he is would be abandoned. This elimination can be brought about in theory by fundamentalist demands on identity and enforced in practice by using force to break another party's will to resist. However, it is a feature of the good sense that makes it possible for human beings to join together in the first place that they cannot be made to submit to this by force. This in turn assumes that it is possible, together with others, to resist the force designed to make one submit by taking counteraction. Vollrath, arguing on similar lines to Wolfgang Sofsky, sees the human capacity to take counteraction, to defend oneself, and to resist as a fundamental condition of the freedom of every society.[151]

4.3.1. Action and Counteraction in Clausewitz's Definition

The distinction between action and counteraction can be illustrated with the help of the initial three-part definition. Clausewitz says that war is an act of force designed to compel our enemy to do our will. This definition operates at the level of the autonomy of one's own action. If we move beyond this conceptualization, the dimension of counteraction is immediately revealed: war involves not just one actor trying to impose his will on another by force, but two opponents fighting each other. Clausewitz uses the image of the duel to make this point. Even before he presents the definition itself, Clausewitz stresses the connection between war and the duel (75).

Within this reciprocal counteraction in a duel, however, there is a fundamental distinction to be drawn: the two sides and the counteractions they take can be either symmetrically or asymmetrically structured. Clausewitz uses the image of two opponents wrestling with one another, each try to floor the other, in order to capture a symmetrical relationship. Here we are at the level of counteraction; the actions of each side, though directed against the other, are of the same type: '*Each* tries through physical force to compel the other to do his will' (75). This symmetrical counteraction needs to be distinguished from another type, asymmetrical counteraction. Let us return to Clausewitz's original definition as a starting point. According to the definition, the idea is to force an opponent to do our will. In a war, though, the opponent does not want to do this and resists. At this level, we have asymmetrical counteraction.

In the second interaction, Clausewitz says that war is not the effect of a living force on a lifeless mass. Rather, because total non-resistance would not be war at all, it is always a collision between two living forces.[152] My interpretation of Clausewitz's Chapter 1 sees the instrumental character of war, force as a means, as resting on the will of one of the opposing sides. In the 'wondrous Trinity', on the other hand, war as a composite made up of different tendencies is explained by the fact that there are two (or more) opponents, both of whom want to assert their (individually isolated) wills in a conflict, in fight and combat. War as an instrument and force as a means rest on action, and this is tied to the relationship between purpose, aim, and means. As a consequence of action and counteraction, however, there comes into being a separate rationality of interaction, which is not in every case subject to the individual will. Clausewitz expresses this theoretically in the 'wondrous Trinity'.

In brief summary, we can say that the difference lies in the fact that war is not just a matter of imposing one's will on the enemy. It is a combat in which two opponents are both trying to impose their will, or one of the two is struggling to prevent the other from imposing his will.

This differentiation of Clausewitz's original definition makes it possible to distinguish between three aspects of the question:

1. Separate consideration of each of the combatants and of instrumental action taken on the basis of each one's free will.
2. Analysis of symmetrical interaction between the opponents. Each of them wants to use force to impose his will on the other. Both of them want to impose their will, but the opponents and their actions are of the same type. Thus a momentum arises, and the consequence of this is that the individual is no longer in control and must even act against his own original will.
3. The asymmetrical relationship within which—according to Clausewitz's definition—the enemy is to be compelled to do one's will. However, this implies the thought that Clausewitz does not express openly at the beginning of this chapter, namely the idea that this opponent defends himself precisely because he does not want to accept being compelled to do the other's will.

Clausewitz begins *On War* by saying that war is nothing more than a duel. Although he then differentiates this original concept by introducing the idea of a 'duel on a larger scale' and the three-part definition, what he is doing here is stressing the symmetrical relationship between opponents. This assumption of symmetry in the concept of the duel has far-reaching consequences. Clausewitz's argument here reflects the political theory of the eighteenth century, according to which every state had the right to wage war. This concept differed from the medieval idea of 'just war' by assuming that the right to wage war was an aspect of every state's sovereignty. This symmetry brings with it a tendency to justify wars, but it has other consequences as well. It includes a recognition in principle that one's opponent is *iustus hostis*—an equal—so the enemy is no longer considered a criminal. This assumption that enemies in war are equal is the basic precondition of respect for the laws of war.[153]

Clausewitz conceptualizes war quite differently in the context of his concept of defence. He argues that when we consider war philosophically, we see that it begins with defence. 'Essentially, the concept of war does not originate with the attack', he says, and notes that it originates with defence rather than attack (377). The immediate purpose of defence is fighting, because defending oneself and fighting are obviously the same thing. Defence is a matter of fighting off an attack, so it presupposes this attack. Attack, on the other hand, is directed towards the occupation of territory, which is its 'positive purpose'. We have, says Clausewitz, now established where to find the 'fixed point' outside the interaction of attack and defence, namely in defence (377). By saying this, Clausewitz introduces a decisive qualification into his account of the symmetry and polarity of the duel. There are political implications here as well. If we establish a close connection between the conceptualization of war and the concept of defence, we have grounds on which to state that war may have a *iusta causa*—a just cause—and also that an attacker may be committing a criminal act.

Wolfgang Sofsky takes up Clausewitz's idea that war begins with defence rather than attack. An invasion or occupation is not fighting, he says; fighting only begins when someone resists the attack. The attack wants to seize and subjugate, to invade and triumph, not to fight. It is only the defence which wants to fight, to resist the invader, to hold on to what it has, to defy the enemy. 'This means that resistance and fighting are one', concludes Sofsky. Anyone who wanted to abolish the violence of fighting would have to take away from human beings their capacity to resist.[154]

Clausewitz translates the categories of compelling the enemy *to do our will* as well as *not allowing the enemy to impose his will upon* us into the antithetical principles of attack and defence. At the level of abstraction at which Chapter 1 operates, he treats attack and defence as opposed principles rather than as strategic, tactical, or operational concepts within warfare. Needless to say, actions in war cannot simply be divided into these tendencies, and this is certainly not the sense or purpose of my distinction here. The point is that this distinction can be used to reconstruct the way in which Clausewitz's first chapter develops. We can then identify a sequence of autonomous action, symmetrical counteraction (the equality of two opponents in the interactions), and asymmetrical counteraction (to impose one's will on the other and to resist attempts to compel one to do the will of the other). I shall now go on to use this distinction in a section-by-section examination of Chapter 1. The objective is to offer an interpretation of the way Clausewitz moves from the definition of war to the 'wondrous Trinity', and so to get a clearer view of the puzzle and to reveal the secret.

4.3.2. Action and Counteraction in Chapter 1

Section 1

Clausewitz begins with the conceptualization of war as a 'duel on a larger scale' (75). The theoretical status of this determination of war probably remains a matter of dispute; here it expresses the most general conceptualization of 'pure' counteraction. No distinctions are drawn between the opponents or their actions.

Section 2: Definition

Clausewitz continues by—initially—looking at each of the two opponents separately. 'Each tries through physical force to compel the other to do his will', and this leads him to conclude: 'War is thus an act of force to compel our enemy to do our will' (75). This definition means that war is an act of force for both sides; the objective is to impose one's own will on the other side, by carrying out an action with purposes, aims, and means one has decided for oneself. Each side's will is initially considered in isolation.

Sections 3–9: Interactions

In the next section, Clausewitz returns to the idea that action in war never occurs in isolation, but is always confronted by another action: the other side does 'the same'. He discusses the consequences of this counteraction in the three interactions to the extreme (sections 3–5) and to moderation (sections 6–9). Up until now, most commentators on Clausewitz have connected the category of interaction with the extreme of force. This has made it more difficult to understand the distinction between action and counteraction. An additional difficulty has been caused by the fact that the way Clausewitz structures Chapter 1 is determined by an initial assumption that there is no difference between the two opponents' respective wills or the purposes of their actions in the duel. This assumption that the opponents are of the same type can lead to the further assumption that all we need is an examination of war in relation to each of the two opponents and their isolated wills. It is true that at this level, it is hard to distinguish between action and counteraction.

Section 10

After the three interactions to the extreme Clausewitz introduces the distinction between theory and reality, but he accounts for this in terms of the interactions to limited war. On the basis of the antithesis of the interactions to escalation and those to limited war, Clausewitz concludes that the laws of probability are in operation: 'From the enemy's character, from his institutions, the state of his affairs and his general situation, each side, using the laws of probability, forms an estimate of its opponent's likely course and acts accordingly' (80).

Section 11: The Influence of Policy on War

Up until this point, Clausewitz has been examining the problems that arise because of the symmetry of counteraction. He now returns to the question of the effects of the interactions on each of the two opponents, and argues that this object has up until now been 'rather overshadowed' by the law of the extremes. As soon as this law 'begins to lose its force' and is replaced by the calculation of probabilities, the political purpose of war must come to the fore again. In this section, therefore, Clausewitz leaves the level of counteraction and returns to the examination of action (80).

In this section there is a passage that can be used to elucidate the distinction between action and counteraction. Clausewitz's argument here uses the idea of war's instrumentality as a means of policy, but he restricts this in a very significant way. The political purpose is only described as the 'original motive' of war. One and the same political purpose can have quite different effects when pursued by different peoples and at different times. The influence of policy on war is limited to the extent to which it influences 'the forces it is meant to move'. It is possible that 'there can be such tensions' and such a 'mass of inflammable material' between two peoples and states that 'the slightest quarrel can produce a wholly disproportionate effect—a real explosion' (81).

This position is diametrically opposed to the statements of the famous formula (in sections 24 and 25), which declares that war is a 'true political instrument'. The only thing that remains as a specific characteristic of war, Clausewitz stresses there, relates purely to the specific nature of the means employed. However strongly war may also, in some cases, affect the political intentions of the actors once it has started, this can only be seen as a modification of those intentions. Clausewitz emphasizes this thought when he says that the political intention is the purpose and war is the means of reaching it; the means can never be thought of in isolation from the purpose (87). Immediately after making this point, Clausewitz even argues that the more violent the tension preceding a war, the closer it comes to its abstract, absolute form; even this kind of war, though, is politically determined (sections 25 and 26, pp. 87–8).

Although Clausewitz sees one case in which the tensions between states are so great that even a trivial quarrel can lead to an explosion (section 11), he argues later that even a war with a tendency to become total remains politically determined (sections 24–6). There is a logical contradiction here, but this antithesis can be resolved. My argument with respect to this point is that in the later sections (24–6), Clausewitz emphasizes that each of the opponents will remain responsible for his own actions, even in a war with a tendency to become total.

However, after his examination of the three interactions as forms of symmetrical counteraction, he moves on to a *first attempt* to analyse their relationship to the initial definition of war, which was oriented towards the autonomous will. Clausewitz says clearly at this point: the political object will determine both the military objective to be reached and the amount of effort it requires, but it cannot 'in itself' provide the standard of measurement because it can do so 'only in the context of the two states at war' (81). In this way it becomes possible for one and the same political purpose to have quite different effects.

Having dealt with the two types of action separately up to this point, Clausewitz turns for the first time in this section to an analysis of the relationship between action and the momentum which arises out of counteraction.

Sections 12–14: An Interruption of Military Activity

Immediately after this, Clausewitz begins to differentiate further the idea of counteraction. He introduces this question with an examination of interruptions in military activity. It is at first glance surprising that Clausewitz should consider an examination of interruptions of military activity to be necessary at the level of abstraction at which Chapter 1 operates. One indication of just how surprising the examination of this topic at this point is can be seen in the fact that up until now, commentators on Chapter 1 have paid absolutely no attention to it. They have evidently seen it as a special military problem which does not fit Chapter 1's level of abstraction. However, as Clausewitz puts it: 'can the process of war be interrupted, even for a moment? The question reaches deep into the heart of the matter'

(81–2). This question becomes interesting at the point where Clausewitz again begins to discuss tendencies to moderation and to escalation. He initially rejects the view that a balance between the warring parties can explain the interruption (82–3). In fact, he says, both parties' striving to avoid a situation of balance would bring with it a new continuity of escalation (section 14, 83).

Sections 15–17: Polarity as Against the Asymmetry of Attack and Defence

The difference between the two forms of counteraction emerges even more clearly in the following sections of Chapter 1. Up until this point, Clausewitz has distinguished between the individual action and individual will of each actor, and the counteraction that results when two equal wills collide with one another and each side seeks to impose its will on the other. Now he differentiates between the symmetrical and the asymmetrical form of counteraction. He starts by explaining once again the specific feature of symmetrical counteraction: 'In a battle each side aims at victory; that is a case of true polarity, since the victory of one side excludes the victory of the other' (83). This symmetry is conceptualized with the help of the category of polarity. Clausewitz then distinguishes it from another form of counteraction, which he discusses by using the example of the relationship between attack and defence.

Clausewitz begins this section by saying that if there were only one form of war in which there was no difference between attack and defence, the forms of fighting would be 'identical'. In this case fighting would be a zero-sum game and a 'true polarity'; one side loses whatever the other side gains. Clausewitz then stresses that attack and defence are in fact very different, and of unequal strength. Defence, he says, is a stronger form of war than attack. This means that the escalatory effect of the equality of the two sides, each of which wants to defeat the other, is lost as a result of the different strengths of attack and defence, and so becomes ineffective. 'I am convinced that the superiority of the defensive (if rightly understood) is very great, far greater than appears at first sight. It is this which explains without any inconsistency most periods of inaction that occur in war' (84).

Here too, one could argue that Chapter 1 is not really the right place for a discussion of attack and defence. However, Clausewitz is drawing attention to a more fundamental problem, that of counteraction in war.

We can shed more light on this problem if we bring in some additional statements about the difference between attack and defence from Chapter 2 in which Clausewitz distinguishes the positive purpose of the attack from the negative purpose of the defence. He describes this positive purpose as the destruction of the enemy forces, but characterizes the negative purpose differently: 'But resistance is a form of action, aimed at destroying enough of the enemy's power to force him to renounce his intentions.' Clausewitz understands this 'pure resistance' as 'fighting without a positive intention' (93), whereas this positive intention involves an action where an attempt is made to impose one's will on an opponent.

On the basis of this distinction between the two kinds of action, Clausewitz concludes that there is a fundamental difference between attack and defence. He formulates this as follows: 'Here lies the origin of the distinction that dominates the whole of war: the difference between attack and defence' (94). The most general aspect of this difference is, says Clausewitz, that while the attack seeks to destroy the enemy's resistance, the defence has a different purpose: 'Preserving our own forces has a negative purpose: it frustrates the enemy's intentions—that is, it amounts to pure resistance' (98). Clausewitz's initial definition of war says that the enemy must be compelled to do one's will, but defence is characterized differently. The content of defence is self-preservation driven by the imperative of not allowing the enemy to impose his will on us.

It is true that this distinction is relative. One could argue that if one of the two sides does not allow the enemy to impose his will, or is trying to prevent him doing so, then this side too is trying to compel the enemy to do his own will. This relative equality explains the possibility, which frequently becomes a reality, that action and asymmetrical counteraction may in practice merge with one another. But this does not mean that the entirely distinctive nature of the two kinds of action, and the difference between them, disappears. I assume that action and asymmetrical counteraction account for different forms of rationality in both physical and political self-preservation. The difference between these two forms of action becomes particularly clear in partisan warfare: partisans who put up 'pure resistance' have already 'won' if they do not allow the enemy to 'defeat' them.[155]

Sections 18–22: Probabilities, Chance, and War as a Gamble

In the next few sections, Clausewitz sets out the conclusions that follow from the antithesis of action and interruption in war. He says that an interruption moves war even further away from the absolute and makes it a calculation of probability in which chance dominates. Because of war's complete unpredictability, its objective nature and subjective appearance make it seem like a game: 'In short, absolute, so-called mathematical, factors never find a firm basis in military calculations. From the very start there is an interplay of possibilities, probabilities, good luck and bad that weaves its way throughout the length and breadth of the tapestry. In the whole range of human activities, war most closely resembles a game of cards' (86). We have reached another of Clausewitz's 'extreme points' here, but this time it is the extreme of chance, of a game of cards, rather than of force. The three interactions to the extreme were determined by the extreme of force and the extreme logic of escalation; now, Clausewitz compares war with the extremes of chance that occur in a game of cards, with its complete unpredictability.

However, Clausewitz does not simply regret this uncertainty, the way warfare depends on good or bad luck, on probabilities and unpredictability.[156] It is only because war is, as Clausewitz understands it, marked by a series of unpredictable factors that moral forces such as courage, self-confidence, and boldness, 'even foolhardiness' acquire their meaning. 'The art of war deals with living and with moral forces. Consequently, it cannot attain the absolute, or certainty; it must always leave a margin for uncertainty' (86). The uncertainty of warfare also means that daring, caution, and shrewdness become more significant. Clausewitz concludes that in general, this suits human nature best (86).

Sections 23–6: The Famous Formula

After this comparison of the unpredictability of war with a game of cards, Clausewitz stresses in the next section that war remains 'a serious means to a serious end' (86). This is an obvious change of subject, which brings Clausewitz back to the political conceptualization of war. The transition between these two sections appears to be a sudden break in the argument. This reveals a characteristic of the account which runs through the whole of Chapter 1. Clausewitz takes each aspect of his subject, and examines it so fully and exhaustively that the internal logic of the account leads to an extreme. Once a full account of one aspect has been given or has reached an extreme, he turns to the antithesis of this question or tries to sum up what he has said so far so that the continuity of the argument is not lost.

To explain this approach very briefly: Clausewitz begins with the definition, which seems to him to be complete. He then introduces the three interactions to the extreme in connection with the aim of the military action, and this leads him to extremes. The account then goes off in a different direction, as Clausewitz suggests that in reality there would never be any such escalation to the extreme. The interactions to escalation and to limitation are focused on the equal wills of both opponents, and identify the question of their contrasting effects. Clausewitz then changes his perspective again, and introduces the idea that opponents in war do not want the same thing; in fact, there are different forms of counteraction. This brings Clausewitz to a new extreme, the comparison between war and a game of cards. This too calls for a new antithesis: war is not a game of cards, but rather 'a clash between major interests, which is resolved by bloodshed' (149).

After Clausewitz has, within the internal logic of Chapter 1, started by examining the action of one of the two sides and then looked at counteraction that can either be symmetrical ('the enemy does the same') or asymmetrical (the desire not to allow the enemy to impose his will on one), he returns once again to the question of action. War should, he says, remain subject to the action of a 'superior intelligence' in order to be able to deal with the unpredictable nature of counteraction (87). The continued influence of the momentum of counteraction, which he examined earlier, becomes clear when one considers the following sentence: 'Policy, then, will permeate all military operations, and in so far as their violent nature will admit, it will have a continuous influence on them' (87).

I would like to suggest that this formulation is where Clausewitz provides his best description both of the influence of policy on warfare and of the limits of its importance. Immediately after this he changes his perspective once again and states the world-famous formula, 'war is merely the continuation of policy by other means' (87). In terms of its content, one certainly cannot say that this conceptualization of war follows from the way the argument has developed in Chapter 1 so far. In fact, the reverse is the case. In particular, the statement that war is 'merely' a continuation of policy has led to numerous misunderstandings in the literature. A complete reduction of war to an instrument of policy would be a contradiction even within Chapter 1, as it would conflict with the 'wondrous Trinity'.

Within the implicit logic of Chapter 1 as I have presented it, however, the formula emerges as Clausewitz returns once again to the level of action. This can be seen in particular in his statement that war must remain subject to the action of a superior intelligence and has a political purpose. What he is therefore doing in the famous formula is stressing action, the responsibility of each of the two opponents for their own actions. Since, with the exception of the initial definition, Clausewitz has concentrated as Chapter 1 progresses on reciprocal counteraction, there is a new break in the argument when he returns to autonomy and the responsibility of each party for his own actions. In order to ensure that this dimension of action is distinguished sharply enough from the counteraction he has just dealt with, he exaggerates this point (probably unconsciously) and says that war is *merely* a continuation of policy by other means.

In the three sections that follow the formula, Clausewitz argues that both limited and unlimited wars are politically determined, whatever appearances may suggest (87–9). This argument is not at all unsurprising, as Clausewitz has explained the expansion of warfare in the French Revolution by referring to changes in political circumstances and has also explained Napoleon's final defeat with reference to changes in domestic political conditions. However, this position contradicts the last sentence before the introduction of the formula, which states that policy only influences military operations 'in so far as their violent nature will admit' (87).[157]

In section 11 of Chapter 1 Clausewitz stresses that even a very minor political quarrel can lead to a real explosion of warfare and that one and the same purpose can have different effects (80–1). Within the context of the formula he says the opposite: even total war remains determined by the political purpose. How can this contradiction be resolved? In my view, this is only possible if we assume that *before* the formula Clausewitz sees the influence of policy as limited by the momentum of counteraction. *After* the formula, though, he develops a position which states that even an unlimited war retains a dimension in which the parties are responsible for their own actions; this dimension does not disappear completely in the imposed reciprocity of counteraction.

Section 27: Consequences for the Theory of War

After Clausewitz has provided an exhaustive account of the influence of the political purpose, he reaches another extreme. Even in an unlimited war with a tendency to become total, he says, warfare is determined by policy. This position obviously strikes him as so extreme that he immediately qualifies it, and there is another sharp break in the argument. The next 'antithesis' is the introduction of the category of the 'wondrous Trinity', in which the instrumentality of war fought for a political purpose is now only one of three tendencies of equal importance.

Section 28: The Result—'Wondrous Trinity'

The three different dimensions of action (action, symmetrical counteraction, and asymmetrical counteraction) are still reflected in the 'wondrous Trinity'. Action appears in the conceptualization of war as a subordinate instrument of policy. The activities of commanders and armies attempting to defeat each other can be interpreted as symmetrical counteraction: 'the scope which the play of courage and talent will enjoy in the realm of probability and chance' depends on the particular character of the commander and his army. (89). The primordial violence of war, as the third dimension of the 'wondrous Trinity', cannot be immediately classified in an unambiguous way as a kind of action.

As I have already indicated, in one of his antitheses Clausewitz derives the actual theory of war from defence: 'Consider ... how war originates. Essentially, the concept of war does not originate with the attack' (377).[158] The absolute purpose of attack is primarily possession, and only secondarily fighting, while defence is determined by fighting and self-preservation. An invasion or conquest is not yet a war. Fighting and war only come about when the side under attack defends itself. Clausewitz is therefore saying that the way war comes into existence, its origin, is primarily a matter of defence, and this in turn is determined by the taking of counteraction so that the enemy cannot impose his will on one. If we combine the category of original violence with Clausewitz's identification of defence as the phenomenon that gives rise to war, we can say that defence is determined by asymmetrical counteraction. This indicates that the three tendencies of the 'wondrous Trinity' provide a systematic reflection of the three dimensions of action—action, asymmetrical counteraction, and symmetrical counteraction.

4.4. CLAUSEWITZ'S 'TESTAMENT': BRINGING TOGETHER THE INITIAL THREE-PART DEFINITION AND THE 'WONDROUS TRINITY'

Let us summarize our findings in relation to the structure of Clausewitz's Chapter 1. War is for Clausewitz a conflict made up of active, reciprocal actions. Chapter 1 of Book I of *On War* is Clausewitz's attempt to bring together his diverse experiences of war and his understanding of its essential dynamism within an analytic synthesis. However, because he has such a realistic view of the world, Clausewitz cannot be satisfied with one-sided conceptualizations of war. He has too much intellectual integrity to derive his theory of war from dogmatic positions. In Chapter 1, whenever he has provided a full account of one elemental conceptualization of war or taken it to its logical conclusion, he then shifts to an antithesis, and from this point begins to investigate a new aspect of his subject.

What this means for the interpretation of Chapter 1 is that Clausewitz conceptualized war as a process developing within the antitheses of the 'wondrous Trinity' and the initial three-part definition. These antitheses are boundary concepts, tendencies or dimensions which characterize every war. Depending on the historical situation, the external circumstances, and the decisions taken in each case, one or other of these poles comes to the fore at the expense of the others. Every war, though, is characterized by the antitheses between the instrumental rationality of force and its 'primordial violence', of an immanent, necessary logic of action and counteraction, and of the play of chance and probability. War as a *continuation of policy* by *other means* itself rests on a tension that can never be overcome. The influence of policy on warfare is, says Clausewitz, very great, but he simultaneously stresses that policy makes use of *other* means when a decision to wage war is taken.

Clausewitz's way of proceeding in Chapter 1 follows the logic of the succession of action, symmetrical counteraction, and asymmetrical counteraction. He sees action as tied to a rationality of purpose, aim, and means; action's relationship to its own means of power and to the enemy is an instrumental one which treats them as objects. However, because there are two opponents who are both doing 'the same thing', a dynamic is set in motion which releases other forms of rationality. Initially, this 'doing the same thing' leads to symmetrical counteraction which gives expression to the fact that each of the two sides is seeking to defeat the other. This counteraction relates primarily to the enemy's actions rather than to the enemy as an object.

In the three interactions to the extreme the reflexivity of this counteraction leads to escalation and the absolute of violence, but in the three interactions to limited war it leads, via communication between the sides and the passage of time, to a moderation of violence. However, this does not mean the end of the dynamic that develops out of the fact that the enemy does the same. Because both sides do the same thing and each wants to compel the other to do its will, it is inevitable that resistance actions arise in the form of a determination not to let the enemy impose his will and to assert one's own will or special qualities. This last concept of asymmetrical counteraction can be connected with the original concept of action: not allowing the enemy to impose his will can equally well be described as the assertion of one's own will, which one is attempting to compel the enemy to accept. In fact, the distinction between action, symmetrical counteraction, and asymmetrical counteraction not only distinguishes between different kinds of action but also makes distinctions within one and the same kind of action.

Clausewitz's contemporary Hegel emphasized that the truth could not be stated in one sentence only. Each of Hegel's statements, like each of Clausewitz's, calls for an antithesis to follow it.[159] As quoted earlier, Carl Linnebach emphasized Clausewitz's way of developing his ideas as follows: 'The statements and counter-statements made by Clausewitz are like "weights and counterweights", and one could say that through their play and interplay the scales of truth are brought into balance.'[160] The statement and counterstatement of Chapter 1 of Book I are the initial three-part definition and the 'wondrous Trinity' at the end of this chapter. In Chapter 1, Clausewitz depicts the contrasting effects of the three conceptual fields of violence/force, fighting, and policy. War is characterized by these 'boundary concepts' (Muenkler), which in Clausewitz's account constitute every war and within which war develops as a form of 'Between'.

5

Polarities and the Asymmetry between Attack and Defence

> And if we are ever to succeed in creating a political theory worthy of the name, this will only be possible in a similar way, by means of an equally harmonious combination of conflicting elements.
>
> Hans Rothfels[161]

Clausewitz's Testament is characterized by the way in which it brings together contrasting tendencies. According to Clausewitz, war is made up of the antitheses that constitute his three-part definition and the 'wondrous Trinity'. My argument so far has been that the antitheses in Clausewitz's political theory can be explained with reference to his own experience of war. This made it possible to explain the antitheses in Chapter 1 by distinguishing between action and counteraction. The subject of the present chapter is Clausewitz's attempt to think systematically about the interaction of antithetical elements.

5.1. ANTITHESES IN THE THOUGHT OF CLAUSEWITZ AND HIS CONTEMPORARIES

Clausewitz was aware that the conceptualization of war in terms of antitheses was problematic, and he made some attempts to solve this problem. Evidence of this can be found in his statement that he intended to write a separate chapter on the principle of polarity (83). He was never able to do this, as was the case with so many of the plans he had at the time of his death. In an article written shortly before he died, Clausewitz says that the 'whole of physical and intellectual nature' is kept in balance by means of antitheses.[162] When he deals with the relationship between attack and defence, Clausewitz even speaks of the 'true logical antithesis' between them, which is of greater significance than a simple logical contradiction (523).

Raymond Aron and Peter Paret, the authors of some of the most important studies of Clausewitz published to date, have both emphasized his 'dialectical' method. Aron assumes that Clausewitz would have disclosed the secret of his method in the chapter he intended to write about polarity. He draws attention in particular to the fact that none of the commentators on Clausewitz has so far undertaken any further investigation of the significance of this remark. The planned chapter on polarity would, says Aron, have covered the different kinds of antithesis, which is to say that it would have dealt with the particular features of Clausewitz's method. Aron assumes that in this chapter, Clausewitz would have revealed the secret of his dialectics.[163] It is this question, the secret of Clausewitz's dialectics, that I now wish to look at more closely.

Aron argues that the narrow concept of polarity could not become a fundamental concept for Clausewitz because it is tied to the idea of a zero-sum game. As Clausewitz puts it, the principle of polarity is only valid in cases where 'positive and negative interests exactly cancel one another out'. In a battle, both sides are trying to win; only this is 'true polarity', since if one wins the other must lose (83). Aron distinguishes between the zero-sum game of the duel and the diverse forms of antithesis which are typical of the pairs of concepts Clausewitz uses. In these antitheses, each concept can be seen as a pole: theory and practice, the scale of success and the risk taken, attack and defence. Aron concludes that if one wanted to identify a fundamental concept in Clausewitz, it would be that of the antithesis.[164]

Peter Paret determines that Clausewitz's general approach is dialectical in character. This was, he says, something shared by Clausewitz's generation, all of whom thought in terms such as contradiction, polarity, the separation and connection of the active and passive, the positive and the negative. The principle of polarity seemed to be the only thing that could overcome the infinite distance between the positive and the negative. Clausewitz's treatments of polarity and of the relationship between attack and defence were, according to Paret, variations on a theme that was very popular at the time.[165]

What was the significance of the concept of polarity in Clausewitz's time? It was a fundamental principle of Goethe's understanding of nature that a force could be divided into polar opposites, but that these would then reunite. Goethe wrote in 1828 that the concepts of polarity and growth were the two great wheels driving the whole of nature. Clausewitz's remarks at the beginning of his first chapter are in accordance with this methodological principle: he infers the natural intensification of force within the three interactions to the extreme from the polarity of the duel (75–7). Hegel stressed that the contemporary discovery of polarity had been of 'enormous significance'.

During this period, a time of fundamental changes in the circumstances of life, ideas, habits of thought, and political conditions, the question of whether an antithesis should be thought of as a unity, or if it was only possible to emphasize the contrast between old and new, was an issue of paramount importance. In 1811, Rahel Levin described this problem in the following terms: 'In this new world that has been broken into pieces, the only thing left to a man who wishes to understand . . . is the heroism of scholarship.'[166]

There are different aspects of polarity which need to be distinguished from one another. Schelling, for example, stressed the idea that behind what appeared to be contrasts there was a hidden identity that must be sought, and understood polarity as a law of the world: 'It is *a priori* certain that . . . real principles opposed to another are at work throughout the whole of nature.' If these opposing principles are united in one body, they give that body polarity, according to Schelling. Goethe, on the other hand, placed more emphasis on the idea that there was a lively tension between the opposites: 'The life of nature divides what is unified and unites what is divided.'[167]

The most important influences on Clausewitz were the rationalist currents of the Enlightenment, Idealism, Romanticism, and the findings of the natural sciences. It was from Kiesewetter, a follower of Kant, that Clausewitz learned about rationalism at an early age. During Clausewitz's time in Berlin, the idealism of Fichte and Hegel was the dominant current of thought in intellectual circles. It has to be mentioned, that Clausewitz also spent a number of weeks in 1829 reading the Goethe–Schiller correspondence. Additionally, he also attended the lectures of the romantic philosopher Heinrich Steffens during the winter of 1824–5, and those of the naturalist Alexander von Humboldt, which were the start of a new flowering of the natural sciences in Germany, in 1827.[168]

Clausewitz took up aspects of all these tendencies within the thought of his contemporaries and used them in his theory of war, to the extent that they helped him to reflect on his own experiences of war. One can say that Clausewitz's own position floats within the field formed by these four currents of thought. Each of them provided him with stimulation, but his own position cannot be traced back to any single one of them. By floating in this way, Clausewitz was able to develop a position of his own which is more than a mere variation on the theme of the significance of antitheses and their unity, which was so widely discussed at the time.

5.1.1. Polarity in Clausewitz's Thought

There are only four places in the whole of Clausewitz's writings where the concept of polarity appears. The first of these is to be found in the title of a section dealing with the simultaneous and the successive use of the armed forces, in a very early text entitled *Leitfaden zur Bearbeitung der Taktik der Gefechtslehre*. In this section, Clausewitz says that it is important to understand the laws of polarity. The two ways in which the armed forces can be used are simultaneously or successively, and these can be understood as a pair of poles which balance each other.[169] The second use of the concept of polarity comes in Clausewitz's report on the Russian campaign. Here he uses the concept to demonstrate that both Napoleon and his opponent Kutuzov had the same desire not to fight another battle after Borodino.[170]

The third appearance of the concept of polarity is to be found in one of the works that was unpublished in Clausewitz's lifetime. This is a preliminary sketch of the chapter on polarity he intended to write. Here, Clausewitz stresses that polarity is by no means restricted to the description of an antithesis and that it also implies equality between the two poles. He says that the rule that one should always do the opposite of what the enemy wants, which is so often found in the works of military writers is no more than a distorted picture of the truth. This rule can easily deceive the unwary. The mistaken, or at least misunderstood, precondition is that the two commanders never want the same thing and always have contrasting desires. It is true that the activities of the two sides are set against one another and tend to cancel each other out. It is seen to follow from this that any advantage gained by one side will *eo ipso* be to the disadvantage of the other. However, this is only true if we look at each individual and fail to consider the whole context.

Clausewitz then subordinates the polarity of the individual elements of a situation ('Elementarteilchen' in German) to the oppositions relating to the whole; he argues that it is not in the end the polarity of the parts that is decisive, but rather that of the unities: 'The most complete and necessary elements are the final goals and the highest unities, which cancel each other out.'[171] In this draft, the main question Clausewitz is addressing is that of why two opponents in war see one and the same thing as being to their advantage, and can in this respect—despite their antagonism—also pursue the same interests. In saying this, he qualifies the opposition within the polarity (though this continues to exist) and places more emphasis on the equality of the poles.

The final occasion on which Clausewitz speaks of polarity is in Chapter 1 of *On War*, where he develops a concept of a 'genuine polarity': 'By thinking that the interests of the two commanders are opposed in equal measure to each other, we have assumed a genuine *polarity*' (emphasis in original). The principle of polarity is only valid, he says, when polarity is thought of in relation to one and the same object, where the positive and negative interests cancel each other out completely. Clausewitz develops this thought further by saying that if there were no defence but just 'attacking the enemy' by both sides, war would always be exactly the same: 'then every advantage gained by one side would be a precisely equal disadvantage to the other—true polarity would exist' (83). Friedrich Engels follows the same train of thought in connection with the relationship between attraction and repulsion, originally emphasized by Kant. These forces, he says, offset each other perfectly, and this situation follows as a matter of necessity from the nature of polar distribution: two magnetic poles would not be true poles if they did not exist in balance with one another. As mentioned, Aron characterizes this form of polarity as a zero-sum game, that is to say a case in which a gain for one side means a loss for the other.[172]

If we look more closely at Clausewitz's text here, we can see that he really does use the concept of polarity in connection with the idea of a zero-sum game; however, he only does this in order to distance himself from this idea immediately afterwards. He argues that when we speak of two different things which have a common relation external to themselves, it is the relationship and not the things themselves which partakes of polarity. Clausewitz put this concept of polarity forward in his analysis of the Russian campaign: 'Polarity refers only to the end, not the means.' The title of section 16 states that attack and defence are different in kind and of unequal strength, so that the idea of polarity seems not to be applicable to them. But it is clear that what Clausewitz means here is that polarity as a zero-sum game would not be applicable to attack and defence. He does, though, explain that the polarity of attack and defence is to be found in the decision, which is what they both seek to achieve (83–4).

Clausewitz thus distinguishes between two elements within polarity. He initially emphasizes that the two poles are united because they are elements of an overarching whole. In this respect there is no difference between attack and defence, both of which are just elements of war. Clausewitz characterizes this aspect by saying that the principle of polarity is only valid when it is thought of as applying to one and the same object. Immediately after this, he stresses that the polarity (of attack and defence) is characterized by the relationship between the poles, not by the poles as 'things'[173] (83–4). If we turn this around, we can say that Clausewitz's concept of polarity is characterized by a high degree of symmetry, and implies the similarity or equal strength of the poles. Clausewitz goes on to argue that true polarity is when the victory of one side destroys the victory of the other. Polarity is present when any advantage one side gains in combat would be an equally great disadvantage to the other (83–4). The equality of the poles is demonstrated by their symmetry, but Clausewitz stresses that these are not 'things', not objects. What does he mean by this distinction?

5.1.2. Polarity Explained, Using the Example of a Magnet

In order to clarify the question of whether polar opposites relate to the poles as 'things' or to their relationship to one another, it is helpful to consider the example of a magnet. Hegel incorporated into his work a finding from natural science, the idea that even filing through a magnet does not lead to a separation of the poles. If we do this what we have is not separate north and south poles, but more than one of each type and more than one magnet. Clausewitz understands polarity as a relationship between opposites rather than one between different 'things'. According to this conception, the unity of north and south poles does make them an inseparable unity as a third entity, the magnet.[174] The equality of the poles in a magnet is not material or concrete. There is no north or south pole as a thing, an object, just their inseparable unity as a magnet. This is the sense in which Clausewitz emphasizes that in polarity, it is the relationship rather than the things themselves which establishes an identity. There is therefore a third entity which goes beyond the two poles and exceeds them. This third entity, though, is by no means located outside the two opposites; it is determined by the opposition in the relationship of the two poles.

One can get a particularly vivid sense of this model by considering not just the opposition between the poles treated as a unity, but also their field formed by a magnet. The dynamic element in the model of polarity, which forms its structure, also discloses its full scope when the extremes are not perceived as things, objects, substances, and so on. This interpretation corresponds to Hegel's position on the philosophical conceptualization of magnetism, which understands it as a purely immaterial form.[175] If the poles in a polar antithesis are understood as objects, the concept of the object entails a separation. It would therefore be a logical contradiction to assign a unity to the antithesis between objects within one and the same relationship. In Clausewitz's treatment of polarity he argues unambiguously that it can only be thought of in relation to one and the same object. This means, quite simply, that the poles in this kind of antithetical relationship cannot themselves be objects.

There was a very similar problem in mathematics during Clausewitz's lifetime, which became a philosophical problem too once Kant had taken it up. This involved the question of how the content of negative numbers could be provided with a philosophical basis. If positive numbers exist and zero is understood as 'nothing', what are negative numbers? Less than nothing? Kant tried to solve this problem by treating positive and negative numbers as relations rather than substances.[176]

Since this is all Clausewitz wrote on the subject of polarity, I shall now try to deduce his likely intentions by looking at the work of one of his contemporaries, Johann Bernhard Wilbrand. Wilbrand taught anatomy, physiology, and natural history in Giessen, and was also the head of the town's botanical garden. In 1819, he identified the following elements of polarity:[177] Polarity is, he says:

1. an opposition between two entities, each of which presupposes the existence of the other, and where one of the two only has its characteristic meaning when opposed to the other;
2. the internal unity of this antithesis within a third entity, which
3. has the antithesis to thank for its own characteristic unity, which could not be in being without the antithesis.

Arguing in a way that is very close to Clausewitz's method in the 'wondrous Trinity' sections, Wilbrand concludes that neither feature takes priority over the other. Summing up the state of natural-scientific knowledge at the time, Wilbrand immediately stresses both the antithesis and the inseparable unity within a higher whole. It has turned out to be the case, he writes, that both electric and magnetic phenomena rest on an internal antithesis. The nature of this antithesis is that the opposing forces are both part of one and the same whole. Wilbrand argues that the most important aspect of the concept of polarity is the fact that it points to an antithesis that only exists within one and the same whole.[178]

For Wilbrand, the concept of polarity corresponds to a 'dynamic view of nature'. This view of nature may treat material as the result of interaction between two opposing forces, or portray natural phenomena as the result of an antithesis. Wilbrand distinguishes his position sharply from atomism. The difference between atomism and dynamism becomes evident, he says, when we ask about the origins of matter. Wilbrand then refers explicitly to Kant, saying Kant has shown that all material can only be thought of as the product of two conflicting forces.[179] Clausewitz's idea of polarity, like Wilbrand's, is dynamic and characterized by an implicit rejection of atomism.

Let us try to summarize what Clausewitz says about polarity. Although polarity involves an antithesis, it constitutes a third entity as a unity. This third entity is the whole, whether it be the magnet determined by the polar relationship, or war, which Clausewitz sees as characterized by the 'true logical antithesis' of attack and defence. This identity of an object can only exist because the poles within such a relationship are not 'things'. Even a violent splitting of the two parts of this relationship of mutual dependency does not lead to a genuine separation of the opposing poles, but rather to the multiplication of their potential. When Clausewitz emphasizes polarity, he is giving expression to his dynamic conception of war.

5.2. THE CONCEPT OF THE 'TRUE LOGICAL ANTITHESIS'

I do not entirely share Raymond Aron's view that Clausewitz would have revealed the 'secret of his method' in the chapter he intended to write about polarity. Although it is true that polarity is an important part of Clausewitz's theory, he does not leave things there. In Clausewitz's view, polarity would only be present if there were just *one* form of war, attacking the enemy, a case in which one side's advantage is always an equally great disadvantage to the other side. In order to explain how varied war can be and how it does not always consist of one and the same battle, Clausewitz introduces the categories of attack and defence. These categories are in one sense polar opposites in their mutual relations, but at the same time they are fundamentally different and are therefore something other than polarity. Clausewitz expresses this tension by saying that polarity cannot be applied to attack and defence as things, but is only in their relationship[180] (83). This means that his conception of attack and defence goes beyond pure polarity. To emphasize the difference, Clausewitz says that polarity lies 'not... in attack or defence, but in the object both seek to achieve: the decision' (84).

Clausewitz stresses that in a 'true polarity', the forms of fighting would be 'identical'. Even though he says some positive things about polarity, he criticizes it because it is a concept that cannot be used to make any further progress in thought (83–4). Clausewitz's criticism of the limitations of 'pure' polarity can be explained with the help of a comparison with G. W. F. Hegel's position.[181] Although Hegel too is extremely positive about polarity, there are some points in his treatment that also lead him to criticize the concept.[182] The most important of these are:

1. Hegel is critical of the fact that in polarity there is no transition from unity to antithesis and back to identity. Polarity thus lacks further development, since the unity of the antithesis is simply presupposed. Clausewitz argues in an analogous way, saying that a purely polar duel always remains one and the same.
2. Hegel argues that in polarity there is no transition between the opposites; they do not mutually interpenetrate one another. On the basis of his own experiences of war, Clausewitz too insists that attack and defence can merge with one another in war.

3. In polarity, the equality of the poles is complete, so that there is no perceptible difference between them in terms of their content; in Hegel's critique, polarity has not yet reached the stage of being a concept.[183] Clausewitz takes up this criticism when he says that attack and defence are very different and of unequal strength.

Clausewitz develops a position that goes beyond the limitations of the idea of polarity, but simultaneously tries to incorporate its positive aspects. He understands the relationship between attack and defence as a polar one that explains the unity of war. However, he argues that the difference between them mainly is responsible for the concrete course taken by wars. The relationship between attack and defence therefore allowed Clausewitz to extrapolate a model that he used to conceptualize (at least implicitly) the unity of antitheses within an identity. The model character of this conceptualization is underlined by the fact that Clausewitz places particular stress on the relationship between attack and defence; he calls attack and defence a 'true logical antithesis'.

Clausewitz's exposition of this concept is as follows: 'Where two ideas form a true logical antithesis, each complementary to the other, then fundamentally each is implied in the other. The limitations of our mind may not allow us to comprehend both simultaneously, and to discover by antithesis the whole of one in the whole of the other. Nevertheless each will shed enough reciprocal light to clarify many of the details' (523). What does Clausewitz mean when, at the beginning of Book VII, he calls attack and defence a 'true logical antithesis'? It is clear that he is not only distinguishing this 'true logical antithesis' from another form, the normal or usual antithesis; in addition, he is characterizing this kind of antithesis as the real or 'true' logical antithesis.

What is the relationship between Clausewitz's conception of the 'true logical antithesis' and the concept of polarity? He argues that attack and defence are different kinds of thing and have different degrees of strength. In the text that Aron calls the 'Second Note',[184] Clausewitz explains that defence is the stronger form of fighting with a negative purpose, while attack is the weaker form with a positive purpose. Aron considers this to be Clausewitz's antithesis *par excellence*. It is noticeable here that the difference between attack and defence is captured in concepts that are themselves not far from being polar opposites: negative and positive purpose, stronger and weaker forms of fighting. In the simple form of polarity, when both poles are absolutely equal, there can be no progress or development. Clausewitz says quite clearly that in this case, fighting is always one and the same. There can only be a development in war, he argues, when other antitheses, which are themselves very similar to polar opposites, are incorporated into the simple polar antithesis.[185] It is this totality formed by the unity of different antitheses that Clausewitz calls the 'true logical antithesis' of attack and defence.

In order to explain the 'true logical antithesis' in more detail, let us begin by identifying its characteristics (at the beginning of Book VII):

If two concepts form a true logical antithesis,

- in which one is complementary to the other,
- each is fundamentally implied in the other.

Let us now ask what Clausewitz means by a complement. One contemporary encyclopedia presents various definitions of the concept of a complement, and one of these comes very close to the way Clausewitz uses the term: 'A complement or supplement is what needs to be added to a quantity in order for it to be equal to another quantity. In pure mathematics, we encounter this expression most frequently in the following connection: the complement of a fraction is what must be added to the fraction for it to be made equal to 1.'[186] An important characteristic of the relationship between attack and defence can be seen clearly here: attack and defence complement each other so that they form a whole (i.e. they equal 1).

The modern concept of complementarity is rather different. It is now understood as the shared element linking alternative ways of *experiencing* the same object. We speak of different forms of knowledge being complementary to the extent that they apply with equal validity to the same object. However, they exclude each other in the sense that they cannot provide knowledge of this object simultaneously and in relation to the same moment. This modern concept of complementarity attained general scientific significance as a result of Niels Bohr's interpretation of wave–particle dualism.[187]

There is a clear difference between this definition and the earlier one. The 'modern' concept of complementarity is characterized by the fact that the antitheses exclude each other to the extent that they cannot be experienced simultaneously and in relation to the same moment; but this does not apply to the complementarity between attack and defence.

Although these complementary characterizations of war are mutually exclusive, they nevertheless constitute the whole of war in relation to the same moment in time and space. Complementary antitheses, unlike polar relationships, also contain numerous forms of coupling and interaction between the two aspects. Clausewitz says that each term is implied in the other.

One modern contribution expresses the limitation of the concept of polarity explicitly. A study of polarity and its significance for the philosophy of modern physics, biology, and psychology specifies the criteria required for polarity and names one feature that can often be observed. The criteria mentioned are those oppositions that follow a regular and necessary pattern, their mutually exclusive nature, and the equally invariable way in which they belong together; it is this last element that would resolve the antithesis in the Hegelian sense. In addition, the absence of any transition between the poles is identified as a special characteristic of polarity. This last relational element is not necessary, but it can be observed in many polar antitheses. There is, it is argued, no dimension that serves as a transition from one pole to the other.[188] The absence of any transition between one pole and the other is thus a crucial characteristic distinguishing polarity in the strict sense from the 'true logical antithesis' of attack and defence.

Let us draw up a preliminary summary of Clausewitz's exposition of the 'true logical antithesis':

1. Like polarity, a 'true logical antithesis' constitutes an identity as an object. The polarity of this antithetical relationship conditions the symmetrical relations between the poles; they are of the same kind, but only in their relationship to one another and not as things.
2. The 'true logical antithesis' goes beyond the limitations of polarity and makes it possible to think in terms of additional forms of interaction and development in this relationship. Each term is implied in the other, and positing one of them entails the other. Clausewitz accounts for development by saying that a 'true logical antithesis' not only implies a single polar relationship, but also includes several such 'antitheses' of the same kind: the polarity of the duel, the positive as against the negative purpose of attack and defence, and their different strengths.

5.3. CLAUSEWITZ ON THE RELATIONSHIP BETWEEN ATTACK AND DEFENCE

Clausewitz's dynamic model is characterized both by the polarity of the duel and by the difference between attack and defence (attack is the weaker form of war with a positive purpose, and defence is the stronger form of war with a negative purpose). This conception enables Clausewitz to think in terms of transitions between and the development of antitheses in war.

Clausewitz's analysis of the relationship between attack and defence is based to a considerable extent on his examination of the Russian campaign. This is where he argues for the first time that attack is the weaker form of war and defence the stronger, but that the former has positive, that is to say greater and more decisive, purposes, while the latter has only negative purposes; it is this that makes it possible for both forms to exist alongside one another.[189] Clausewitz's historical analyses directly influenced both the formation of his theory and his methodological reflections, for '[a]nalysis and observation, theory and experience must never disdain or exclude each other' (61). I have argued that Clausewitz's 'true logical antithesis' goes beyond polarity. There are two respects in which it can be compared with Hegel's conception. Firstly, in both cases the antitheses are opposed to one another, but each also defines its own identity in relation to its opposite. Secondly, there are many forms of transition between attack and defence, and this is excluded in polarity. Let us now look more closely at the various relations of and transitions from attack to defence and from defence to attack.

5.3.1. Different Concepts of Defence

Clausewitz distinguishes between two fundamentally different forms of defence. The first of these is defence in opposition to an attacker; the attacker seeks to overcome the defence, and the defender resists. The second is a quite different form of defence, which is transformed into an element of attack.

The first form of defence is distinguished from attack with the help of the antithesis between a negative and a positive purpose. This distinction is derived from Clausewitz's definition of war. He says that the positive purpose is the desire to impose one's will on the enemy. The content of defence, on the other hand, is self-preservation and resistance to the enemy's intentions. The main concern of the defender is to prevent the enemy imposing his will on one. This is the antithesis, imposing one's will on the enemy (the positive intention) as distinct from frustrating the enemy's intentions (the negative action), which lies at the root of Clausewitz's distinction between the positive and negative purpose of attack and defence (98).

There is a distinction between this concept of defence and a quite different one that constitutes a second form of defence. In the chapter on 'The Nature of Strategic Attack', Clausewitz argues that '[t]he act of attack' is 'a constant alternation and combination of attack and defense'. Defence is not just an effective preparation for attack, he says, but simultaneously its 'impending burden', 'original sin', and 'mortal disease'. Clausewitz describes the transition to defence in terms of the diminishing force of attack: 'The object of strategic attack, therefore, may be thought of in numerous gradations, from the conquest of a whole country to that of an insignificant hamlet. As soon as the objective has been attained the attack ends and the defence takes over' (524–6).

Clausewitz uses quite different concepts of defence in this short passage:

- Firstly, we find a concept of defence that is completely subordinated to attack: defence is nothing more than an effective preparation for attack.
- This concept of effective preparation for attack can be contrasted with a second notion of defence, which places the emphasis on different aspects: 'original sin', 'mortal disease', 'impending burden'. Defence is an element of attack here as well, but it is no longer its effective preparation. It is rather to be understood as something that is attached to attack, but weakens it because it is by nature opposed to it.
- Clausewitz also uses a third concept of defence, as something that takes over when the attack has attained its purpose. This last form of defence is hardly part of war any more, and could be described as the state of affairs after the end of military action, but it is nevertheless assigned to defence.

Although these three concepts of defence are very different, the characteristic they share is the fact that they are a mere tendency within attack. Attack therefore has its own antithesis within itself, but for this very reason, defence, which originally confronts an attack, is transformed into a tendency of the latter. It is vital to appreciate that this process of transformation leads to a change in the content of the concept of defence. When characterized as a tendency within attack, this form of defence differs fundamentally from the one that has an adversarial relationship to attack. Clausewitz says that when an attack comes to an end because the objective has been attained (i.e. its limited or more comprehensive aim) or because it has exhausted its strength, this leads automatically to defence. This defence, which comes about automatically and which is attached to attack or is the consequence of attack, is a fundamentally different kind of defence from the one that is opposed to attack in the strict sense. This latter kind of defence stands opposed to attack, and the aim of attack is to overcome it. This is where attack and defence clash with one another, repulse each other, and are in 'conflict' (Kiesewetter) with each other.

Clausewitz goes on in this section to ask what defence is, and answers his own question: it is nothing but the more effective form of war, by means of which one seeks to attain victory in order to go onto the attack after gaining the upper hand—in other words, to move on to the positive purpose of war. He also emphasizes that: 'A sudden powerful transition to the offensive—the flashing sword of vengeance—is the greatest moment for the defense'[190] (370–1). A further differentiation in the concept of defence emerges here. Defence is nothing less than a more effective form of war; it is only chosen as a preferred way of fighting because it improves the prospects of victory. When Clausewitz puts this argument forward he dispenses almost completely with the difference between attack and defence, so that they are treated as no more than temporary differences in the symmetry of the duel.

Overall, we can distinguish three fundamental concepts of defence in Clausewitz's work:[191]

- Defence is characterized by the purpose of self-preservation and parrying the enemy's blow. With this in mind, Clausewitz argues that the real concept of war only begins with defence, and he stresses the asymmetry between attack and defence. The point of departure for these conceptualizations of defence is the antithesis of the negative and the positive purpose.

- However, defence for Clausewitz is at the same time nothing other than the 'more effective form' of combat, which is selected temporarily so that one can be surer of winning the war. As a consequence of the polarity between them, attack and defence are only different elements within warfare.
- Finally, defence is attached to its own antithesis, defence as a delaying factor and also as an effective preparation; this changes the original concept of defence.

The combination of his various determinations explains the numerous differentiations put forward by Clausewitz in his treatment of the relationship between attack and defence and their respective conceptual expressions. When Clausewitz argues, for example, that defence is a more effective way of preparing an attack, he combines the 'positive purpose' of attack with the greater strength of defence. When, on the other hand, he claims that defence is the original sin of attack, he brings together the positive purpose of attack and the negative purpose of defence on the attacker's side. In one famous passage, Clausewitz says that the 'flashing sword of vengeance' is the greatest moment for the defence. Here he combines the greater strength of defence with the positive purpose of attack.[192]

5.3.2. Different Kinds of Transition: Highest Intensity (Immediacy) and Declining Strength (Mediacy)

In Clausewitz's theory, a standstill within a military activity is a form in which an attack changes into a defence of one's own position. The reason for this transition to defence is either the 'diminishing force' of the attack or the resistance put up by the enemy. For Clausewitz there is a point at which the attack culminates: 'where [the attack's] remaining strength is just enough'. 'Beyond that point the scale turns and the reaction follows.' The force of this kind of reaction is usually much greater than the strength of one's own attack (527–8). Elsewhere, Clausewitz argues in an analogous way when he says that going beyond this culminating point is not just a useless expenditure of energy but also a damaging one. Experience has shown, he says, that the reactions that follow always have disproportionate effects[193] (570). In this way, attack changes initially into a standstill within a military action and subsequently into defence. What is involved here is not the form of defence that is incorporated into the effectiveness of attack; rather, a real change from attack to a state of defence comes about via a standstill within a military activity.

The transition from defence to attack is something quite different, the 'greatest moment' for the defence, as Clausewitz puts it (370). Every defender does all he can to find a way of going over to the attack (600). During the most intensive stage of combat, the differences between attack and defence initially become blurred; it is no longer possible to distinguish between them, so that a direct transition to attack can take place. In concrete reality one certainly encounters quite different, mixed forms of this mutual transition; but if we distinguish between attack and defence by formulating ideal types, they look like this:

- Attack becomes defence via a standstill within a military action—either because the attack has exhausted itself, or because it has reached its culminating point, or because there is no longer any way to attain further political goals on the basis of a reasonable calculation of costs and benefits. A standstill within a military action is the point of medi-acy, the point half way between attack and defence when we consider the transition from attack to defence.
- Defence becomes attack directly via combat, when the intensity of combat has reached a level at which the antithesis of attack and defence is blurred. Defence is therefore transformed *directly* into attack, because this is a change at the highest level of intensity.

Clausewitz gives two explanations of the difference between the transition from attack to defence and the transition from defence to attack. The first of these relates to a standstill within a military action, the second to the highest level of intensity.

5.3.3. Attack and Non-Attack, Defence and Non-Defence

For Clausewitz, the relationship between attack and defence is a 'true logical antithesis'. This raises the question of the relationship between this 'true logical' antithesis and the traditional conception of a logical antithesis. What is the relationship between the attack–defence antithesis and the logical contradiction of attack–non-attack or defence–non-defence? Clausewitz draws a fundamental distinction between the true logical antithesis and one formed by mere negation. At no point does he formulate explicitly the concepts of either non-attack or non-defence, but one can certainly deduce them from the context.

If attack and defence were a simple logical antithesis, this would mean that attack would be the same as non-defence and defence the same as non-attack.[194] What Clausewitz means by non-attack, though, is not defence but rather a standstill within a military action, the absence of the positive element of attack. In Chapter 4 of Book VII, Clausewitz deals with the diminishing strength of the attack and the way in which this is brought about by a variety of factors. These include the purpose of the attack, i.e. the goal of occupying the enemy's country, and the need to occupy territory one has already conquered in order to secure one's lines of communication. The attack is weakened further by losses in action and through sickness, the increasing distance from sources of replacements, sieges and the investment of fortresses, relaxation of efforts, and the defection of allies (527).

All these factors, which weaken the attack with its 'positive' purpose, help to bring about a standstill within a military action. As early as Chapter 1 of *On War*, Clausewitz emphasizes the efforts that have to be made to overcome the standstill: war is the effect of forces that sometimes expand sufficiently 'to overcome the resistance of inertia or friction; at others they are too weak to have any effect' (86–7). In war, the resistance of inertia or friction must be overcome. It is completely justified to describe this standstill within a military action (and before it) as 'non-attack', because the 'positive purpose' of attack is missing. Attack and non-attack are, in their mutual relationship, characterized by the positive purpose that one has and the other lacks. Attack and non-attack differ by virtue of the 'positive purpose' of *overcoming* 'inertia' which determines attack and is absent from non-attack.

This also applies in principle to defence, though in reverse and in a different form. If a state, nation, or community does not defend itself when an attack is launched against it, this is scarcely the equivalent of a 'counterattack'. But this is what non-defence would have to be if attack and defence were a logical antithesis. Clausewitz uses a concept that makes this clear: defence is not simply passive endurance. We could add that it is not just a matter of putting up with an attack (379). Passive endurance of an attack could be characterized as non-defence, and non-defence could in no circumstances be understood as a form of attack. Here too, non-defence lacks something—the negative purpose of defence, which may be negative but is still a purpose. It is this purpose that Clausewitz conceptualizes with reference to attack as winning and to defence as preservation, and which he uses to distinguish attack from non-attack and defence from non-defence (357).

5.4. SUMMARY: POLARITY AND THE TRUE LOGICAL ANTITHESIS

We can sum up Clausewitz's conception of the unity of and difference between antitheses in the following terms. The unity of antitheses, in the duel and in the relationship between attack and defence, rests on polarity. Both polarity and the true logical antithesis are only valid when they apply to one and the same object. The relationship between the opposing poles in polarity is a symmetrical one. However, Clausewitz does not restrict himself to characterizing polarity, and he goes on to consider its limits. He develops his own model in the true logical antithesis of attack and defence.[195]

The following characteristics should be noted:

1. In a true logical antithesis, as in polarity, the polar opposites are not things or objects. They are antithetical tendencies within a single identity. Within this identity, the opposites cannot be separated from one another. In addition, in a true logical antithesis each of these tendencies is implied in the other. This is not dualism, since polarity ensures the maintenance of an inseparable unity. Nor is it monism, since this identity, its 'essence', can only be characterized by the two opposites. This kind of opposition and its unity is clearly distinguishable from a binary code, in which there is only one sequence of antitheses as substances. The field of action in warfare is structured and given dynamism via this kind of opposition, and this is quite different from how a binary code works.

2. Each pole of the pair in such a 'true logical' antithesis is attached to its own opposite, though these take different forms. Defence is attached to attack, which leads to changes in the content of the concept and form of defence as an element of attack. The transition from attack to defence therefore needs a mediacy, because it is tied to the standstill in the military action. This non-attack (standstill) is the point located half way between attack and defence, the moment when a transition from attack to defence occurs. Defence, on the other hand, has its direct antithesis within itself, since—as the metaphor of the flashing sword of vengeance expresses it—it shifts to its antithesis directly at the most intensive stage of combat.
3. The true logical antithesis of attack and defence cannot be characterized as a double negative. It contains different kinds of antithesis within itself: the polarity of the duel, the positive and the negative purpose, and the weaker and stronger form. The logical antitheses of attack and non-attack and of defence and non-defence are integrated into this more comprehensive antithesis.

This means that Clausewitz's model of the true logical antithesis incorporates polarity and at the same time, in contrast to this determination, makes it possible to account for the development of and transition between opposites within this unity. With the help of Clausewitz's treatments of polarity and of the true logical antithesis, we can conclude that his different conceptualizations of war in Chapter 1 of Book I of *On War* are antithetical tendencies within every war. The antitheses of his initial definition of war at the beginning and of the 'wondrous Trinity' at the end of Chapter 1 can be understood as poles of one and the same object. These poles are not separate 'things'. They provide the basis for the unity of war by functioning as antithetical tendencies within it, and as its borders. We can elucidate the diversity of the antitheses and the transitions that can often be observed in war with the help of the model of the true logical antithesis. Just as this specific antithesis contains within it a unity made up of different antitheses, so Clausewitz articulates in Chapter 1 a variety of polar antitheses which, taken together, make up war as a whole.[196]

6

The Formula: Politics in War

> The readiness to fight and the readiness to compromise lie at the core of politics.
>
> Peter Paret[197]

'War is merely the continuation of policy by other means' (87). Attempts to reduce complex social phenomena to simple formulae have seldom been successful in human history. However apt they may be, they can never do more than express one aspect of reality. '*L'état, c'est moi*', the famous sentence attributed to Louis XIV, the 'Sun King', expressed one aspect of absolutist reality in the eighteenth century. Clausewitz's formula, too, captures only one aspect of war. However, it has been the fate of this sentence to be treated as the definition of the whole of war, its totality. Clausewitz cannot be entirely absolved of blame for the history of this misinterpretation. He wanted to stress the great and significant influence of policy on war, but in doing so he gave this question an excessively privileged place and, in some of his formulations, reduced war, as he says, 'merely' to a continuation of policy.[198] It is therefore necessary to consider how this famous formulation should be understood in relation to the development of Clausewitz's overall argument?

Let us begin by recapitulating the argument that has been put forward in this study in respect of the relationship between politics and war. In his early work, Clausewitz traced the revolutionary transformation of warfare back to changes in political conditions in France. During this period, though, he still thought of war as a self-contained whole: 'In this way, every war is raised to a whole which is complete in itself.'[199] In these terms Napoleon's way of waging war appeared at first to be the realization of the idea of true war. As a result of Moscow and especially of Waterloo, however, he came to appreciate the fundamental contrast between limited and unrestrained war. In the Note of 1827, Clausewitz made the existence of these 'two types of war' one of the two principles on which his planned revision of the book was to be based (69–70).

Once he had arrived at the antithesis of limited and unrestrained war, Clausewitz could no longer see war as an autonomous unity. From now on, he considered it to be only part of a *more comprehensive* whole. Although Clausewitz is uncertain about what exactly he wants to say in Book VIII, this is where he identifies this particular problem with great clarity: the practice of war is 'incomplete and self-contradictory'. It therefore cannot simply follow its own laws but must be 'treated as a part of some other whole; the name of which is policy' (606). Treating war as part of a larger whole provides the basis for the formula, Clausewitz's statement that war is *merely* a continuation of policy.

However, both the critics and the admirers of Clausewitz's formula have usually failed to see that there is a tension here, a tension that cannot be overcome, between the conceptualization of war as a *continuation* of policy and the final part of the sentence, which states that policy uses *other* means. If we look more closely we can see that the world-famous formula, even though it appears to be unambiguous, actually contains three aspects, and that there are tensions between them. Firstly, Clausewitz emphasizes the influence of policy on warfare. War is a continuation of policy, but this does not mean that war can be reduced to policy. Secondly, he stresses that in this continuation, the means used differ from those employed in policy as such. Thirdly, the formula says that war is 'merely' a continuation, which means that Clausewitz is treating war as part of a more comprehensive whole, as part of politics in general.

In conceptual terms, we can once again trace this distinction back to Clausewitz's reflections on Jena, Moscow, and Waterloo. He explains the triumphal progress of the Napoleonic armies by referring to Bonaparte's own military genius, but he also refers to changes in political conditions in France and to the mistaken policies of France's enemies (609). In Moscow, it became clear that warfare also operated according to its own laws. Even without any changes in the social-political conditions of the Russian Empire, the 'pure resistance' (98) of the Russian army led to a military disaster for Napoleon (as did the guerrilla war in Spain). Napoleon attempted to use military force to create a political fait accompli, and failed when he reached the limit of what was militarily possible. The formula states the conclusion Clausewitz arrived at: war is a continuation of policy, but by other means. In its internal workings, war continues to operate according to its own rules. War does not have a logic of its own, because it is part of a larger whole, but it does have its own grammar (605). Finally, after Waterloo Clausewitz saw that war was not an independent whole itself, but something that must be understood as part of a more comprehensive whole, politics.

However, there is a difference between Chapter 1 and Book VIII together with the Note of 1827. In the 'wondrous Trinity' of Chapter 1, the influence of policy is only one of three tendencies, any one of which may prevail over the others. As far as the overall logic of *On War* is concerned, this difference can be explained as Clausewitz's attempt to explain how his contrasting experiences of war—Jena, Moscow, and Waterloo—could be accounted for within one unified conception. We can grasp the contrast between the formula and the 'wondrous Trinity' by distinguishing between action and counteraction. In the formula, Clausewitz emphasizes the autonomy of human (political) action, which is always limited but can never be abandoned. In the 'wondrous Trinity', he tries to conceptualize action and counteraction together.

The inherent tension within Clausewitz's formula is investigated in the following sections.

6.1. DIFFERENT CONCEPTS OF POLITICS IN CLAUSEWITZ

6.1.1. The 'Subjective' Understanding of Policy Versus Political Intercourse

Raymond Aron distinguishes between two dimensions of Clausewitz's concept of politics. The first of these is objective politics as the totality of socio-political conditions, and the second is subjective policy; the state is 'thought of as a person, and policy as the product of its brain' (88).[200] Dan Diner argues on similar lines when he speaks explicitly of a doubling of the concept of politics in Clausewitz. The first form of the concept, says Diner, should be understood as an instrumentally sought after framework of goal-oriented behaviour involving the organized use of force. This instrumental rationality is involved in every act of warfare. But, he argues, the concept also has another meaning for Clausewitz: the expression of the whole range of societal conditions, as something relevant to action; these conditions are always present before force is used, and they cannot be manipulated by the actors in any way that suits them. The political in this sense is thus a 'substance' removed from the concept of means and purpose that can be steered by the will, and it stands in an analogous relationship to the prevailing form of societal interaction.[201]

Kondylis generalizes this second concept of politics in Clausewitz even further. He argues that it is so broad as to mean something like 'the societal unit', 'the political whole', or 'the polity'. The concept of politics in Clausewitz, says Kondylis, does not have the sense of a single-minded action; rather, it expresses the idea of public interaction within a given societal unit. This is such a broad interpretation of Clausewitz that it becomes almost impossible to distinguish between politics and society or culture.[202] In terms of the overall logic of the argument, we can see the contrast between the two concepts as the result of the range of Clausewitz's own experiences. The absolutist idea of the state that prevailed during the eighteenth century saw it as a living whole, a sovereign actor with clear aims equipped with a 'personified intelligence'. However, this idea of the state collapsed as a result of the Prussian defeat at Jena and Auerstedt. Clausewitz took the view that it was precisely the mistaken policy pursued by the personified intelligence of the Prussian state that had led to this disaster.

After this, Clausewitz's thought developed within the parameters set by the ideas of the constitutional government and national interest.[203] Within this framework, he argued in a number of military and political memoranda that national unity should take precedence over the special interests of individual sections of the population. Finally, Napoleon got himself into an impossible situation at Waterloo: for domestic political reasons, he was forced to wage war with inadequate military forces against an alliance of hostile powers. This strengthened Clausewitz's conviction that the concept of politics should not be restricted to the actions of a political intelligence. He now saw politics as determined to the same degree by political intercourse between the states, which placed limits on the autonomy of their actions (87–8, 605–7). The antithesis that resulted from the autonomy of the actor and the limits to this autonomy set by existing conditions, which Clausewitz expressed in his treatment of warfare in the ideas of action and (asymmetrical) counteraction, also lies at the heart of his understanding of politics.

6.1.2. The Antithesis of Political and Military Leadership

The tension between the subjective and objective concepts of politics becomes especially clear when Clausewitz formulates his recommendations for action. Throughout *On War*, he provides numerous instructions to commanders and political leaders. 'If war is to be fully consonant with political objectives, and policy suited to the means available for war', then there is only one means available: the supreme commander must be made a member of the cabinet, so that the cabinet can be involved in the most important decisions he takes (608). If war were, for Clausewitz, always and in every case merely a continuation of policy, there would be no need for advice on the best way to bring about a unity of war and policy. We can see the inherent importance of this factor in Clausewitz's statement that it is justified for the art of war and the commander to demand that the goals of policy should not be inconsistent with the means used to wage war (87).

Clausewitz argues on similar lines in Book VIII, saying that it would be senseless to subordinate political considerations to military ones. The only possible way of proceeding is to subordinate the military to the political. The supreme standpoint for the war leadership, the place where decisions are taken on the main priorities, must be the political perspective. He goes on to say that leaving a major military action, or the plan to carry out such an action, to be decided by military criteria alone involves drawing an inadmissible distinction, a distinction which is harmful in itself. In fact, it would be nonsensical to ask the military for advice on war plans in order to come to purely military judgements on these plans (606–8). Clausewitz is certainly not saying here that war is always, from the very start, a continuation of policy by other means. What he is doing is using his general *postulate* about the primacy of policy as the basis for a recommendation that it should *in practice* always be given priority.

If we look more closely, we can see that Clausewitz is introducing a new differentiation between military and political leadership here. As Clausewitz sees it and expresses his recommendation, this primacy of the political leadership must and should be re-established every time. This reflects an element of tension in Clausewitz's understanding of theory. There are two senses of theory in Clausewitz. On the one hand, theory involves an effort to develop a structured and dynamic image of the whole of war. On the other hand, *On War* is just as much an attempt to develop a guide to the art of war for the time in which it was written. Theory has to provide knowledge about its object, but it also has to furnish guidance for action. For Clausewitz, true knowledge leads to creative action based on a mastery of theory. In Clausewitz's work, this dual sense of theory provides the basis for the antithesis of subjective and objective politics.[204]

We can see the subjective element in Clausewitz's conceptualization of politics clearly in the concepts of government and commander, political and military bodies (609–10). With reference to this understanding of politics, we can note that the famous formula is almost a paradox. War *is* the continuation of policy by other means (i.e. the objective concept of politics), and it *should* therefore be waged in accordance with the requirement that policy be given primacy (i.e. the subjective concept of politics). An examination of Clausewitz's analysis of the Prussian defeats shows the correspondence and difference between fact and recommendations for action most clearly. In his later writings, Clausewitz's position differs from arguments put forward by other authors at the time. He argues that it was not the influence of the political leadership as such that was harmful, but only the policy mistakes made by the Prussian government and its allies (607–8). Policy can only have a harmful effect on war when it misunderstands certain possibilities in warfare. If this happens, the political leadership can issue orders 'that defeat the purpose they are meant to serve' (608). In this subjective dimension of policy recommendations, the primacy of policy is therefore something that needs to be established.

Clausewitz's position on this point can be more clearly understood if we consider a comparable argument found in Hegel. Throughout his work, Hegel set himself the task of developing a practical philosophy that would turn Kant's idea of individual autonomy into something more than a mere normative demand. He succeeded in doing this by treating the idea as an element of social reality that was already historically effective.[205] In an analogous way, the primacy of policy expressed in Clausewitz's formula could be understood as an unconditional demand. This already affects the reality of war, but it does not come to complete fruition in every individual case.

6.1.3. Objective Politics as a Political Intercourse in the Nuclear Age

The possibility of a fundamental reversal in the relationship between means and the political purpose of war played a major role in the discussion about Clausewitz in the nuclear age that was conducted not so very long ago. Aron, in his book first published in 1976, says that these days one only needs to quote Clausewitz's formula about the primacy of policy in order to receive the seemingly illuminating response: nuclear war is no longer a continuation of policy by other means. How could the destruction of cities, the blind wiping out of millions of people by thermonuclear weapons, be considered a means like others employed to achieve goals such as those normally pursued by states?

Aron argues that war is only one phase in interstate relations. If nuclear weapons were actually used, the human significance of this relationship, the trial of wills, would disappear and only the raw trial of strength would remain. The peace researcher Dieter Senghaas wrote a programmatic paper in which he said a premature farewell to Clausewitz's work. He posed the question of the relationship between war and policy in a nuclear war, in which the reality of war would be identical with the philosophical concept of the absolute of war. In such an eventuality, argued Senghaas, war can no longer be a continuation of policy.[206]

It is quite clear that an answer to the question of whether war in the nuclear age can still be a continuation of policy by other means depends on which of Clausewitz's concepts of politics one uses. If we proceed on the basis of a subjective concept of politics, we can say that during the period of the nuclear arms race there were no political goals that could have been attained with the help of military action that would have destroyed the planet many times over. Things look different if we follow Kondylis and attribute to Clausewitz an extremely broad concept of politics: in this case, there is a continuity between politics and war which rests on their homogeneity. If any act of warfare carried out by 'civilized peoples' must be political, the concept of politics has become so broad that even a nuclear war is by definition a political act.[207]

Another way in which it was possible to continue to employ Clausewitz's formula, in spite of the fundamental changes that took place in the means of warfare, was by establishing a link between the concept of politics and class struggle, an element that transcended both war and politics to the same degree. According to an article on basic concepts which summarized the debate in a Soviet military journal: 'We assume once again that the unchanging formula, which states that war is a continuation of policy by violent means, is correct. We also assume that the unity of the political, class-determined content of war and armed force represents the relatively permanent and general basis of the nature of all wars, without exception.'[208] The conceptualization of war as a continuation of politics depends here on a category that extends beyond both (subjective) policy and war to the same degree.

Clausewitz's position in his later writings is located between the two extremes of policy conducted by autonomous subjects and an objectified political intercourse. This tension expresses the antithesis of action and counteraction, the consciousness that there is a sphere of autonomy and responsibility that is always present, however limited it may be. Simultaneously, however, one's own actions can be influenced by the political actions of others and the surrounding conditions to such an extent that this autonomy appears to be pure fiction. For Clausewitz, Jena and Waterloo are antitheses in warfare which provide a contrast but cannot be considered separately from one another.

At the same time, though, war was in both cases a continuation of the policy that had gone before. In the first case it reflected the failure of the Prussian political leadership, and in the second case it reflected the fact that every aspect of Napoleon's action was influenced by the domestic and external conditions in which France found itself. Although Jena and Waterloo formed an antithesis, they could also be treated as battles of the same type. In each case, it was the political dimension that decided the outcome of the battle. By identifying the parallels between Jena and Waterloo in this way, Clausewitz was able to see the overlapping whole of politics that brought the internal contradictions within war together into a unity once again.

Clausewitz's argument returns to its starting point here. In his analysis of the successes of the French armies (before Napoleon), he emphasized that fundamental political changes resulting from the Revolution had made these victories possible. Around the time of Jena, he stressed the subjective aspects of the Prussian leadership's political failure and of Prussia's political self-assertion as a state. There was a direct connection between the

Prussian state's ability to re-establish its honour and regain international recognition through once again taking up the struggle against Napoleon. Moscow showed that there were limits to the political changes that could be brought about by the use of military force. Finally, Waterloo demonstrated the dominant influence of political conditions on success in warfare.

6.1.4. Politics between Power and Freedom

Clausewitz's dual concept of politics also articulates a further, even more fundamental antithesis. According to the formula war is a continuation of policy, but the means employed are different. This implies that the formula rests on two inherently contrasting concepts of politics. War is a continuation of policy in the sense of an understanding of politics characterized by power—gaining power, using power, and fearing the loss of power. In this respect, Clausewitz is part of a tradition stretching from Niccolò Machiavelli to Max Weber. At the time of Jena, Clausewitz took the view that the essence of politics was to be found in Napoleon's demonstration that a policy based on military power was superior to inadequately armed political ideals.[209] There is, however, a quite different concept of politics that can be found in the history of political thought. Seen from this perspective, Clausewitz's formula treats war as a continuation of politics with the emphasis placed on the different quality of the means employed.

From the Ancient period up until the eighteenth century, the concept of politics reflected efforts to create a just way of exercising power that was oriented towards the common good. The common good was the central point of reference for the natural law doctrine of the late eighteenth century. However, this doctrine differed from the Christian-influenced medieval understanding of politics in so far as it associated this sphere more strongly with autonomous ideas of the goals action was intended to achieve in *this* world. We have still not seen any resolution of this debate: which is the more important of the two contrasting elements of the conceptual field of politics, power or agreement? Since Ancient times, there has been an unbroken series of discussions about the essence of the political—is this a matter of 'power or order'?[210] The concept of politics has been most positively charged when it has been equated with peace: 'The object and the goal of politics is peace. Peace is definitely *the* political category.'[211]

Clausewitz's formula articulates these contrasting concepts of politics within one unified context. But Clausewitz is well aware of the problems raised by this tension, as can be seen from an examination of three passages from *On War*. In Chapter 1, Clausewitz uses a concept of politics based on the capacity to achieve one's goals through the exercise of power. He distinguishes his own position from another idea, the conventional idea of a 'cautious, devious, even dishonest, shying away from force' (88). As a result, Clausewitz's own concept of politics is revealed: it expresses force rather than turning away from it. Clausewitz never got over his experience of the failure of Prussia's political leadership, which wanted to avoid war by using 'diplomatic cleverness', which led the country into the catastrophe of Jena. He reacts in an almost knee-jerk way to anything that reminds him of this experience.

Whenever Clausewitz observes anything that might present the slightest threat to the existence of Prussia as a state, his political reaction to it reflects a concern that a repetition of Jena is imminent.[212] After Jena, Clausewitz sees the preservation of a position of military power as the essence of politics, because a state's own military power is the only thing that can guarantee its existence as a state confronting other states: 'Because it guarantees the state's existence, power in relation to other states is the ultimate standard by which the internal affairs of the state must be measured.'[213]

In Book VIII, on the other hand, Clausewitz characterizes politics in a different and more complex way. Here, he says: 'The conduct of war, in its great outlines, is therefore policy itself, which takes up the sword in place of the pen, but does not on that account cease to think according to its own laws' (610). The metaphor of exchanging the pen for the sword expresses the contrast between the two concepts of politics particularly well. The pen stands for civil policy and diplomacy, and the sword for military self-assertion and the exercise of force. However, Clausewitz is saying that even if politics exchanges the pen for the sword, it does not stop thinking in terms of its own laws. In this context, politics is to be understood as a category including action with both the pen and the sword. This concept of politics cannot be equated with and thus restricted to the institutional contrast between political and military leadership, but is a general concept of political action. The metaphor treats politics as both a subjectively determined civil policy and a sphere where political and military leadership overlap: 'In short, at the highest level the art of war turns into policy—but a policy conducted by fighting battles rather than by sending diplomatic notes' (607).

Kondylis argues that we cannot read Clausewitz as saying that politics must be conceptualized within the antithesis of civil and military action. This antithesis, says Kondylis, only developed gradually during the course of the nineteenth century, as a result of the growing professionalization and specialization of military affairs and the early stages of the industrialization of warfare—or, to be more specific, of war waged with mass-produced weapons and the rise and consolidation of the liberal ideas of popular sovereignty and the state governed by the rule of law. But Kondylis fails to see that Clausewitz does not have just a single concept of politics containing the general elements of war. He also has a second concept that provides a contrast with war and the military. Kondylis practically contradicts himself when he says that military authority is self-evidently subordinate to political authority because the latter gives expression to the priority of the political point of view. If this is the case, this civil authority must at least have a stronger affinity with the political than the military authority does.[214]

The contrast between a civil concept of politics and one based on military power is emphasized by Clausewitz in the following passage: 'It can be taken as agreed that the aim of policy is to unify and reconcile all aspects of internal administration as well as of spiritual values, and whatever else the moral philosopher may care to add. Policy, of course, is nothing in itself; it is simply the trustee for all those interests against the outside world.' Policy may sometimes move in the wrong direction, or it may serve the ambition, private interests, or vanity of rulers, but these are secondary considerations. Commenting on this point, Clausewitz says that 'we can only treat policy as representative of all interests of the community' (606–7). Clausewitz's understanding of politics is characterized here by the idea of a sense of balance of interests and compromise between adversaries. There can be few conceptualizations of politics so far removed from an understanding based on force and power. Although this conception could at first glance only be applied meaningfully *within* a state and community, and Clausewitz therefore seems to express only the well-known 'realist' position, this contrast between the two concepts of politics transcends the opposition of internal and external. As Peter Paret emphasizes in the above quotation with regard to Clausewitz's concept of politics: *The readiness to fight and the readiness to compromise lie at the core of politics.* These contrasts not only constitute an unresolvable tension within the concept of politics, a further 'Between'. The 'floating' between these contrasts is additionally one of the driving forces of history and is therefore articulated again and again in the history of political ideas.[215]

We can turn to Hegel once again in order to render visible the complex nature of this concept of politics. Hegel's concepts of the state as the consciousness of freedom, and of law as the rule of freedom, are the counterparts of the conceptualizations of politics as force. Hegel writes: 'It is often said that force keeps the state together, but in reality it is only the basic feeling of order shared by all that does this.' At another point, Hegel says that force is by no means the basis of law; it is only the external or apparent starting-point of states, not their substantive principle. Hegel therefore sees a fundamental difference between force as the apparent starting-point of states and order as their substantive principle. We can say that Clausewitz's concept of politics places him somewhere 'between' Machiavelli and Hegel, between the conceptualization of politics as an inherently violent sphere where force and power enjoy primacy, and one in which politics is an expression and means of freedom, intelligence, and hence reason.[216]

We can sum up by saying that the basis of Clausewitz's conceptualization of war as a continuation of policy by other means is a contrast within the concept of politics. Unless we are aware of this, we cannot assess the famous formula adequately.[217]

6.2. ON CLAUSEWITZ'S CONCEPT OF THE LOGIC AND GRAMMAR OF WAR

We can arrive at a more concrete understanding of the relationship between politics and war by looking at Clausewitz's statement that war has no logic of its own, but does have its own grammar (605). If war has no logic of its own, what does it mean to say that it has a grammar? Clausewitz's emphasis on the concept of grammar probably reflects the fact that he was acquainted with Wilhelm von Humboldt, who was an important philologist and politician. Von Humboldt's works are among the most significant in the history of the study of grammar. Of particular importance for the development of linguistics was his view that every language expresses its own unique view of the world.[218] Clausewitz rejected the idea that war has its own logic with the argument that this would imply the conceptualization of an independent whole, which in his later works after Moscow and Waterloo, he dismissed totally. The concept of grammar, on the other hand, illustrates both war's unity with a greater whole and its relative autonomy.

An article in the *Encyklopädie der Wissenschaften und Künste*, (Encyclopedia of the Sciences and Arts), expounds in detail the concept of grammar in use at the time. If one substitutes 'war' for 'language', much of the content of Clausewitz's conceptualization of war can be found in this article.[219] Clausewitz makes this comparison explicit, and argues initially that political intercourse does not end when war breaks out, it is not transformed into something quite different. He then asks whether war is not 'just... another form of speech or writing', a way of expressing the thoughts of different peoples and governments. In this context, Clausewitz then stresses that while war has no logic of its own it does, as the 'speech or writing' of thought, have its own grammar (605). According to the *Encyklopädie*, grammar is the meaning of a scientific embodiment of the laws of language. Everything about language that is lawful belongs to grammar. Grammar is complete when it encompasses in itself the complete extent of these lawful elements in language.

The *Encyklopädie* goes on to say that something of a double nature is united in the concept of language, just as man is made up of body and soul: the sensory body of the way audible sounds are put together and the contents of thought, the soul of these sounds. Both man and language are said to be a living combination or unified synthesis of a double element, something that in itself is completely diverse, the real and ideal or sensory and spiritual. In the formula, in an analogous way, Clausewitz understands the concept of politics as a synthesis made up of quite heterogeneous elements.

The *Encyklopädie* then describes how language is understood as the expression of the intellectual nature of man. If we apply this characterization to the relationship between politics and war, it corresponds to a position in which war is only an expression, something corresponding to a concept of politics based on relations that take a violent form. In this understanding of the relationship, war can do no more than modify the pre-existing general phenomenon of politics. It cannot change it in any significant way. The *Encyklopädie* also says, however, that the unity of language and thought is limited by the fact that thought is more comprehensive than language. Thought cannot be separated from language, which is its external form or reality, but thought has a completely specific, objective nature. For Clausewitz, politics too is more comprehensive than war.

What consequences does the *Encyklopädie* draw from the unity of language and thought and from the independence and specificity of thought? It argues that the relationship between them is frequently understood as external, in the sense that language is seen as nothing but a means of imparting information (here one can emphasize Clausewitz's analogous characterization of force as a means). Thought is the earlier, primary phenomenon, and expression comes later. On the other hand, it is also stated that this dependence of language on thought applies the other way round too, because thought itself cannot be expressed in any other way than at the level of language. Language is, in one sense, the expression of thought, as war is for Clausewitz the continuation of policy. But precisely because language is an expression of thought, the actual act of speech can in turn have an effect on this thought, just as the course of a war can affect politics and can also change it in a fundamental way.[220]

If the relationship between language and thought were to be reduced to nothing more than correspondence, the reversal would mean that the grammar of language would simultaneously be the logic of thought. And indeed, the core of the linguistic turn of the twentieth century does amount to just such a reversal, in which the grammar of language generates the logic of thought. The *Encyklopädie* article also assumes that language and thought more or less correspond to one another, but it also stresses that thought is more comprehensive than language. Clausewitz takes the same position, but it is noticeable that he is applying an implicit description of politics and war that is dynamic: war is part of politics, which is a more general phenomenon, but for this very reason, the conduct and outcome of war can change the original underlying aims and ends of politics.

6.3. IS THERE A CONFLICT BETWEEN POLITICS AND WAR?

The formula's apodictic way of making its point seems to say that there can, as a matter of principle, be no disagreement between politics and war, so that any possibility of warfare operating according to its own laws and dynamic would be excluded. This assumption is strengthened when we note Clausewitz's argument that, although things may look different on the surface, he considers both unrestrained war with a tendency to become absolute and limited war to be influenced by policy to the same degree. But what exactly is Clausewitz's argument here? 'The more powerful and inspiring the motives for war, the more they affect the belligerent nations', the closer war comes to its absolute form.[221] In this case the military aim and the political purpose would be identical, and 'the more military and less political will war appear to be'. The weaker the motives leading to war and the tensions between the opponents are, the greater would be the distance between the political purpose and the goal of 'ideal war', and so war would appear to be more political (87–8).

Two factors need to be borne in mind in interpreting this passage. Clausewitz speaks here of the aim of an 'ideal war', meaning Napoleon's way of waging war from the time of Jena, the search for a decisive encounter in battle, and the tendency towards unrestrained violence in war. A limited way of waging war can only appear more strongly political against the background of this comparison with an 'ideal war'. Furthermore, Clausewitz's own concept of politics in this context is a general, objectified one which expresses the political circumstances. The formulations he uses make this clear: the more inspiring the motives for war are and the more they affect the belligerent nations, the closer war comes to its absolute form.

In a letter written at almost the same time, Clausewitz explains that in this kind of war politics and enmity are the same thing: the more policy functions on the basis of considering the whole and the existence of the state, the more the question posed on both sides is 'to be or not to be?'[222] We can decipher these statements of Clausewitz's by recalling his dual concept of politics. As war draws closer to its absolute form, it seems to become more and more apolitical in the sense of a concept of politics based on force. What about limited war? The further war deviates from its 'natural' direction, the more it seems to be influenced by policy in the sense of Clausewitz's 'conventional' concept of politics. Both types of war, though, are—despite appearances—characterized to the same extent by a correspondence, as military aim and political purpose coincide with one another.

When Clausewitz assumes that the political purpose and the military aim coincide, is he thereby ruling out any possibility of a conflict between them? Does he think war is always and everywhere nothing more than a continuation of policy? Clausewitz qualifies this correspondence when he introduces a distinction between *some* cases and *most* cases. In some cases, the 'morale and emotions of the combatants' mean that they can only with difficulty be restrained within the framework of the political purpose. In most cases, though, this kind of conflict would not arise because in war the 'emotions' are usually tied up with an associated policy (88). By contrasting 'some' and 'most' cases in this way, Clausewitz makes it clear that he admits the possibility of a conflict between political purpose and warfare or military aim. This qualification of the correspondence between war and policy is general, and is not affected by the question of whether the conflict arises because of the stimulation of the 'emotions' of the combatants, as in this case, or, as Clausewitz stresses elsewhere, as a result of societal, national, or other differences and tensions (86–7).

The most important point must be emphasized once again. Within Clausewitz's formula stating that war is merely the continuation of policy by other means, there is a tension between different concepts of politics. According to the first of these, war is merely a continuation against the background of a quite general understanding of politics on Clausewitz's part, political intercourse between men and states. There are no clear boundaries between this understanding of politics and categories such as society and culture. In the second sense, the formula understands politics as a struggle for power and for political existence, one of the central components of Clausewitz's political thought after Jena. In the third sense, though, war is a continuation of policy by *other* means. This stress on the fact that these means are different implies both a concept of politics that can be approximately characterized with the help of categories such as 'civil' or the capacity for compromise and peace, and the relative autonomy of warfare (war can change the policy being pursued in a reflexive way).

The central problem posed by the formula is not only that it articulates these different conceptualizations of politics as such. This is not a problem in itself. The real difficulty that arises does so as a result of the fact that Clausewitz summarized these different aspects in an undifferentiated way, in a short formula which left a great deal of room for misinterpretation. Because Clausewitz only identified these different characterizations of politics implicitly and never stated them directly, each individual interpretation of the formula has singled out only one aspect. For example, if the formula is interpreted as stating that war is *merely* a continuation of politics, the grammar of war becomes the logic of policy. This would be reductive, and it would even lead to a reversal of the formula.[223]

If politics is no more than something general which is by nature violent, it becomes a continuation of war by other means (as in Foucault's work). The way in which words are assigned to new developments in warfare is reflected in one's own behaviour. This is nowhere clearer than in the case of Michel Foucault, who thought of society exclusively in terms of conflict, violence and power. Foucault stated that war was not the continuation of politics, but politics the continuation of war by other means. Although he was able to achieve impressive research results, Foucault's one-dimensional view led him to problematic conclusions. For Foucault, the inversion of Clausewitz's formula means three things: he understands politics as the sanctioning and preservation of an imbalance of power, as demonstrated in war. Within this 'civil peace', conflicts in a political system, clashes with respect to power, and shifts in the balance of power can only be understood as a continuation of war.

Even if Foucault were right about this, a fundamental and insurmountable problem for this position would arise: how could one escape this ubiquitous balance of power, the result of a previous struggle or war, if not through a new struggle? Foucault logically accentuates a third meaning of the inversion of Clausewitz's formula. The 'last decision' can only result from war, he emphasizes. The whole point of politics would be the final battle, and 'only the last battle would eventually stop the execution of power as incessant war'. To dispel any doubt about this position, Foucault emphasizes that war must not just be rediscovered for society as a principle of explanation. It must be revived in order to 'fight it until the decisive battle'; 'we must prepare to emerge from this battle as victors'. Starting out from the critique of the modern age and its violence, Foucault's argument 'tilts' and results in the substantiation of new battles, even in the 'decisive battle'.[224]

If, on the other hand, we only conceive of politics in connection with categories such as 'civil' and the capacity to compromise, we deny that it can also take violent forms. If we do this, we have no way of capturing the influence of politics and of political conditions on warfare. War would then appear to be an independent whole which could not be influenced by politics. In the field of politics, Clausewitz articulates a fundamental antithesis which is similar to the ones he identifies in the two other conceptual fields of the 'wondrous Trinity', each of which is itself antithetically structured: politics understood as a power relationship, and an understanding of politics in categories such as law, the capacity to compromise, and the capacity for order and freedom. The most revealing insight of Clausewitz's treatment of the relationship between war and politics, as well as of the history of its understanding, is that neglecting this tension between contrasting principles always leads to a primacy of the military and violent means. This is the case with respect to the German military in both world wars, and also in utopian conceptions like Marxism and finally in an approach like that of Foucault, too.[225]

6.4. PRIMACY OF POLITICS OR CULTURE?

Does Clausewitz's thesis of 'war as a continuation of policy by other means' actually amount to 'war, all against all'? In *A History of Warfare*, the British military historian Sir John Keegan suggests this idea. Keegan denounces Clausewitz as 'the apostle of a revolutionary philosophy of war making' that derived from the French Revolution. The British military author Sir Basil Liddell Hart had already interpreted Clausewitz between the two world wars as 'the Mahdi of the masses and mutual massacres'. Following this tradition, Keegan states that there are places in the world riven by tribal wars and saturated with cheap weapons, where the 'war of all against all' takes place. He insists that it teaches us to what afflictions war may subject us if we accept the Clausewitzian idea of 'war as a continuation of policy'.[226]

Keegan refers to two different and controversial themes, which he regards as being directly combined in Clausewitz's theory. First, 'absolute warfare' and the 'concept of war' are both absolute and extreme. Second, the primacy of policy dominates over warfare. We have to concede to Keegan that there are some positions Clausewitz conveys in *On War* which seem at first hand to confirm a part of his criticism. But Clausewitz's idea of 'two kinds of war' does not allow a connection between the concept of absolute war and his famous formula of war being a continuation of politics by other means. But in Chapter 1 of Book I, Clausewitz mentions that unlimited war, as well as limited war, is determined by politics in every case. If this is Clausewitz's position, there can be no question that his famous formula does not lead directly to the idea of 'war, all against all'.

We can conclude that Clausewitz's formula has certain limitations; nevertheless, it retains its validity within these limits. At this point of our discussion we must question the status of the formula. At the beginning of Chapter 1 of Book I, Clausewitz defines war as an act of force to compel our enemy to do our will. If we relate the formula to Clausewitz's 'definition' of war, we find the political intention is the object and war is the means of achieving this political intention. In this way, the 'definition' corresponds to the formula.

However, it must be emphasized again that the paragraph at the end of Chapter 1, where Clausewitz refers to the 'consequences of theory', has a totally different outcome, as demonstrated before. Even though he describes war as an instrument of policy that is subject to pure reason, politics is only one of three tendencies that affect war. The other two are 'primordial violence' and 'chance and probability within which the creative spirit is free to roam'. Clausewitz argues that these three tendencies are like three different codes of law.

Keegan and many others perceive the Clausewitzian formula of war as a total phenomenon. Keegan declares that war is not the continuation of politics by other means.[227] This is correct if we take the entire war into account, as well as referring to a special concept of politics. Clausewitz also takes exactly the same position, without paradox. He declares that war is an instrument of policy, but this is only one of three tendencies in war within his concept of the trinity. Clausewitz clearly pointed out that war as a total phenomenon is composed of three tendencies, of which politics is only one part.

6.4.1. 'Primitive Warfare' and the Inherent Contradictions of Modern War

Both Keegan's and Clausewitz's position is strongly influenced by the French Revolution, which initiated the evolution of warfare towards the tendency of absolute war. Keegan highlights this one factor in the historical evolution of warfare in the nineteenth and twentieth centuries. Other factors are, in my view, the 'industrial revolution of warfare', as Michael Geyer has called it, and the historical evolution and costs of imposing discipline on soldiers.[228]

Until now, there has been no sign of a simple way out or a reliable possibility for a change away from these tendencies to absolute war. Following the argument of Kant, some authors believe in an internationally ordered peace and in the link between democracy and cooperation and interdependence in the international community. Unfortunately, even the strategy of limitation is not always easily obtainable. Wars that seem limitable are more likely to be waged than those that cannot be calculated. The occurrence of a totally destructive nuclear war has thus far been prevented, but only for as long as the opponents act rationally.[229]

Keegan's description has nothing in common with these concepts. He argues that, over the course of 4,000 years, war-making has become a habit of mankind. 'In the primitive world this habit was circumscribed by ritual and ceremony. In the post-primitive world human ingenuity has ripped away ritual and ceremony and the restraints they imposed on war-making, empowering men of violence to press the limits of tolerability to, and eventually beyond, the extreme.'[230]

As an example, Keegan quotes Clausewitz's opinion extracted from the first 'interaction to the extreme', where war is described as an act of violence pushed to its utmost bounds. Here, Keegan does not consider that Clausewitz's three cases of 'interaction to the extreme' only describe true forms of unlimited violence; they do not legitimate them. Clausewitz must be interpreted in the following way: 'War is an act of force and there is no logical limit to the application of that force' (76), because violence is exceeding the limits itself, little by little. Keegan strangely concludes: 'To turn away from the message Clausewitz preached', we need not ponder 'the means of altering our genetic inheritance' or 'break free of our material circumstances'. All we need to accept is that war-making has become a habit. If we hope to survive, the habits of primitive civilizations containing 'restraint, diplomacy and negotiation deserve relearning'. Keegan presents Clausewitz as he is—the snake that tempts Adam to eat the apple of knowledge, who, as a result, is driven out of the 'paradise' of 'primitive warfare'.[231]

In the first of the three cases of 'interaction and extreme', Clausewitz formulates the main contrast that is contained in 'modern' warfare. On the one hand, he argues that wars between savages are more cruel and destructive than those between civilized nations. Clausewitz experienced the cruelty of primitive warfare in Russia, when the Cossacks slaughtered the French army at the Beresina River. On the other hand, he mentions that intelligence provides civilized nations with more effective ways of using force than the crude expression of instinct. We can conclude from Clausewitz that the cruelty of warfare is more closely associated with primitive cultures and life-and-death battles as in a natural state (*pace* Hegel and Hobbes). But in recent history there has also been an increase in more effective ways to use force due to developments in science, technology, politics, and society (76). This is the main antithesis of Clausewitz's assessment, formed by the same development of rational and civil affairs and ways of thinking. The limitation on the use of force is contrasted with the exceeding of its bounds by the same modern evolution.

In spite of the contradictory evolution of modern warfare, Keegan only makes a clear distinction between 'primitive' and 'modern' warfare. This type of distinction enables him to cover over the contradiction in his own theory. On the one hand, he argues that war has become a scourge and we need a new culture that leaves no room for war. Such a cultural transformation would demand a break from the past for which there are no precedents. 'Charting the course of human culture through its undoubtedly warlike past towards its potentially peaceful future is the theme of this book.'[232] On the other hand, he states that a world 'without armies—disciplined, obedient and law-abiding armies—would be uninhabitable'. Armies of that quality are an instrument but also a mark of civilization, and without their existence mankind would have to reconcile itself either to life at a primitive level below 'the military horizon' or to a lawless chaos of masses warring, in Hobbesian fashion, 'all against all'.[233] Again, we must question Keegan's polemics against Clausewitz. Keegan looks at armies as instruments of civilization; Clausewitz considers war an instrument of politics.

We fully agree with Keegan that preserving the existence of mankind by avoidance of war, or at least by limiting it, is one of the most important tasks of the twenty-first century. We can also agree with Keegan that a basic cultural transformation has become necessary to accomplish this task. Nevertheless we must challenge Keegan when he turns away from Clausewitz and advocates a return to 'the habits of the primitives and their warfare' to reach this goal. Clausewitz has a different goal. Even though he admired Napoleon, whose strategy was based on unlimited warfare and the decisive battle, Clausewitz sought to restrain this kind of warfare. Clausewitz was not a pacifist, and his aim was not the avoidance of war. His interest was warfare and the theory of war. But he repeatedly emphasized the balance of purposes, aims and means of war, and pointed out that if this equilibrium were tilted, it would be necessary to limit or end warfare, or possibly not even start it in the first place. 'Once the expenditure of effort exceeds the value of the political object, the object must be renounced and peace must follow' (92, similarly 81). After experiencing war himself and its unlimited effects, Clausewitz concluded, towards the end of his life, that war must be balanced between purposes, aims and means in order to restrict the new style of unlimited warfare.

What is Keegan's perspective concerning a return to primitive warfare? He describes this form of warfare at the end of his book with concepts such as: 'restraint, diplomacy and negotiation', but these are only a few features of 'primitive warfare'. Keegan could have referred to elements of international law, which are also respected today in modern warfare, to develop his ideas. But Keegan separates the limiting aspects of 'primitive warfare' from the excessive violence involved. An example of this excessive violence is evident in regards to the Cossacks, who indulged in indiscriminate destruction, pillage, rape, murder, and numerous other outrages.

Keegan says that the Cossacks' way of waging war was not politics, but a culture and a way of life.[234] He describes how much cruelty the Cossacks displayed during the retreat of Napoleon's army, inhumane behaviour that was a reminder of the Steppe People's invasion. When the Cossacks caught the remnants of the French army (those that had failed to cross the Beresina River before Napoleon burned the bridges), the slaughter became wholesale. Clausewitz told his wife that he had witnessed ghastly scenes. 'If my feelings had not been hardened it would have sent me mad.'[235]

Of course, we do not want to suggest that Keegan means these negative aspects of war when he endorses a return to primitive warfare. He himself stresses the ambivalence of this type of conflict. But when he separates the limiting aspects of primitive warfare from its opposite effects of excessive violence, he separates warfare from its cultural context. His desire to integrate warfare into its related culture does not allow a civilization with high technical standards to conduct primitive warfare. In order to associate modern cultures with primitive warfare, it would first be necessary to separate the limitations of primitive warfare from its use of excessive violence.

Keegan implies, in his detailed description of primitive warfare, that those limitations can only take place between equal opponents. Cruelties are unlimited when directed towards civilians and persons not regarded as equal. Keegan could argue that he did not mean this kind of association, but when we follow his arguments closely we find that limits in primitive warfare belong only to their associated culture. One of these limits is the weapons of those cultures, as Keegan recognizes. Today's sophisticated and destructive weapons do not allow the same limitations of warfare as when bows and arrows were used. If we transposed 'primitive warfare' (e.g. as the nomads practised it) into the era of highly developed technology and weapons of mass destruction, there would be no end to the suffering.

6.4.2. Primacy of Culture or of Politics?

Contrary to his main argument, Keegan assumes a separation between culture and warfare. Without this separation, an association between *primitive* warfare and *modern* culture would not be possible. This conclusion contradicts Keegan's own argument of associating every form of warfare with its dependent culture. Keegan tries to solve this contradiction by suggesting the creation of an aristocratic warrior class subculture with its own kind of warfare. He emphasizes this aristocratic aspect in his criticism of the French Revolution. The purpose of the French Revolution, Keegan tells us, was 'to confer on the majority what hitherto had been the privilege of a minority—the title to full legal freedom represented by the aristocrat's warrior status'. Without denying the ambiguous character of the French Revolution, the claim for full legal freedom cannot be perceived as a 'frenzy to equalize'.[236]

Keegan describes other aspects of this subculture. He learned from his students, who had done military service, how the time in uniform had introduced them to an entirely different world. The afterglow of that experience had also cast its spell on him. The glittering array of medals and uniforms entranced him and he perceived the British Army to be under a 'tribal spell', whose men had values and skills which were quite different from those of the civilian society. This 'culture of warriors' could never be the culture of civilization, Keegan tells us. It 'reaches into the most secret places of the human heart, places where self dissolves rational purpose, where pride reigns, where emotion is paramount, where instinct is king'.[237] But there is no passage in Keegan's description of warfare where it is plausibly argued that such a 'culture of warriors' has contributed to a limitation of war in general.

What does it mean if there really exists a parallel culture of warriors, different from the civilian society? Keegan's argument is by no means new; it is generally accepted that all armies must have different values from those in civilian society. This is one reason for separating armies from civilian societies. The problem is how these different cultures can coexist. Because modern society does not belong to one culture alone, it is necessary to combine some, and sometimes many different, 'cultures' into one. For this reason, policy is a relatively independent part of society with the function of bringing together the different subcultures. Therefore, warfare is connected with culture (in the meaning Keegan gives the term) only in uniformed societies, in a strict sense, and only in primitive societies.

Towards the end of his book, Keegan argues that politics must continue and war cannot. This statement does not mean that the role of the warrior is over. More than ever, the world community needs skilful and disciplined warriors who are ready to put themselves at the service of its authority. Such warriors should be properly seen as the protectors of civilization, not its enemies. The style in which they fight for civilization—against ethnic bigots, regional warlords, ideological intransigents, common pillagers, and organized international criminals—cannot derive from the Western model of war-making alone. Keegan proposes that future peacekeepers and peacemakers have much to learn from alternative military cultures, not only that of the Orient but also from the primitive world.[238]

We must question how the concept of 'primitive warfare' can serve the world community. Keegan describes natural battle behaviour as: 'Nature argued for flight, for cowardice, for self-interest; nature made for Cossacking, whereby a man fought if he chose and not otherwise, and might turn to commerce on the battlefield if that suited his ends.'[239] Such a primitive means of warfare stands in stark contrast to armies serving civilization which are characterized, according to Keegan, by obedience, discipline, and abiding by the law. In another passage, Keegan refers to the Greek Klephts: 'They lived to fight another day, but not to win the war, a point they simply could not grasp.'[240] Of course, such an attitude entails some reductions and limitations in warfare; but should the warriors serving the world community practise such warfare? The main problem with Keegan is that he recommends that 'warriors in service of the world community' should proceed with the forms of primitive warfare. This opinion actually opposes his own argument of associating the forms of warfare with their own culture. According to his claim, only primitive cultures could practise primitive warfare, as long as war was not the continuation of politics.

Keegan's discussion about returning to primitive forms of warfare serves as an attempt to dissociate the actions of armies in democratic societies from the primacy of political leadership. Here is the political truth in Keegan's dispute with Clausewitz. His polemics concerning Clausewitz are overstated and excessive, since only Keegan's caricature of Clausewitz seems to provide justification for his position. Keegan's perspective of the warrior serving the world community is contradictory. He points out that these soldiers would have to fight for civilization against 'ethnic bigots, regional warlords, ideological intransigents, common pillagers, and organized international criminals'.[241] But the main question is, should these soldiers act according to the political order of the world community, or should they function independently, in the manner of state police?

In his examples, Keegan simply overlooks the different tasks of police and military actions. He does this in order to preserve his idea that 'warriors' must be independent from politics. Police act when rules and regulations are broken or infringed, without receiving direct political orders; but this would not be sensible with armies. As long as corresponding laws and rules do not exist, as they would in a 'world state', armies can only function according to their political orders. For example, Keegan states that a battle against 'regional warlords' can only be carried out by political orders in contradistinction to the other tasks.[242] In this case Keegan's postulated battle of 'warriors', in the service of the world community, would be a continuation of community politics by other means.

One of the most common criticisms is that Clausewitz's theory only applies to state-to-state wars. But Clausewitz's concept of the state must be understood as any kind of community. This interpretation is based on an often-neglected chapter in *On War*, in which Clausewitz deals with the warfare of the 'semibarbarous Tartars, the republics of antiquity, the feudal lords and trading cities of the Middle Ages, 18th Century kings and the rulers and peoples of the 19th Century' (586). Despite this variability, Clausewitz stresses that war is also in these cases a continuation of their politics by other means. However, this makes it impossible to express the difference between the policy of modern states and the values of the various communities waging war. Therefore, it would make sense to supplement the primacy of state policy as a general category by the affiliation of the belligerents to a warring community. If these communities are states, one can speak of policy in the modern sense; if they are racial, religious or other communities, the value systems of these communities are the more important factors. Although we would replace Clausewitz's term of 'state' through that of a 'warring community', we would remain much more faithful to his understanding of what a state embodies.

Apparently without noticing, Keegan returns (in his perspective of a more peaceful world) to the strongly criticized Clausewitzian formula of war as a 'continuation of politics by other means'. The only difference is that he does not mean the continuation of politics of independent states, but the continuation of world community politics. There could hardly be a stronger substantiation of Clausewitz's theory and its relevance for our times if even his most emphatic critics unconsciously return to his conception. What they are implicitly endorsing is just a new interpretation of Clausewitz, in contradiction to their own intentions—nothing more and nothing less. The pieces of the puzzle for such a new interpretation have been collected and composed; the portrayal of Clausewitz's theory is finished. It is not 'the start of the end' but nothing else than a new 'beginning'.

Notes

1. Clausewitz, Carl von, *On War*. Translated and edited by Michael Howard and Peter Paret. Princeton University Press: Princeton, NJ, 1976, 1984 (emphasis added by Herberg-Rothe). All direct quotations from *On War* in this book are taken from this edition; subsequent references given in the body of the text take the form of page numbers placed in parentheses immediately after the quotation (or, in some cases, paraphrase). I prefer to use this edition despite the fact that there are some shortcomings in the translation. The cited text of the Trinity has been taken from the edition of 1984, p. 89. I have only changed 'reason alone' into 'pure reason' because Howard and Paret's translation leads to a misunderstanding of the Trinity which has far-reaching consequences. For further discussions of problems of translation, see the contributions of Jan Willem Honig and Christopher Bassford in: Herberg-Rothe, Andreas and Strachan, Hew (eds.), *Clausewitz in the 21st Century*. Oxford University Press: Oxford, 2007; cited as *Clausewitz in the 21st Century*. When I refer to the German text of *On War*, I always use the 19th edition, edited by Werner Hahlweg, Bonn, 1980 (reproduced 1991 and 2003); cited as *Vom Kriege*.
2. This book was originally published in German in 2001 by Wilhelm Fink Publishers, Munich; Hew Strachan has now written a very revealing historical overview of the importance of Clausewitz's analysis of war campaigns: Strachan, Hew, *Clausewitz On War*. Atlantic Books: London, 2007 (forthcoming).
3. This differentiation is derived from Muenkler, Herfried, *Gewalt und Ordnung*. Fischer: Frankfurt, 1992; cited as *Muenkler, Gewalt und Ordnung*.
4. In German, Clausewitz uses the term 'Resultat', which is a little stronger than 'consequence'; *Vom Kriege*, p. 212.
5. Gat, Azar, *A History of Military Thought*. Oxford University Press: Oxford, 2001, pp. 257–65.
6. Heuser, Beatrice, *Reading Clausewitz*. Pimlico: London, 2002.
7. It may be that the relationship between war as a continuation of politics, but with other means, could be best described as a non-linear correlation. This assumption is derived from a suggestion made by Alan D. Beyerchen in *Clausewitz in the 21st Century*.

8. Keegan, John, *A History of Warfare*. Alfred E. Knopf: New York, 1993; cited as Keegan, *History of Warfare*; van Creveld, Martin, *The Transformation of War*. Free Press: New York, 1991.
9. Summers, Harry G. Jr., *On Strategy: A Critical analysis of the Vietnam War*, Presidio Press: Novato, CA, 1982; see for the contrary position: Bassford, Christopher and Villacres, Edward J., 'Reclaiming the Clausewitzian Trinity', *Parameters*, 1995, pp. 9–19. In German, Clausewitz uses the word *mehr* (more or mainly in English), for each part of these examples of use of the Trinity, whereas in Howard and Paret's translation it is only mentioned once (89); *Vom Kriege*, p. 213.
10. van Creveld, Martin, *Die Zukunft des Krieges*. Gerling: Munich, 1998, chapter *Der trinitarische Krieg*; cited as van Creveld, *Zukunft des Krieges*.
11. See Peter Waldmann in his foreword to the German edition of van Creveld's book, *Zukunft des Krieges*.
12. Howard and Paret translate: 'that maintains a balance between these three tendencies' (89). In German we find the expression: 'dass sich die Theorie wie zwischen drei Anziehungspunkten schwebend erhalte' (*Vom Kriege*, p. 213). I therefore prefer 'floating', following a suggestion by Christopher Bassford, which is a better way of expressing Clausewitz's determination of the relation between the three tendencies as dynamic than the term balance.
13. Kaplan, Robert D., *Warrior Politics*. Vintage Books: New York, 2002.
14. Macan Marker, Marwaan, 'Sun Tzu: The Real Father of "Shock and Awe"', *Asia Times*, 2 April 2003.
15. Peters, Ralph, 'A New Age of War', *New York Post*, 10 April 2003.
16. Echevarria, Antulio II, *Fourth-generation Warfare and Other Myths*. Carlisle, 2005; Lonsdale, David, *The Nature of War in the Information Age. Clausewitzian Future*. Frank Cass: London, 2004.
17. Clausewitz: 'und nicht der politische Zustand, welcher ihm (dem Krieg, Herberg-Rothe) folgen wird, durch den Kalkül schon auf ihn zurückwirkte', *Vom Kriege*, p. 196.
18. McNeilly, Mark, *Sun Tzu and the Art of Modern Warfare*. Oxford: Oxford University Press, 2001.
19. Huai-nan tzu, *The Book of Leadership and Strategy*. Translated by Thomas F. Cleary. Shambhala: Boston, MA, 1990.
20. I have made this concept the decisive basis of a philosophical examination in Herberg-Rothe, Andreas, *Lyotard und Hegel*. Vienna, 2005; here I would just like to recall that the 'Between' is also the decisive basis for the ideas of Eric Voegelin and Hannah Arendt.

21. Gray, Colin S., *Another Bloody Century. Future Warfare.* Weidenfeld & Nicholson: London, 2005.
22. Carl Linnebach, quoted by Werner Hahlweg in *Vom Kriege*, p. 1361; translated by Gerard Holden.
23. 'In the beginning there was Napoleon' is the first sentence of Thomas Nipperdey's multi-volume history of Germany: *Deutsche Geschichte 1866–1918, 1: Arbeitswelt und Bürgergeist.* Munich, 1990.
24. Förster, Stig, *Ein alternatives Modell? Landstreitkräfte und Gesellschaft in den USA 1775–1865*, in Frevert, Ute (ed.), *Militär und Gesellschaft im 19. und 20. Jahrhundert.* Stuttgart, 1997, pp. 94–118; cited as Frevert, *Militär.*
25. Clausewitz, letter from 28 January 1807. In: Clausewitz, Carl von, *Politische Schriften und Briefe.* Munich, 1922, edited by Hans Rothfels, p. 12; translated by Gerard Holden; cited as Clausewitz, *Politische Schriften.*
26. Frederick the Great, speaking after the Prussian victory at Hohenfriedberg (1745), quoted by Muenkler in *Gewalt und Ordnung*, p. 55; translated by Gerard Holden.
27. Paret, Peter, *Clausewitz und der Staat.* Duemmler: Bonn, 1993; cited as Paret, *Staat.*
28. Hagemann, Karen, 'Heldenmütter, Kriegerbräute und Amazonen', in Frevert, *Militär*, pp. 174–200, on this point pp. 182–3.
29. Ritter, Gerhard, 'Revolution der Kriegführung und der Kriegspolitik. Napoleon und Clausewitz', in Dill, Guenther, *Clausewitz in Perspektive.* Ullstein: Frankfurt, 1980, pp. 291–333; cited as Dill, *Clausewitz in Perspektive.*
30. Clausewitz in a letter dated 9 January 1807 to his fiancée Marie, in Clausewitz, *Politische Schriften*, p. 10: 'Verwaist irren wir Kinder eines verlorenen Vaterlandes umher und der Glanz des Staates, dem wir dienten, den wir bilden halfen, ist erloschen'; translated by Gerard Holden.
31. Clausewitz, 'Historische Briefe über die großen Kriegsereignisse 1806–1807', in Clausewitz, Carl von, *Verstreute kleine Schriften.* Osnabrück, 1980, pp. 93–125; this passage at pp. 124–5: 'Wir haben die schönsten Hoffnungen in uns genährt; denn nie hat wohl eine Armee einen edleren Ruhm mit ihrem Blut erkauft, als der gewesen wäre, die Ehre, die Freiheit, das Bürgerglück der Deutschen Nation gerettet zu haben'; translated by Gerard Holden; cited as Clausewitz, *Verstreute kleine Schriften.*
32. An inspiring overview about national mobilization since the French Revolution can be found in Moran, Daniel and Waldron, Arthur (eds.), *The People in Arms.* Cambridge University Press: Cambridge, 2003.
33. Quoted Muenkler, *Gewalt und Ordnung*, pp. 54–6.

34. Clausewitz, 'Über das Leben und den Charakter von Scharnhorst', in Clausewitz, *Verstreute kleine Schriften*, pp. 205–50; see also Clausewitz's reflections on the respective national characters of the French and Germans, which can be found in his essays, 'Aus dem Reisejournal von 1807' and 'Die Deutschen und die Franzosen', both from 1807, in Clausewitz, *Politische Schriften*, pp. 23–34 and 35–51. These comments are not in themselves of any great significance, but they do demonstrate the way in which Clausewitz's conception of the political subject shifted from the Prussian state to the German nation.
35. Clausewitz, *Politische Schriften*, p. 75; Muenkler, *Gewalt und Ordnung*, pp. 103–4.
36. Clausewitz, 'Politisches Rechnen', in Rothfels, Hans, *Carl von Clausewitz. Politik und Krieg*. Bonn, 1980, p. 216: 'Sie wollen eine Revolution—ich habe nichts dagegen; aber wird diese Revolution in der bürgerlichen und Staatenverfassung sich nicht weit leichter machen in der Bewegung und Schwingung aller Teile, welche der Krieg hervorbringt?' Translated by Gerard Holden. In the following sentence Clausewitz admits that no revolution is likely at present, but this does not change his basic view that such a revolution could and should be brought about via war.
37. Clausewitz, Letter of 2 January 1809, in Schwartz, Karl, *Leben des Generals Carl von Clausewitz und der Frau Marie von Clausewitz geb. Gräfin Brühl*, 2 vols. Berlin, 1878, pp. 330–1: 'Einer großen und allgemeinen Revolution kann Europa nicht entgehen, es mag da Sieger bleiben, wer will.... Von dieser großen und allgemeinen Revolution... würde selbst eine allgemeine Insurrektion der deutschen Völker nur ein Vorläufer sein'; translated by Gerard Holden; cited as Schwartz, *Leben*; Aron, Raymond, *Den Krieg denken*. Propylaen: Frankfurt, 1980; p. 56; cited as Aron, *Den Krieg denken*.
38. Muenkler, *Gewalt und Ordnung*, pp. 104–7. The idea of violence and war as a medium for abandoning self-restraint of man, as an expression of the 'mania for immortality', is described in a very graphic way by Sofsky, Wolfgang, *Traktat über die Gewalt*. Fischer: Frankfurt 1996; cited as Sofsky, *Traktat*; and by Berghoff, Peter, *Der Tod des politischen Kollektivs. Politische Religion und das Sterben und Töten für Volk, Nation und Rasse*. Akademie: Berlin, 1997.
39. Frevert, Ute, 'Das jakobinische Modell: Allgemeine Wehrpflicht und Nationsbildung in Preußen-Deutschland', in Frevert, *Militär*, pp. 17–47; on this point pp. 25–6. One would need to look more closely at the question of whether someone like Gneisenau was simply employing 'political rhetoric', as Frevert believes, when he called for a free constitution.

40. These points, and the Clausewitz quotation, are taken from Aron, *Den Krieg denken*, pp. 56–7, and from Schwartz, *Leben*, pp. 330–1; translated by Gerard Holden.
41. John Fuller doubts whether Clausewitz really used Napoleon's conduct of war as the basis for his formation of concepts, and suggests instead that he may have formed these concepts just in an abstract way; see John Fuller, *Die entartete Kunst Krieg zu führen*. Cologne, 1964, p. 65.
42. Fuller, *Die entartete Kunst*, op. cit., pp. 78–9; the whole of Book IV of *On War* is in essence an examination of the unleashing of violence as a way of achieving military goals.
43. Clausewitz, *On War*, pp. 263–70, the chapter on 'Strategic Means of Exploiting Victory'. With respect to this statement, there is no greater difference between Clausewitz and Sun Tzu.
44. All these points are taken from Sofsky, *Traktat*, the chapter on 'Jagd und Flucht', here pp. 159–67.
45. Kleßmann, Eckart, *Napoleons Russlandfeldzug in Augenzeugenberichten*. Düsseldorf, 1965, p. 304; translated by Gerard Holden; see also Sofsky, *Traktat*, p. 236.
46. Ritter, Gerhard, 'Revolution der Kriegführung und der Kriegspolitik. Napoleon und Clausewitz', in Dill, *Clausewitz in Perspektive*, pp. 291–333; on this point p. 297.
47. Muenkler too sees Clausewitz as a follower of Machiavelli; see Muenkler, *Gewalt und Ordnung*, p. 62.
48. Clausewitz, *Schriften, Aufsätze, Studien, Briefe*, edited by Werner Hahlweg, 2 vols., Göttingen 1966 and 1990, pp. 686–7; cited as Clausewitz, *Schriften*.
49. Clausewitz, 'Briefe an die Braut', in Schwartz, *Leben*, Vol. I, pp. 233 and 288: 'mit Peitschenhieben würde ich das träge Tier aufregen und die Kette zersprengen lassen, die es sich feig und furchtsam hat anlegen lassen. Einen Geist wollte ich in Deutschland ausströmen, der wie ein Gegengift mit zerstörender Kraft die Seuche ausrottete, an der der ganze Geist der Nation zu vermodern droht'; translated by Gerard Holden.
50. Paret, *Staat*, p. 220.
51. In some of his later remarks on this point, however, Clausewitz also says that violence is the highest form of politics.
52. Clausewitz, *From the Campaign in Russia*, in: Paret, Peter and Moran, Daniel (eds.), *Carl von Clausewitz. Historical and Political Writings*. Princeton University Press: Princeton, NJ, 1992, pp. 110–204; cited as Clausewitz, *Russian Campaign*, here pp. 201–2; Clausewitz expressed this statement quite similarly in *On War*, pp. 166–7.

53. Clausewitz, *Russian Campaign*, p. 201.
54. Aron, *Den Krieg denken*, pp. 207–8.
55. Clausewitz, *Russian Campaign*, pp. 202–3 and 169.
56. Ibid. p. 169.
57. Ibid. p. 167.
58. Clausewitz, *Der russische Feldzug von 1812*. Essen, 1984, p. 64: 'Wer die Sache gründlich durchdenkt, wird sich sagen, dass die Angriffsform die schwächere und die Verteidigungsform die stärkere im Krieg ist, dass aber die erstere die positiven, also die größern und entscheidendern, die letztere nur die negativen Zwecke hat, wodurch sich die Dinge ausgleichen und das Bestehen beider Formen nebeneinander erst möglich wird.' Translation Gerard Holden; cited as Clausewitz, *Der russische Feldzug*. Unfortunately, this passage is missing in the Paret/Moran edition of the Russian Campaign; Clausewitz repeats this analysis of the 'dialectical' relationship between offence and defence in almost the same words in the first chapter of *On War*, pp. 83–4.
59. Clausewitz, *Gedanken zur Abwehr*, in *Verstreute kleine Schriften*, pp. 493–527, on this point pp. 497–8; Muenkler, *Gewalt und Ordnung*, the chapter on 'Die instrumentelle Auffassung des Krieges und die Relativierung des Vorbildcharakters der napoleonischen Strategie', pp. 94–8, on this point p. 96.
60. Aron, *Den Krieg denken*, p. 211.
61. Clausewitz, *Russian Campaign*, p. 204.
62. Ibid. p. 179
63. Ibid. p. 202.
64. Aron, *Den Krieg denken*, p. 208; translation Gerard Holden from the German edition.
65. For all references and citations in this paragraph see Clausewitz, *Russian Campaign*, p. 202.
66. Clausewitz, Feldzug von *1815*, in *Schriften II*, pp. 936–1118; in the following I cite the (unpublished) translation of this text by Moran, Daniel: Clausewitz, *Carl von The Campaign of 1815. Strategic Overview.* Translated and edited by Daniel Moran, unpublished manuscript, Monterey 2005; cited as Clausewitz, *The Campaign of 1815.*
67. Clausewitz, *The Campaign of 1815*, p. 89; Clausewitz, *Schriften II*, pp. 1087–8.
68. Ibid. p. 11; Clausewitz, *Schriften II*, p. 961.
69. Ibid. pp. 83–6; Clausewitz, *Schriften II*, pp. 1076–81; on Blücher's pursuit and Gneisenau's contribution, see Clausewitz, *Campaign of 1815*, pp. 81–3; Clausewitz, *Schriften II*, pp. 1072ff.

70. Ibid. pp. 8–9; Clausewitz, *Schriften II*, pp. 956–8.
71. Clausewitz argues that Napoleon's victory at Ligni, the battle that preceded Waterloo, was made possible by the greater experience of the French veterans; Clausewitz, *The Campaign of 1815*, pp. 44–5; Clausewitz, *Schriften II*, p. 1014.
72. Clausewitz, *The Campaign of 1815*, pp. 8–9; Clausewitz, *Schriften II*, pp. 956–8.
73. Clausewitz, *The Campaign of 1815*, p. 87; Clausewitz, *Schriften II*, pp. 1085–6.
74. Clausewitz, *The Campaign of 1815*, p. 80; Clausewitz, *Schriften II*, p. 1070.
75. Ibid. p. 80; Clausewitz, *Schriften II*, p. 1070.
76. Ibid. When reading these analyses, one must bear in mind that the destruction and disintegration of the French army, in the strict sense of these terms, was only brought about by the pursuit of Blücher.
77. Clausewitz, *The Campaign of 1815*, p. 61; Clausewitz, *Schriften II*, p. 1040.
78. Clausewitz, *From Observations on Prussia in Her Great Catastrophe*, in Paret, Peter and Moran, Daniel (eds.), *Carl von Clausewitz. Historical and Political Writings.* Princeton University Press: Princeton, NJ, 1992, pp. 30–84; cited as Paret/Moran, *Clausewitz. Historical and Political Writings.*
79. Bredow, Wilfried von and Noetzel, Thomas, *Lehren des Abgrunds. Politische Theorie für das 19. Jahrhundert,* Part 1. Münster, 1991, p. 83; translated by Gerard Holden.
80. There is only one exception, as far as I am aware—Muenkler's book *Gewalt und Ordnung.*
81. Clausewitz, *Schriften I*, pp. 733–4: 'als ob wir nicht so gut grausam seyn könnten als der Feind' and 'Lassen wir es darauf ankommen Grausamkeit mit Grausamkeit zu bezahlen, Gewaltthat mit Gewaltthat zu erwiedern! Es wird uns ein leichtes seyn den Feind zu überbieten, und ihn in die Schranken der Mäßigung und Menschlichkeit zurückzuführen'; translated by Gerard Holden.
82. Ibid.: 'die Sache nicht so arg, als man sie sich denkt'; translated by Gerard Holden.
83. Goya, Francisco, *Sämtliche Radierungen und Lithographien.* Vienna, 1961.
84. Clausewitz, *Schriften I*, p. 734.
85. Muenkler, *Gewalt und Ordnung*, the chapter on 'Partisanen der Tradition'.
86. Stephan, Cora, *Das Handwerk des Krieges.* Rowohlt: Berlin, 1998, p. 156.
87. The German word *Gewalt* can be translated into English as either 'force' or 'violence'. In some cases, however, the German term can also indicate a field of meaning that cannot be unambiguously translated using

either of these words. In these cases, we have indicated this by saying 'violence/force'.

88. Clausewitz had in 1809 written Fichte a letter about the latter's essay on Machiavelli: Clausewitz, Letter to Fichte, in Paret/Moran, *Clausewitz Political and Historical Writings*, pp. 280–4; Engfer, Hans Juergen, *Triebtheorie und Dialektik in Schillers Briefen über die 'ästhetische Erziehung des Menschen'*, in Becker, Werner and Essler, Wilhelm, K. (eds.), *Konzepte der Dialektik*. Frankfurt, 1981, pp. 30–41.
89. A UN report documents the effects of war on children as victims who both suffer and use violence: Graca, Marcel, *The Impact of Armed Conflicts on Children*. New York, 1997; Kant quoted by Muenkler in *Gewalt und Ordnung*, pp. 56–7: 'Der Krieg ist darin schlimm, dass er mehr böse Leute macht als er deren wegnimmt'; translated by Gerard Holden.
90. Poiesis has its purpose outside this process, while praxis—on the basis of Aristotle's definition, finds its meaning in the action itself; Sofsky, *Traktat*, pp. 62 and 53.
91. Hirschfeld, Gerhard et al. (eds.), *'Keiner fühlt sich hier als Mensch...' Erlebnis und Wirkung des ersten Weltkrieges*, Essen 1993; Geyer, Michael, *'Eine Kriegsgeschichte, die vom Tod spricht'*, in Lüdtke Alf and Lindenberger, Thomas (eds.), *Physische Gewalt*. Frankfurt 1995, p. 160.
92. Clausewitz, *Schriften II*, p. 631. Clausewitz formulates these sentences in one of the last draft versions of the first chapter of *On War*. Self-preservation as a motive is a central aspect of Hobbes's thought and of his conception of the disarming of the citizen and the state monopoly of force (which the citizens agree to because of their interest in self-preservation), which is a fundamental concept of modern political theory.
93. Grossman, Dave, *On Killing: The Psychological Costs of Learning to Kill in War and Society*. Boston, 1995.
94. Berghoff, Peter, *Der Tod des politischen Kollektivs. Politische Religionen und das Sterben und Töten für Volk, Nation, Rasse*. Akademie: Berlin, 1997, pp. 178–9.
95. The third interaction to the extreme is also the one to which Clausewitz devotes significantly less attention in quantitative terms. The first interaction takes up 68 lines of text (52 in the English translation), the second 29 (21 in the translation), and the third no more than 18 (13 in the translation); Clausewitz, *On War*, pp. 75–7. The third interaction also appears abstract because Clausewitz does not explain what causes the escalation in this case; he only argues that the intensification to the

extreme occurs in 'pure theory' (77). However, one can use the example of the arms race during the Cold War period to show that the third interaction too, and the tendency to escalation to which it gives rise, do not remain limited to pure theory.

96. Weber, Max, *Economy and Society: An Outline of Interpretative Sociology*, edited by Guenther Roth and Claus Wittich. New York, 1968, vol. 3, p. 942. At another point, Weber says: '*Power* is the probability that one actor within a social relationship will be in a position to carry out his own will despite resistance', ibid. vol. 1, p. 53. See also the entry for 'Power' (*Macht*) in *Pipers Wörterbuch der Politik*, München & Zürich, vol. 1, pp. 521–5.
97. Here I follow Muenkler, *Gewalt und Ordnung*, pp. 81–4.
98. Thucydides, *Der Peloponnesische Krieg*. Essen, 1993, section 23, p. 20, I, sections 140–1, pp. 106–8; Muenkler, *Gewalt und Ordnung*, pp. 81–4.
99. The contrast between the absolute and extreme as the 'pure' concept of war and real war is the subject of the next chapter.
100. One should also mention that the concept of 'duration' used by Clausewitz in his second moderating interaction is, for Hegel, the unmediated unity of space and time; see Hegel, *Enzyklopädie II*, §260, p. 56; in Hegel, Georg Wilhelm Friedrich, *Werke*. Suhrkamp: Frankfurt, 1980ff.; cited as Hegel, *Enzyklopädie* and Hegel, *Werke*.
101. Clausewitz, *Schriften II*, p. 672.
102. Keith Ronald Kernspecht, an advocate of the Wing Tsun method of (unarmed) self-defence, has provided a brief treatment of the most important differences between Clausewitz's definition of war and his own view of the duel; see Kernspecht, Keith Ronald, *Vom Zweikampf. Strategie, Taktik, Physiologie, Psychologie, Philosophie und Geschichte der waffenlosen Selbstverteidigung*, 4th edn., 1994, on this point p. 51.
103. Ibid. p. 51.
104. This interpretation is shared by, among others, Baumann, Timo. 'Friktion und Chaos. Clausewitz und das naturwissenschaftliche Weltbild', *Zeitschrift für Geschichtswissenschaft*, 8: 1997, pp. 677–95.
105. This section on the battle comes much later in the text, but it was written much earlier than the first chapter.
106. Maengel, Manfred, 'Vernunft keilförmig, auf sinnlosem Kampf. Kleist, Krieg und Clausewitz', *Tumult. Schriften zur Verkehrswissenschaft*, Vol. 21, 1995, p. 81.
107. Geyer, Michael, *Deutsche Rüstungspolitik 1860–1980*. Frankfurt, 1984.
108. Howard, Michael, *War in European History*. Oxford, 1984, p. 132.

109. Muenkler, Herfried, 'Menschenrechte und Staatsräson', in Gustenau, Gustav (ed.), *Humanitäre militärische Intervention zwischen Legalität und Legitimität*. Baden-Baden, 2000, p. 157; Genschel, Philipp and Schlichte, Klaus, 'Wenn Kriege chronisch werden: der Bürgerkrieg', *Leviathan* 4, 1997, pp. 501–17.
110. The escalation during the First World War seems also to have been influenced by the fact that in a fully formed system of states the entire system can collapse as a result of disruption to one part of the system. In addition, one cannot exclude the possibility that an exclusive focus on the maintenance of peace through balance might lead to an immanent pressure to upgrade weapons systems, because no balance can be completely stable in the long run.
111. There is a voluminous literature on these contradictions within the category of power. In particular, the end of German fascism led to a debate about the demonic aspects of power; see, among other works, Ritter, Gerhard, *Die Dämonie der Macht*, 6th edn. Munich, 1948. Among more recent contributions, the volume edited by Greven, Michael Th., *Macht in der Demokratie* is especially worthy of mention, Baden-Baden, 1991.
112. Ehrenreich, Barbara, *Blood Rites. Origins and History of the Passions of War*. Metropolitan Books: New York, 1997. Because rifles, submachine guns, and machine guns are now easier to use, small arms are increasingly becoming an outlet for aggression. Modern rifles and submachine guns can even be considered *the* symbols of contemporary civil war.
113. Muenkler, *Gewalt und Ordnung*, p. 60.
114. Ibid. 60–1; translated by Gerard Holden.
115. Howard and Paret usually translate Clausewitz's German term 'Begriff' as 'theory', though they occasionally use 'concept' as well. To mark the difference between 'Begriff' and 'Theorie', which is a differentiation employed by Clausewitz, I always use 'concept' for 'Begriff' and 'theory' for 'Theorie'.
116. Aron, *Den Krieg denken*, p. 111; translated by Gerard Holden.
117. Quoted by Rothfels, Hans, *Clausewitz*, in Dill, *Clausewitz in Perspektive*, pp. 261–90, quotation from p. 262; translated by Gerard Holden; cited as Rothfels, *Clausewitz*.
118. Quoted in Michalka, Wolfgang (ed.), *Deutsche Geschichte 1933–1945. Dokumente zur Innen- und Außenpolitik*. Frankfurt, 1993.
119. Kondylis, Panajotis, *Theorie des Krieges: Clausewitz–Marx–Engels–Lenin*. Stuttgart, 1988, p. 14; cited as Kondylis, *Theorie*.
120. Rothfels, *Clausewitz*, pp. 273–5.

121. Kondylis, *Theorie*, pp. 11 and 19.
122. Ibid. p. 17.
123. In the three interactions to the extreme, in *On War*, pp. 75–7.
124. Clausewitz, *On War*, pp. 87–8; Note of 1827, ibid. pp. 75–7. Clausewitz says something similar in his *Gedanken zur Abwehr* ('Thoughts on Defence'), in *Verstreute Kleine Schriften*, pp. 497–9.
125. On human inhibitions about killing others, see Grossman, Dave, *On Killing*. New York, 1996. Oskar Negt and Alexander Kluge emphasize social distance, as the difference between a struggle involving individuals and a subject–object relationship in which the enemy becomes an object within range of a weapon, in their book *Geschichte und Eigensinn*. Frankfurt 1981, p. 809ff.
126. Clausewitz, *Gedanken zur Abwehr*, in *Verstreute kleine Schriften*, p. 498; translated by Gerard Holden.
127. Aron, *Den Krieg denken*, p. 31 and p. 108; translated by Gerard Holden.
128. Ludendorff's formal rank was only that of Quartermaster General, but he was, together with Hindenburg, the Chief of General Staff, responsible for the general conduct of the war. The quotations from Ludendorff are taken from Wehler, Hans-Ulrich, *'Absoluter' und 'Totaler' Krieg. Von Clausewitz zu Ludendorff*, in Dill, *Clausewitz in Perspektive*, pp. 474–510, quotations from pp. 492–493; translated by Gerard Holden. Ludendorff was also of the view that 'the striving for power of the Jewish people and the Catholic Church' should share the responsibility for the trend towards total war; see ibid.
129. The proceedings of five international conferences devoted to the development of total war have drawn attention to the problems associated with the concept. At the 1996 conference, Roger Chickering reported that his review of the literature on 'total war' had revealed an almost unprecedented conceptual chaos. Many authors were, he said, only able to cover up their heuristic difficulties with the help of 'imprecise, bombastic rhetoric'. Chickering's remarks are quoted in Montani, Marco, *Im Zeitalter innerer und äußerer Mobilmachung*, Frankfurter Allgemeine Zeitung, 23.10.96, p. 6.
130. Freyer, Hans, *Der Staat*, Leipzig, 1925, p. 20 and pp. 140–3; translation Gerard Holden.
131. Clausewitz, *On War*, Book I, Chapter 1, Section 6, p. 78; Section 8, pp. 79–80; Section 10, p. 80.
132. Clausewitz, *Schriften II*, pp. 33–4.
133. Clausewitz, *Der russische Feldzug*, p. 129.

134. Baumann, Timo, *Friktion und Chaos, Clausewitz und das naturwissenschaftliche Weltbild.* In Zeitschrift für Geschichtswissenschaft 8, 1997, pp. 677–95, on this point pp. 679–80; Wolff, Michael, 'Hegel und Cauchy. Eine Untersuchung zur Philosophie und Geschichte der Mathematik', in Horstmann, R. P. and Petry, M. J. (eds.), *Hegels Philosophie der Natur.* Stuttgart, 1986, pp. 197–263, on this point pp. 197–8.
135. Keegan, *History of Warfare*, p. 75; Clausewitz, *On War*, pp. 119–21. It is, however, troubling to see that in his book on command Keegan has some surprisingly positive things to say about the capacities as a commander of, of all people, Hitler; Keegan, John, *The Mask of Command.* London, 1987.
136. It must be mentioned again that in the German original there is no equivalent to the term 'preliminary', which Howard and Paret have inserted themselves.
137. Stumpf, Reinhard, *Kriegstheorie und Kriegsgeschichte. Carl von Clausewitz. Helmuth von Moltke.* Deutscher Klassiker Verlag: Frankfurt, 1993, pp. 693–4; cited as Stumpf, *Kriegstheorie*; Stumpf stresses Clausewitz's 'subjective feeling that he had failed', thus seeking to challenge Peter Paret's verdict in his *Clausewitz and the State*, Princeton University Press: Princeton, NJ, 1976, pp. 431–40. Aron, on the other hand, emphasizes the importance of Clausewitz's intention to revise *On War* in order to account for the difference between early and late Clausewitz; see Aron, *Den Krieg denken*, p. 92ff.
138. In Chapter 1, at p. 87, Howard and Paret translate this as '*by* other means', though the German text says '*mit* anderen Mitteln' in both cases.
139. It is consistent with Stumpf's argument that he places the Note of 1827 and the text known as the unpublished Note, in which Clausewitz says that his work has not been completed, in an appendix. Almost all the editors who preceded Stumpf had followed Marie von Clausewitz's instructions and placed the two notes before the main body of *On War.* Stumpf also accounts for his selection of texts in a strange way. He omits Books IV–VII, saying that they are outdated; however, he prints Chapter 3 of Book I precisely in order to demonstrate that Clausewitz is not only outdated but also militarily 'antiquated', 'sometimes dry as dust', and 'tedious' (ibid. p. 679). In Books VI and VII, which Stumpf omits, Clausewitz addresses the fundamental problem of attack and defence and argues that defence is superior. A similar argument to Stumpf's can be found in Hepp, Robert, *Der harmlose Clausewitz, Zeitschrift für Politik* 25, at pp. 303ff. and 390ff. Both of these authors seek to reduce Clausewitz's theory of war to a conception of fight and combat.

140. Aron, *Den Krieg denken*, pp. 103–15.
141. See also Clausewitz, *Gedanken zur Abwehr*, 22.12 and 27.12.1827, in *Verstreute kleine Schriften*, pp. 493–525, and Clausewitz, *Schriften II*, p. 630ff.
142. Clausewitz, *Schriften II*, pp. 630–6; compare this with *On War*, pp. 75–89.
143. We have already mentioned that, contrary to Howard and Paret's translation, 'wondrous Trinity' is perhaps the best expression of 'wunderliche Dreifaltigkeit', and also that the term 'floating' might express the dynamic nature of this relationship better than 'balance'.
144. Aron, *Den Krieg denken*, pp. 103–15.
145. Stumpf takes the view that the 'wondrous Trinity' is no more than a religious extravagance, and so considers it to be of no particular significance; Stumpf, *Kriegstheorie*, p. 769.
146. Krug, Wilhelm Traugott, *Allgemeines Handwörterbuch der philosophischen Wissenschaften*, 2nd edn. Leipzig, 1832–8; 1st edn. from 1827; facsimile edn., Stuttgart, 1972, Vol. 1, p. 645ff., this entry pp. 645–6. In the winter of 1824–5, Clausewitz attended the lectures of the romantic philosopher Heinrich Steffens, who had been invited to Berlin by Gneisenau to deliver them. Steffens's lectures on anthropology were probably based on the two-volume work of the same title which he published (in Breslau) in 1822. This work ends with a very emotional paean of praise to the idea of the religious Trinity; Clausewitz, *Schriften II*, pp. 470 and 535.
147. Aron, *Den Krieg denken*, pp. 106–11.
148. Aron, *Den Krieg denken*, p. 104: 'The main point in this chapter is the transition from a two-part definition of war', ('War is thus an act of force to compel our enemy to do our will'), to a 'three-part definition', which Aron identifies as the 'wondrous Trinity'. He continues: 'the sentences at this initial stage of the analysis, at the conceptual level, do not apply to the whole'; ibid. 105; translated by Gerard Holden.
149. See, e.g. the work of Dan Diner, Raymond Aron, Herfried Muenkler, and Panajotis Kondylis.
150. Vollrath, Ernst, 'Neue Wege der Klugheit. Zum methodischen Prinzip der Theorie des Handelns bei Clausewitz', in *Zeitschrift für Politik* 31,1, 1984, pp. 53–76, and Vollrath, Ernst, 'Überlegungen zur neueren Diskussion über das Verhältnis von Praxis und Poiesis', in *Allgemeine Zeitschrift für Philosophie* 1, 1989, pp. 1–26.
151. This paragraph relies on Vollrath, *Theorie des Handelns*, pp. 56–8 (see previous footnote); Buck, G., 'Über die Identifizierung von Beispielen', in *Hermeneutik und Bildung*, München, 1981, p. 101; and Sofsky, *Traktat*, p. 137ff.

152. Both here and in Clausewitz's numerous references to the interactions, friction, and so on, Vollrath's distinction is confirmed unambiguously. There is nothing to add on this point, but I disagree with Vollrath's assumption that all action in war is counteraction and that Clausewitz's treatment of the instrumental character of war can be incorporated directly into a theory of counteraction.
153. Schmitt, Carl, *Der Begriff des Politischen*, 6th edn. Berlin, 1996, p. 29ff. See also Muenkler, *Gewalt und Ordnung*, p. 71ff. Schmitt's theory of war seems at times to be something like a further differentiation of the basic antithesis of symmetry and asymmetry between the opposing sides; see also Diner, Dan, 'Anerkennung und Nicht-Anerkennung. Über den Begriff des Politischen in der gehegten und antagonistischen Gewaltanwendung bei Clausewitz und Carl Schmitt', in Dill, *Clausewitz in Perspektive*, pp. 447–64; cited as Diner, *Anerkennung und Nicht-Anerkennung.*
154. Sofsky, *Traktat*, p. 139.
155. Muenkler, *Gewalt und Ordnung*, chapters on 'Der Partisan', pp. 111–26, and 'Partisanen der Tradition', pp. 127–41.
156. At another point, however, Clausewitz speaks of 'tremendous friction' (120).
157. In the German original, Clausewitz stresses this statement even more strongly and writes: 'Die Politik wird also den ganzen kriegerischen Akt durchziehen und einen fortwährenden Einfluß auf ihn ausüben, soweit es die Natur der in ihm explodierenden Kräfte zulässt'; *Vom Kriege*, p. 210. Howard and Paret translate: 'violent nature' of war (87), but this statement by Clausewitz would be better translated as: 'the nature of the exploding powers in war'.
158. I have eliminated in this quote the term 'in the abstract', because in German Clausewitz uses the expression 'philosophisch', which is not necessarily thinking 'abstractly': 'Wenn wir uns die Entstehung des Krieges philosophisch denken'; Clausewitz, *Vom Kriege*, p. 644.
159. Hegel argued that 'a sentence in the form of a judgement is not the best way of expressing speculative truths'; Hegel, *Wissenschaft der Logik*, Part 1, in Hegel, *Werke*, Vol. 5, p. 93; translated by Gerard Holden. He bases this argument on the contention that a sentence like 'Being and non-being are one and the same' is incomplete; the idea of 'one and the same' is stressed here, which would seem to mean that the difference directly expressed in the sentence is simultaneously denied.
160. Carl Linnebach, quoted by Hahlweg in Clausewitz, *Vom Kriege*, p. 1361.
161. Rothfels, Hans, *Politik und Krieg*, Berlin 1992, Preface.

162. Clausewitz, *Die Verhältnisse Europas seit der Teilung Polens*, in Schwartz, *Leben*, pp. 401–17; Clausewitz uses the expression: 'ganze physische und geistige Natur'; translated by Gerard Holden.
163. Aron, *Den Krieg denken*, p. 623. Clausewitz seems to use the concept of polarity for the first time at a late stage in his work. Stumpf has noted that the categories of polarity and continuity are still absent from the 1817 article on progress and interruptions to progress in military affairs, which deals with a closely related topic; see Stumpf, *Kriegstheorie*, p. 759.
164. Aron, *Den Krieg denken*, p. 623.
165. Paret, *Staat*, p. 187.
166. In a letter to Gneisenau, Clausewitz mentions the books he is returning and notes that he still has the correspondence between Goethe and Schiller, published in 1828–9, which he is still working on; see Clausewitz, *Schriften II*, p. 550; *Briefwechsel zwischen Schiller und Goethe in den Jahren 1794–1805*, 6 vols., Stuttgart, 1828 and 1829. See also Stumpf, *Kriegstheorie*, p. 761. Hegel, *Vorrede zur zweiten Auflage der Wissenschaft der Logik von 1831*, in *Werke* 5, *Wissenschaft der Logik I*, p. 21. Rahel Levin is quoted by Paret in *Staat*, p. 14; all translations Gerard Holden.
167. *Historisches Wörterbuch der Philosophie*, Vol. 4, I–K, Basel, 1976, p. 934.
168. Clausewitz, *Schriften II*: on Steffens, pp. 470 and 535; on Humboldt, p. 534; on the Goethe–Schiller correspondence, p. 550. See also Paret, *Staat*, for a more general discussion.
169. Clausewitz, *Vom Kriege*, p. 1146 (not translated in the Howard and Paret edition).
170. Clausewitz, *The Russian Campaign*, p. 157: 'the usual polarity of interests'. See also Aron, *Den Krieg denken*, p. 622.
171. In his *Logic*, Hegel emphasizes a very similar approach; Hegel, *Logik I*, *Werke* 5, p. 112; Clausewitz, *Schriften II*, pp. 661–2: 'Ganz ausgemacht und nothwendig sind es die letzten Ziele und die höchsten Einheiten, welche einander aufheben.'
172. Friedrich Engels, in Marx, Karl and Engels, Friedrich *Werke*, MEW 20, Berlin 1961 ff., p. 361; Aron, *Den Krieg denken*, pp. 622–3. The concept of the zero-sum game can be represented as: $(+A) + (-A) = 0$.
173. It is worth remembering Paret's assessment that in this period, it was believed that only polarity could overcome the infinite distance between the positive and the negative; Paret, *Staat*, p. 187.
174. Hegel, G. W. F., *Enzyklopädie der philosophischen Wissenschaften II*, §312–13, in *Werke* 9 ('for example, the north pole cannot be cut off'; 'if one cuts the magnet into two pieces, each of these pieces is a complete

magnet'; p. 205). On the general question of polarity; see Hegel, ibid. pp. 202–17. Karl Marx, on the other hand, understands the problem of determining the poles in a magnet in such a way that their unity consists of being a pole; *Marx–Engels–Werke, MEW 1*, p. 29.

175. Hegel, *Enzyklopädie II*, *Werke* 9, 'Zusatz' to §312, p. 205. Stumpf, on the other hand, completely misses the point when, dealing with Clausewitz's conception of war in the first of the three interactions, he interprets it as 'thinking in the category of substance'; Stumpf, *Kriegstheorie*, pp. 742–3.
176. Kant, Immanuel, *Versuch, den Begriff der negativen Größen in die Weltweisheit einzuführen*, in *Vorkritische Schriften bis 1768*, Vol. II of the Werkausgabe, edited by Wilhelm Weischedel, 2nd–7th edition. Frankfurt, 1991, pp. 799–819.
177. Wilbrand, Johann Bernhard, *Das Gesetz des polaren Verhaltens in der Natur*, Giessen 1819. Introduction.
178. Ibid., §19, p. 12, §6, p. 4, and §12, p. 5; all translated by Gerard Holden.
179. Ibid., §22, pp. 13–14 and §7, p. 5. Wilbrand also deals briefly with the correspondence between the polar antithesis and the mathematical antithesis between plus and minus. Clausewitz too speaks of 'positive' and 'negative' interests (83). Michael Wolff places particular emphasis on the connection between the conceptualization of conflicting quantities in mathematics and Hegel's conception of contradiction; see Wolff, Michael, *Der Begriff des Widerspruchs: eine Studie zur Dialektik Kants und Hegels*, Königstein, 1981.
180. Stumpf, on the other hand, argues that because of the difference between attack and defence one cannot apply the term polarity to them; Stumpf, *Kriegstheorie*, p. 761.
181. On the relation of Clausewitz and Hegel see Herberg-Rothe, Andreas, 'Clausewitz und Hegel. Ein heuristischer Vergleich', in *Forschungen zur brandenburgischen und preußischen Geschichte*, 1, 2000, pp. 49–84.
182. As I have already noted, Hegel argues that the discovery of polarity was of the greatest importance ('von unendlicher Wichtigkeit'); Hegel, *Wissenschaft der Logik*, *Werke* 5, Preface, p. 21; for Hegel's positive remarks and critique, see *Enzyklopädie II*, §312 and §313, *Werke* 9, pp. 203–17.
183. One must, however, bear in mind the fact that for Hegel, interaction as one of the decisive criteria of polarity falls into the last and highest category before that of the concept; Hegel, *Wissenschaft der Logik II*, *Werke* 6, pp. 237–40.

184. This is the second part of the text published in *On War* as the Note, in which Clausewitz says that he only considers Chapter 1 of the book to have been completed; it is also known in English versions and descriptions as the 'undated note' (70–1).
185. For the purposes of this presentation of the argument, I do not distinguish here between polar, contrary, subcontrary, and other antitheses; on this point, see the entry on *Gegensatz* in *Historisches Wörterbuch der Philosophie*, Vol. 3, G–H, Darmstadt, pp. 105–19.
186. *Allgemeine Encyklopädie der Wissenschaften und Künste*, edited by Ersch and Gruber; second section, H–N, edited by Hoffmann, part 19, Leipzig, 1828, p. 390; translated by Gerard Holden. Stumpf underestimates the importance of what Clausewitz says about the mutual relationship between attack and defence in a way that is almost systematic. This can be seen both in his selection of extracts and in the sketchy nature of his commentaries. His only remark relating to the concept of a complement reads: '(French) equivalent'; Stumpf, *Kriegstheorie*, p. 847.
187. *Historisches Wörterbuch der Philosophie*, Vol. 4, I–K, Basel, 1976, p. 934.
188. Bloch, Werner, *Polarität. Ihre Bedeutung für die Philosophie der modernen Physik, Biologie und Psychologie*. Berlin, 1972, pp. 12–13.
189. Clausewitz, *Der russische Feldzug*, p. 64 (this paragraph is not incorporated into Clausewitz, *The Russian Campaign*).
190. Aron quite rightly points out that Clausewitz does not distinguish sufficiently clearly between defence with the negative purpose of resisting attack and defence as no more than the stronger form of war; Aron, *Den Krieg denken*, p. 247.
191. Aron identifies three different characteristics of defence in Clausewitz: parrying as a concept, awaiting the blow as a distinguishing feature, and preservation as the purpose of defence; parrying includes the other two. See Aron, *Den Krieg denken*, pp. 216–17.
192. Aron criticizes Clausewitz's conceptualization of attack and defence in Book VI as a 'balanced play of forces'. He contrasts this with the dialectic of attack as the weaker form of war with a positive purpose and defence as the stronger form with a negative purpose. The substance of Aron's criticism is that Clausewitz has not succeeded in finding a synthesis of these two forms. As we have seen, however, the 'dialectic' of stronger–weaker, positive–negative is only hinted at and not developed in detail, and Clausewitz has a reason for not doing this. We must therefore be content with Clausewitz's basic remarks and with the treatment of defence and attack in Books VI and VII; see Aron, *Den Krieg denken*, pp. 246–7.

193. Here too, the analysis of the Russian campaign provides the background to Clausewitz's assessment. See Muenkler, Herfried, *Clausewitz' Beschreibung und Analyse einer Schlacht: Borodino als Beispiel*; lecture delivered at a conference at the Humboldt University, Berlin, 31.5.–3.6.2000, unpublished manuscript.
194. In a logical antithesis, A differs from non-A. If attack and defence were a logical antithesis, defence would have to be identical to non-A. This, though, would mean that the principle of *duplex negatio affirmat* would hold: the negation of the negation is once again the original identity, that is to say A is identical to non-(non-A). Thus if defence were understood as non-A, this would mean that non-(non-A) = A and hence that non-defence = attack.
195. Clausewitz's implicit model is so important that it even goes beyond Hegel's conception; see, Herberg-Rothe, *Lyotard und Hegel*. Passagen: Vienna, 2005.
196. I have tried to use this approach to develop a general theory of war in Herberg-Rothe, 'Clausewitz's trinity as a general theory of war and violent conflict', in *Theoria*, 2007 (forthcoming).
197. Paret, 'Clausewitz's Politics', in Paret, Peter, *Understanding War*. Princeton University Press: Princeton, NJ, 1993, p. 169.
198. The other formulations Clausewitz uses in *On War* to make a similar point read as follows: 'war is simply a continuation of political intercourse, with the addition of other means' (605); 'war is nothing but the continuation of policy with other means' (69); 'only a branch of political activity' (605).
199. Clausewitz, *Schriften II*, p. 67: 'Dadurch ist ein jeder Krieg zu einem in sich vollständigen Ganzen erhoben', translated by Gerard Holden.
200. In German, Clausewitz uses the expression: 'Intelligenz des personifizierten Staates'; *Vom Kriege*, p. 212. However, he also uses the idea of the state 'as a person' in order to explain why both limited and unrestrained war are influenced by policy to the same extent (88). The status of this category is therefore not altogether clear. My own use of it is intended to express the subjective autonomy of the political actor.
201. Diner, *Anerkennung und Nicht-Anerkennung*, pp. 447–8; Aron, *Den Krieg denken*, p. 389.
202. Kondylis, *Theorie*, p. 28. John Keegan in particular fails to notice Clausewitz's use of this comprehensive concept of politics; see Keegan, John, *Die Kultur des Krieges*. Rowohlt: Berlin, 1995, p. 21. (This is the German edition of Keegan, *History of Warfare*.)

203. Dill, Günter, 'Einleitung', in Dill, *Clausewitz in Perspektive*, p. xiv; Paret, Peter, 'Clausewitz' politische Schriften', in Dill, *Clausewitz in Perspektive*, pp. 380–406.
204. Türpe, Andrée, *Die Theorie von Clausewitz in den geistigen Auseinandersetzungen unserer Epoche*, unpublished Habilitation thesis, library of the Humboldt University, Berlin, 1986, pp. 125 and 130. Stumpf, on the other hand, tries to resolve this tension in Clausewitz's concept of theory between a guide to waging war and an analysis of war in a one-sided way, by concentrating on the instructional element; see Stumpf, *Kriegstheorie*.
205. Honneth, Axel, *Kampf um Anerkennung*. Zur moralischen Grammatik sozialer Konflikte. Frankfurt 1992, p. 11; cited as Honneth, *Anerkennung*.
206. Aron, *Den Krieg denken*, 455; Senghaas, Dieter, 'Rückblick auf Clausewitz', in Dill, *Clausewitz in Perspektive*, p. 351. As I have explained, this connection between the concept and the absolute of war is only one element in Clausewitz's conceptualization of the question.
207. Kondylis, *Theorie*, pp. 30 and 32.
208. Quoted in Türpe, Andrée, *Carl Gottfried von Clausewitz, ein Philosoph des Krieges*, Ph.D. thesis, Library of Humboldt University, Berlin, 1977, p. 141, translated by Gerard Holden.
209. Paret, *Staat*, p. 220; Muenkler, *Gewalt und Ordnung*, p. 62.
210. *Politikwissenschaft*, eds. Iring Fetscher and Herfried Muenkler, Editors' Preface, Reinbeck bei Hamburg, 1985, p. 8.
211. Sternberger, Dolf, *Begriff des Politischen. Der Friede als der Grund und das Merkmal und die Norm des Politischen*. Frankfurt, 1961; Vollrath, entry for *Politik* in *Historisches Wörterbuch der Philosophie*, Vol. 7, pp. 1038–72; see also Schmitt, Carl, *Der Begriff des Politischen*, 1932, 6th edn. Berlin, 1996; Weber, Max, *Politik als Beruf*, 6th edn., 1977; a comparison between the two historical traditions can be found in my article: Herberg-Rothe, *Hannah Arendt und Carl Schmitt. Vermittlung von Freund und Feind*. In Der Staat, 1/2004, cited as *Arendt und Schmitt*.
212. Clausewitz, Letter to Graf von der Gröben, 26.12.1819, in *Verstreute kleine Schriften*, p. 261.
213. Paret, *Clausewitz's Politics*, p. 169.
214. Kondylis, *Theorie*, pp. 103–5.
215. For further details, see Herberg-Rothe, *Arendt und Schmitt* and Herberg-Rothe, *Clausewitz and a New Containment*. In: Herberg-Rothe and Strachan, *Clausewitz in the 21st Century*.
216. Avineri, Shlomo, *Hegels Theorie des modernen Staates*. Frankfurt 1976, pp. 211ff. and 226. Hegel's basic conceptualization of the state as the

consciousness of freedom, and of law as the rule of freedom, does not rule out the possibility that in some cases force may have a 'progressive' meaning; see Avineri, p. 272; Hegel, *Rechtsphilosophie*, Zusatz to §262, and *Enzyklopädie III*, §433, p. 223. Hegel describes the state as 'reason, as it is realized in the element of self-consciousness', Hegel, 'Rechtsphilosophie', *Werke* 7, Preface, pp. 11–28. Paret comments: 'From the most elevated perspective, policy and war appear to be segments of a single continuum; but on the human level peace and war are very different'; Introduction to the Symposium 'The History of War as Part of General History', *The Journal of Military History* 57:5, 1993, p. 10.

217. Kondylis underestimates the emphasis Clausewitz places on the differentness of means in warfare in a systematic way. He quotes correctly Clausewitz's statement that war does not have its own logic, but quotes only half of the sentence in question. In the other half, Clausewitz says that war does have its own grammar: 'Its grammar, indeed, may be its own, but not its logic' (*On War*, p. 605), see Kondylis, *Theorie*, p. 32.
218. Scurla, H., *Wilhelm von Humboldt*, 1976.
219. It is noticeable, and important for the significance of the concept of grammar at that time, that this treatment extends over almost eighty pages; hardly any other concept is examined as comprehensively as this. *Allgemeine Encyklopädie der Wissenschaften und Künste*, eds. Ersch and Gruber, First Section A–G, ed. H. Brockhaus, Leipzig 1865, pp. 1–80.
220. *Allgemeine Encyklopädie*, pp. 1–4.
221. In German, Clausewitz uses the term *abstrakte Gestalt*, which Howard and Paret translate as 'abstract concept'. But what Clausewitz is referring to in the sentence in question is war's absolute form.
222. Clausewitz, *Brief zur Abwehr*, in *Verstreute kleine Schriften*, pp. 498–9.
223. Heuser, Beatrice, *Clausewitz lesen!* (extended German version of the original English text). Oldenbourg: Munich, 2005, p. 60.
224. Foucault, Michel, *In Verteidigung der Gesellschaft*. Suhrkamp: Frankfurt, 1999, pp. 26–7 and pp. 308–9; Foucault, Michel, *Society Must Be Defended* (translation of Foucault 1999). London, 2003.
225. See Herberg-Rothe, 'Die Umkehrungen Hegels im Marxismus [The reversal of Hegel in Marxism]. Methodologie und politische Theorie. Erweiterter Habilitationsvortrag', in *Jahrbuch für politisches Denken*. Edited by Karl Graf Ballestrem, Volker Gerhardt, Henning Ottmann, and Martyn Thompsen. Stuttgart, 2002, pp. 128–51.

226. Keegan, John, *A History of Warfare.* Hutchinson: London, 1993, pp. 384, 18 and 22; cited as Keegan, *History of Warfare.* Liddell Hart; cited Aron, Raymond, *Erkenntnis und Verantwortung*, Munich 1985, p. 416. Keegan, *History of Warfare*, pp. 384–5.
227. Keegan, *History of Warfare*, p. 3.
228. For all his reductionism, Foucault is right to highlight these aspects.
229. For a comprehensive approach see Herberg-Rothe, *Clausewitz and a New Containment*, in Herberg-Rothe and Strachan, *Clausewitz in the 21st Century*.
230. Keegan, *History of Warfare*, p. 385.
231. Ibid. p. 185.
232. Ibid. pp. 59–60.
233. Ibid. p. 384.
234. Ibid. p. 7.
235. Clausewitz, cited by Keegan, *History of Warfare*, p. 8.
236. Keegan, ibid. pp. 364–5.
237. Ibid. pp. xiii–xvi; p. 3.
238. Ibid. p. 16.
239. Ibid. p. 10.
240. Ibid. p. 392.
241. Ibid.
242. Ibid.

Bibliography

Aron, Raymond (1980). *Den Krieg denken*. Frankfurt: Propylaen.

Bassford, Christopher (1994). *Clausewitz in English: The Reception of Clausewitz in Britain and America, 1915–1945*. New York: Oxford University Press.

—— and Edward J. Villacres (1995). 'Reclaiming the Clausewitzian Trinity', *Parameters*, pp. 9–19.

Baumann, Timo (1997). 'Friktion und Chaos. Clausewitz und das naturwissenschaftliche Weltbild', *Zeitschrift für Geschichtswissenschaft*, 8.

Clausewitz, Carl von (1976, 1984). *On War*. Translated and edited by Michael Howard and Peter Paret. Princeton, NJ: Princeton University Press.

—— (1980). *Vom Kriege*. Edited by Werner Hahlweg, Bonn (reproduced 1991 and 2003).

—— (1980). *Verstreute kleine Schriften*. Osnabrück.

—— (1966 and 1990). *Schriften, Aufsätze, Studien, Briefe*, 2 Vols. Edited by Werner Hahlweg. Göttingen.

—— (1992). *Politische Schriften und Briefe*. Edited by Hans Rothfels, Munich.

Creveld, Martin van (1991). *The Transformation of War*. New York: Free Press.

Dill, Guenther (1980). *Clausewitz in Perspektive*. Frankfurt: Ullstein.

Duyvsteyn, Isabelle (2004). *Clausewitz and African War. Politics and Strategy in Liberia and Somalia*. London: Routledge.

Echevarria, Antulio II (2005). *Fourth-Generation Warfare and Other Myths*. Carlisle.

Ehrenreich, Barbara (1997). *Blood Rites. Origins and History of the Passions of War*. New York: Metropolitan Books.

Foucault, Michel (2003). *Society Must Be Defended*. London.

Frevert, Ute (ed.) (1997). *Militär und Gesellschaft im 19. und 20. Jahrhundert*. Stuttgart.

Gat, Azar (2001). *A History of Military Thought*. Oxford: Oxford University Press.

Gray, Colin S. (2005). *Another Bloody Century. Future Warfare*. London: Weidenfeld & Nicholson.

Grossman, Dave (1995). *On Killing: The Psychological Costs of Learning to Kill in War and Society*. Boston, MA: Little, Brown.

Herberg-Rothe, Andreas (1998). 'Opposizioni nella teoria politica della guerra di Clausewitz', *Scienza & Politica*, 19: 23–45.

——— (2000). 'Clausewitz und Hegel. Ein heuristischer Vergleich', *Forschungen zur brandenburgischen und preußischen Geschichte* 1. Berlin: Duncker & Humblot.

——— (2001). *Das Rätsel Clausewitz. Politische Theorie des Krieges im Widerstreit.* Munich.

——— (2001). 'Primacy of "Politics" or "Culture" Over War in a Modern World: Clausewitz Needs a Sophisticated Interpretation', *Defense Analysis*, 17(2): 175–86.

——— (2001). 'Clausewitz oder Nietzsche. Über den gegenwärtigen Paradigmenwechsel in der politischen Theorie des Krieges', *MERKUR* 3: 246–51. Berlin, March. (Version in Italian: 'Clausewitz oder Nietzsche. Sul mutamento di paradigma nella teoria politica della guerra', *futuri. Osservatorio stampa tedesca.* Berlin, July 2001; Version in Swedish: 'Clausewitz eller Nietzsche', *Res Publica* 54; pp. 17–22. Stockholm, March 2002.)

——— (2002). 'Die Umkehrungen Hegels im Marxismus. Methodologie und politische Theorie. Erweiterter Habilitationsvortrag', in Karl Graf Ballestrem, Volker Gerhardt, Henning Ottmann, and Martyn Thompsen (eds.), *Jahrbuch für politisches Denken.* Stuttgart.

——— (2003). *Der Krieg. Geschichte und Gegenwart.* Frankfurt: Campus.

——— (2004). 'Hannah Arendt und Carl Schmitt. Vermittlung von Freund und Feind', *DER STAAT* 1, pp. 35–55.

——— (2005). *Lyotard und Hegel. Dialektik von Philosophie und Politik.* Passagen: Vienna.

——— (2006). 'Privatized Wars and World Order Conflicts', *THEORIA*, August.

——— (2007). 'Clausewitz's Trinity as a General Theory of War and Violent Conflict', *THEORIA*. Forthcoming.

——— (2007). 'Clausewitz and a New Containment', in Herberg-Rothe and Strachan (eds.), *Clausewitz in the 21st Century.* Forthcoming.

——— and Hew Strachan (eds.) (2007). *Clausewitz in the 21st Century.* Oxford: Oxford University Press. Forthcoming.

Heuser, Beatrice (2002). *Reading Clausewitz.* London: Pimlico.

——— (2005). *Clausewitz lesen!* (extended German version of the original English text). Munich: Oldenbourg.

Hirschfeld, Gerhard et al. (eds.) (1993). 'Keiner fühlt sich hier als Mensch . . .'. *Erlebnis und Wirkung des ersten Weltkrieges.* Essen.

Howard, Michael (1983). *Clausewitz.* Oxford: Oxford University Press.

——— (1984). *War in European History.* Oxford: Oxford University Press.

Huai-nan tzu (1990). *The Book of Leadership and Strategy.* Translated by Thomas F. Cleary. Boston: Shambhala, MA.

Kaplan, Robert D. (2002). *Warrior Politics.* New York: Vintage Books.

Keegan, John (1987). *The Mask of Command.* London.
____ (1993). *A History of Warfare.* New York: Alfred E. Knopf.
____ (1995). *Die Kultur des Krieges.* Berlin: Rowohlt.
Kondylis, Panajotis (1988). *Theorie des Krieges: Clausewitz–Marx–Engels–Lenin.* Stuttgart.
Lonsdale, David (2004). *The Nature of War in the Information Age. Clausewitzian Future.* London: Frank Cass.
McNeilly, Mark (2001). *Sun Tzu and the Art of Modern Warfare.* Oxford: Oxford University Press.
Moran, Daniel and Arthur Waldron (eds.) (2003). *The People in Arms.* Cambridge: Cambridge University Press.
Muenkler, Herfried (1992). *Gewalt und Ordnung.* Frankfurt: Fischer.
Paret, Peter (1976). *Clausewitz and the State.* Princeton, NJ: Princeton University Press.
____ (1992). *Understanding War. Essays on Clausewitz and the History of Military Power.* Princeton, NJ: Princeton University Press.
____ (1993). *Clausewitz und der Staat.* Bonn: Duemmler.
____ and Dan Moran (eds.) (1992). *Carl von Clausewitz. Historical and Political Writings.* Princeton, NJ: Princeton University Press.
Rothfels, Hans (1980). *Carl von Clausewitz. Politik und Krieg.* Bonn.
Schmitt, Carl (1996). *Der Begriff des Politischen*, 6th edn. Berlin.
Schwartz, Karl (1878). *Leben des Generals Carl von Clausewitz und der Frau Marie von Clausewitz geb. Gräfin Brühl.* 2 vol. Berlin.
Smith, Hugh (2005). *On Clausewitz: A Study of Military and Political Ideas.* New York: Palgrave/Macmillan.
Sofsky, Wolfgang (1996). *Traktat über die Gewalt.* Frankfurt: Fischer.
Sternberger, Dolf (1961). *Begriff des Politischen. Der Friede als der Grund und das Merkmal und die Norm des Politischen.* Frankfurt.
Strachan, Hew (2007). *Clausewitz—On War.* London. Atlantic Books. Forthcoming.
Stumpf, Reinhard (1993). *Kriegstheorie und Kriegsgeschichte. Carl von Clausewitz. Helmuth von Moltke.* Frankfurt: Deutscher Klassiker Verlag.
Summers, Harry G. Jr. (1982). *On Strategy: A Critical Analysis of the Vietnam War.* Novato.
Vollrath, Ernst (1984). *Neue Wege der Klugheit. Zum methodischen Prinzip der Theorie des Handelns bei Clausewitz.* In *Zeitschrift für Politik* 31:1.
Wilbrand, Johann Bernhard (1819). *Das Gesetz des polaren Verhaltens in der Natur.* Giessen.

Index